THE PARTY
FOOD BIBLE

THE PARTY
FOOD BIBLE

565 RECIPES FOR AMUSE-BOUCHES, FLAVORFUL CANAPÉS, AND FESTIVE FINGER FOOD

Lisa Eisenman Frisk & Monica Eisenman

Photography by Roland Persson

Translated by Anette Cantagallo

SKYHORSE PUBLISHING

CONTENTS

FOREWORD

As children growing up in a suburb of Washington, DC, we often found ourselves perched at the top of the foyer staircase, captivated by the stylish guests who arrived for one of our parents' many dinner parties. This being the 1970s, hip-hugging slacks and splashy wide-collared shirts abounded. Our Swedish mother and American father came from different backgrounds and customs, but one thing they shared was a gift for entertaining friends—from cocktail parties to outdoor barbecues to formal dinners. Once, they even hosted a backwards soirée, kicked off with dancing, port wine, and dessert, followed by a three-course meal, and concluding with appetizers and aperitifs! These festivities instilled in us a similar passion for food and entertaining, and it's this love that inspired this book. Featuring 565 recipes from around the world, here you will find savory and sweet hand-held treats for virtually any occasion—from baby showers, to graduation parties, or simply potluck gatherings with family and friends.

PARTY PLANNING

Planning ahead makes for a successful party. The small details are what add up to a festive whole, and advance preparations will make the event more enjoyable for both you and the guests. Here are some tips on how to best organize a fantastic gathering.

WHAT KIND OF PARTY?

What sort of event are you hosting? Will it be casual, formal, simple, or extravagant? Will finger foods and drinks be the main event, or will there be seating for dinner afterward?

There are many enticing ways to invite people to a party—from fancy cards on elegant paper to whimsical emails. Be clear about the nature of the event, so guests know what to expect. It can also be fun if the gathering has an overarching theme, which can be introduced in the invitation.

WHERE WILL THE PARTY BE HELD?

Regardless of where the party will be located, it's important to know the conditions of the premises. They should be neither too compact nor so roomy that the space feels empty. Is there a good kitchen with heating and cooling appliances? If the location is difficult to find, provide clear directions in the invitation.

If the party is outdoors, make contingencies for bad weather. Large tents can protect against sun, wind, and rain. For chilly evenings, consider renting propane heaters or buying inexpensive blankets to keep guests warm. Also, keep in mind that there may be uninvited intruders, such as mosquitoes, flies, and wasps!

Many people appreciate knowing whether a garden party will be held on the lawn or on a wooden deck, so they can choose suitable shoes and won't risk destroying their delicate high heels.

If the party will inconvenience neighbors, consider notifying them in advance and letting them know how long it will last.

WHAT TO SERVE?

An essential feature of a successful party is a well-considered and composed menu, including a range of flavors, aromas, consistencies, and colors. Mix things up and avoid repeating the same seasonings and ingredients in different dishes. Strive for a balance between sweet and savory, mild and spicy. *See* PROPOSED MENUS *on page 306.*

Offer a variety of dishes that will appeal to all guests: meat, fish, and vegetarian. Some people are adventurous eaters, whereas others are more conservative. Also bear in mind common food allergies.

For large gatherings, try to avoid preparing completely untested recipes. With that said, don't be afraid to try new dishes combined with classic favorites.

Let the season inspire the menu. Fresh, local ingredients usually taste best, and are often the cheapest and easiest to obtain.

Serve hot and cold dishes. In winter, steaming food warms the belly, and in summer, cool dishes are refreshing.

What kind of cooling and warming appliances are available? How long will the food be left out? Consider serving a few dishes that do not need to be refilled and can stay out for a couple hours.

Serve something sweet for dessert. Even if handheld snacks are the primary food (rather than a seated dinner) desserts are always appreciated!

HOW MUCH TO PREPARE?

As long as there is plenty to eat and drink, the party will be a hit. It's always better to have too much than too little, and it all too often happens that hosts or hostesses underestimate guests' appetites! But determining how much food is needed can be difficult. There are several things to consider.

→ WHAT SEASON IS IT? Generally, we eat more in winter than in summer.

→ WHAT TIME IS THE PARTY? When did guests last eat? Are they coming straight from work, or have they traveled from far away? Is the party being held during a traditional mealtime?

→ HOW ARE THE PARTY PREMISES? If the space is crowded, it can be difficult for serving staff to move and for guests to access food tables, resulting in people eating less.

→ WHO ARE THE GUESTS? Close friends and family will often have no difficulty indulging in the food you serve, whereas acquaintances and professional colleagues may be more reserved. At a formal event, people tend to be more restrained and eat less. Men consume more than women, and the elderly tend to eat less than the young.

Calculate at least one serving per guest for each dish—but preferably more, because guests are sure to want to taste each dish and will happily take second and third helpings.

Keep finger food, such as roasted nuts and dried fruit, available as a backup; they're easy to serve and are quite filling.

Don't try to impress your guests by offering as many kinds of foods as possible—there's always the risk that you'll take on more than you can handle.

Rather, select a few dishes, do them well, and prepare more than enough.

PLATING AND SERVING

Consider how colors, shapes, and choices of food and drink can be combined, and how to arrange the dishes and the table settings. Everything looks more appetizing on attractive plates, serving trays, and in beautiful bowls. If possible, match glassware, china, cutlery, and napkins, and make sure you have enough—if not, you may need to rent or borrow from friends.

Arrange the food neatly, and garnish with fresh herbs and spices. A well-designed table setting creates a festive atmosphere. Decorate according to season, and ensure that the lighting suits the room.

It is preferable to place a label listing the ingredients beside each dish. If you are hiring waiters, it is important that they know what is in each dish, so they can inform any guests who may have allergies.

Catering companies often rent heating and cooling plates, which are perfect to use when food is to be left out for a long period.

Remember to choose recipes that are appropriate for the physical constraints of the locale. How will the food and drinks be consumed? Is it possible to sit, or will everybody stand? Will guests eat with their hands or with cutlery, and is there a place to put down a glass or plate? Glass holders affixed to the plate are essential for when there are no tables at which to stand. Also consider providing small tables where guests can put down their plates.

If there are numerous guests, be sure to have staff that can help serve, refill dishes, and clean up. The party will be best for everyone involved if the host and hostess have time to socialize instead of running in and out of the kitchen.

HOW MANY HORS D'OEUVRES WILL BE NEEDED?

Here is an estimate of how much food is required for different types of events.

PRE-DINNER COCKTAIL	3–5 hors d'oeuvres/guest, 3 different varieties
2–3-HOUR GATHERING	3–5 hors d'oeuvres/guest/hour, 5–8 different varieties
FULL EVENING EVENT	10–15 hors d'oeuvres/guest, about 8 different varieties

BEVERAGES

Choosing beverages can be difficult. Are your guests real wine connoisseurs? Do they enjoy a simple beer, or do they appreciate a well-mixed drink? The beverages you choose should also combine well with the food you are serving. If the event has a particular theme, such as tapas, choose spanish wine or sangria. If it is a brunch, consider bloody marys or mimosas.

If guests may be pregnant, driving, or do not drink alcohol, well-conceived non-alcoholic refreshments other than soda and water are always appreciated. In addition to recipes for alcoholic drinks, this book also offers several refreshing non-alcoholic options. Stores may also carry various kinds of non-alcoholic beer and wine from which to choose.

The number of drinks required depends on several factors. How long is the party? What time of day is it being held? Is it on a weekday or a weekend? Are the majority of guests older or younger? How much food will be served? The season also affects consumption. In summer, beer, white wine, and rosé are often preferred; red wine is more popular in winter. If guests are to be served, they will likely drink less than if they serve themselves.

Serve champagne, sparkling wine, white wine, and beer well chilled. Be sure to have plenty of ice for storing bottles and cooling drinks.

In the box below, we have estimated the number of drinks needed to guide beverage planning. As usual, it is better to buy too much than too little.

HOW MANY GLASSES DOES ONE BOTTLE CONTAIN?

BEVERAGE	NUMBER OF GLASSES
CHAMPAGNE/SPARKLING WHITE WINE	7–8
RED WINE	5–6
WHITE WINE/ROSÉ	6–7
BOX WINE (4 BOTTLES)	APPROX. 24
DESSERT WINE	APPROX. 12
BEER (11 OZ)	1–2
BEER (17 OZ)	APPROX. 2
LIQUEURS (1 OZ)	17–18

HOW MANY DRINKS PER GUEST?

Here is an estimate of how many drinks may be consumed at events of various lengths.

LENGTH OF EVENT	WINE/CHAMPAGNE/SPARKLING	LIQUEUR	BEER
1 HOUR	2–3	APPROX. 2	APPROX. 2
2 OR MORE HOURS	APPROX. 4	3–4	3–4

1 PASTRY CUTTERS
2 MINI PIE FORMS
3 ZESTER
4 PASTRY BAG
5 PASTRY TIPS
6 MINI MUFFIN PAN
7 DIGITAL THERMOMETER
8 DIGITAL SCALE

ADVICE & TOOLS

HOW TO USE THIS BOOK

RECIPES Read each recipe carefully before you start, so you know you have the required ingredients and are aware of how long it will take to prepare.

AMOUNT AND TIME Because this book is about hors d'oeuvres, the recipes are sized for smaller portions, but of course almost everything can be served in larger portions as well. Each recipe provides estimated preparation times to facilitate planning. In recipes where we refer to another recipe that is included in the dish, please go to that page for the preparation time.

IN ADVANCE Although most dishes taste best when freshly made, there are several that can be prepared in advance, as you would rather not be stuck in the kitchen when guests arrive. To facilitate planning, we have indicated how far in advance each recipe can be prepared. If we don't say anything about the time, the dish can be plated approximately one hour before serving. Note that almost everything should be stored in a cool place or in the refrigerator until served.

STORING Food that needs to be stored in the refrigerator or in the freezer should be put away as soon as possible. However, it is important to let heated foods cool first. Remember to always keep food covered in the refrigerator; otherwise it may dry out or take on the flavor of other dishes. Food that is to be frozen should also be wrapped in plastic or aluminum foil.

DEFROSTING Everything that is frozen should be removed from the freezer approximately one day before serving. Defrost slowly in the refrigerator. Bread and pastry should defrost in their bag or container at room temperature.

BAKING TIMES These times may vary for different ovens, so read the instructions carefully and keep an eye on the dish while it is baking. Make sure the oven is the right temperature before inserting anything. Unless we note otherwise, bake in the middle of the oven.

FRYING Remember that frying can create an unpleasant odor. Serving fried food is only appropriate if you have good ventilation, and if the event is not held near the kitchen.

HELPFUL TOOLS

PASTRY CUTTERS Are used to cut out different shapes—bread, for example—and are available in different sizes and forms.

MINI PIE FORMS Can be used for both savory and sweet dishes, and to make small bowls or baskets of biscuit dough. Stainless steel or silicone baking trays are also available in various shapes.

ZESTER Used to grate fruit peels, such as lemon and lime.

PASTRY BAGS AND TIPS Piping can be both simple and decorative. Single-use bags are available, as well as those that can be cleaned and reused. Tips come in different sizes and materials and with different nozzles. You can also use bags without the tip if the hole is the right size and if you do not want a particular pattern.

MINI MUFFIN PAN Used not only for mini muffins, but also for mini cupcakes, mini pies, for shaping breadbaskets, and more. Available in both steel and silicone.

DIGITAL THERMOMETER Simplifies deep-frying by displaying the oil temperature.

DIGITAL SCALE A good investment because we often specify quantities by weight. Remember to get a scale that has the tare function, which means that it can deduct the weight of the vessel that holds the raw material.

UTENSILS ONLINE

If you can't find a certain tool in your local kitchenware store, you can always look online. There are many websites that sell well-crafted and useful utensils.

EGG HALVES WITH TOPPINGS

SHRIMP & MAYONNAISE

CAVIAR & SOUR CREAM

CRAYFISH & MAYONNAISE

DEVILED EGGS

SALMON, DILL & CRÉME FRAÎCHE

PARMESAN CREAM & PROSCIUTTO CHIPS

The recipes are available on page 26

**FLATBREAD WITH AJVAR RELISH
& CREAM CHEESE**

ROAST BEEF WITH SWEET CHILI & AVOCADO

**FLATBREAD WITH HAM
& SPINACH**

SALMON WITH AVOCADO & LIME

SALMON WITH WASABI CREAM

**CARPACCIO WITH PARMESAN
& ARUGULA**

**CRÊPE WITH MUSHROOM
& BLUE CHEESE SPREAD**

**SPINACH OMELET
WITH CAVIAR**

**PROSCIUTTO WITH ROASTED
BELL PEPPERS & BASIL**

**OMELET WITH SALMON
& CHIVES**

**SALMON WITH MUSTARD &
DILL CREAM CHEESE**

**FLATBREAD WITH FETA, OLIVES, &
SUN-DRIED TOMATOES**

CARROT OMELET WITH FETA

**BEETROOT OMELET WITH
CHÈVRE & WALNUTS**

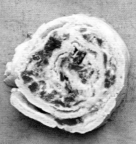

**FLATBREAD WITH SMOKED
MEAT & HORSERADISH**

**SALMON WITH
CHIVE CREAM**

The recipes are available on pages 30–33

SCRAMBLED EGGS WITH CAVIAR

The recipe is available on page 26

BAKED NEW POTATOES

GREEN TAPENADE
WITH ARMAGNAC

SOUR CREAM,
MAYONNAISE &
SHRIMP

FETA, OLIVES &
SUN-DRIED
TOMATOES

SOUR CREAM &
PROSCIUTTO CHIPS

SOUR CREAM &
CAVIAR

SOUR CREAM &
DEEP-FRIED CAPERS

The recipes are available on pages 33 and 200 (Green Tapenade with Armagnac)

PÂTE À CHOUX PUFFS & GOUGÈRES

The recipes are available on page 27

PUFF PASTRY
PALMIERS

STUFFED
PÂTE À
CHOUX PUFFS

PUFF PASTRY
STICKS

PUFF PASTRY WHEELS

21

The recipes are available on pages **27** and **29**

SALMON TERRINE

**CHICKEN LIVER &
FIG TERRINE**

**CHICKEN, APRICOT &
PISTACHIO TERRINE**

**CAULIFLOWER TERRINE WITH
SMOKED MEAT & HORSERADISH**

The recipes are available on pages 24–25

MUSHROOM & COGNAC FILLING

BRIE & CRAB FILLING

The recipes are available on page 28

MODERN CLASSICS

In this chapter, you will find classic hors d´oeuvres, such as vol-au-vents and puff pastry canapés, as well as modern finger foods like flatbread rolls filled with salmon and wasabi cream and new potatoes topped with sour cream and prosciutto chips.

SALMON TERRINE

MAKES approx. 40
TIME approx. 30 min. + 8 hrs. in the refrigerator

- ¾ cup + 2 tbsp (200 g) butter, room temperature
- 7 oz (200 g) cream cheese
- 1 ½ oz (40 g) anchovies, finely chopped
- 1 lemon, zested
- 1 lb (500 g) smoked salmon, thinly sliced
- ½ cup (100 ml) finely chopped dill for garnish

Beat the butter and cream cheese into a creamy mixture. Add the anchovies and lemon zest.

Line a rectangular baking pan with enough plastic wrap so that at least 2 inches (5 cm) hang over the edge.

Cut a piece of cardboard to fit the pan.

Cover the bottom of the baking pan with a layer of salmon. Spread a thin layer of the butter cream mix on top. Repeat with the rest of the salmon and the butter cream mix. Top with a layer of salmon and cover with plastic wrap. Place the piece of cardboard on top of the terrine and put a few cans on the cardboard for weight. Let the terrine sit in the refrigerator overnight or for about 8 hours.

Gently lift the terrine from the pan using the plastic wrap. Gently press the dill down on the top and the bottom.

Slice and then cut each slice in half. Serve on toast.

See photo on page 22.

IN ADVANCE Can be stored in the refrigerator for 2 days.

CHICKEN LIVER & FIG TERRINE

MAKES approx. 20
TIME approx. 30 minutes + 2 hours in the refrigerator

- 7 oz (200 g) chicken liver
- 2 tbsp butter
- ½ cup (100 ml) crème fraîche or sour cream
- salt and pepper
- 8–10 slices prosciutto (approx. 4 oz [100 g])
- 1 fresh fig, cut into 8 wedges

Brown the chicken liver in butter. Let cool slightly, and then chop the liver finely. Mix with the crème fraîche, and season with salt and pepper.

Cover a cutting board with plastic wrap. Layer the slices of prosciutto in the shape of a rectangle, slightly overlapping one another. Spread half of the chicken liver mixture on the longer edge so that it covers half of the prosciutto rectangle. Top the mixture with the fig wedges and cover the figs with the rest of the mixture. Starting with the edge covered with the filling, roll the terrine into a cylindrical shape. Squeeze the roll tightly and shape into a triangle. Refrigerate for at least 2 hours.

Slice and serve on toast.

See photo on page 22.

IN ADVANCE The terrine can be stored in the refrigerator for 1 day.

CAULIFLOWER TERRINE WITH SMOKED MEAT & HORSERADISH

MAKES approx. 40
TIME approx. 30 minutes + 4 hours in the refrigerator

3 tsp unflavored gelatin powder
6 tbsp water
2 cups (approx. ½ lb [250 g]) cauliflower, grated
4 oz (100 g) smoked meat, finely chopped
1 cup (250 ml) sour cream or crème fraîche
2 tbsp finely chopped chives
1 tbsp grated horseradish
salt and pepper
½ cup (100 ml) finely chopped chives
   for garnish

Line a rectangular baking pan with plastic wrap, using enough so that several inches hang over the edge.

Soften the gelatin in a bowl with 6 tbsp cold water.

Mix cauliflower, smoked meat, sour cream, chives, and horseradish. Season with salt and pepper.

Place the bowl with the gelatin in a pan with simmering water until the gelatin melts. Stir into the mixture and blend well. Pour mixture into the pan and cover it with foil. Let sit in the refrigerator for at least 4 hours or until the terrine has set.

Gently lift the terrine from the pan. Divide it in half lengthwise. Roll the lengths in the chives and cut into slices. Serve on toast.

See photo on page 22.

IN ADVANCE The terrine can be stored in the refrigerator for 2 days.

CHICKEN, APRICOT & PISTACHIO TERRINE

MAKES approx. 40
TIME approx. 2 hours + 1 hour in the refrigerator

½ lb (225 g) ground chicken
½ lb (225 g) chicken breasts, cubed
½ lb (250 g) ground pork
1 clove garlic, pressed
1 ¾ oz (50 g) pistachios
10 dried apricots, chopped
1 egg, lightly beaten
½ cup (100 ml) mascarpone
1 tsp salt
1 tsp dried sage

Preheat the oven to 300°F (150°C). Grease a rectangular baking pan.

Mix the ground chicken, chicken cubes and ground pork with the rest of the ingredients.

Spread the mixture evenly into the pan. Cover carefully with aluminum foil, and bake in the oven for approx. 40 minutes or until the temperature of the terrine reaches 160°F (70°C).

Gently remove the terrine. Allow to cool. Slice and serve on toast.

See photo on page 22.

IN ADVANCE The terrine can be stored in the refrigerator for 2 days or in the freezer for about 2 months.

EGG HALVES

MAKES approx. 12
TIME approx. 30 minutes

  6 eggs, cooked, peeled, and halved
  optional toppings or fillings *(see recipe below)*
  fresh herbs for garnish
  See photo on page 16.

WITH SHRIMP/CRAYFISH & MAYONNAISE Top
the egg halves with 12 pieces of shrimp or cooked
crayfish meat and about 3 tbsp mayonnaise.

WITH CAVIAR & SOUR CREAM Top the egg halves
with approximately 1 ¾ oz of caviar (50 g), about 3 tbsp
of finely chopped red onion, and about 3 tbsp of sour
cream. Garnish with fresh herbs.

WITH SALMON, DILL & CRÈME FRAÎCHE Top the
egg halves with about 4 oz (120 g) of sliced smoked
salmon and about 3 tbsp of crème fraîche (or sour
cream). Garnish with fresh dill.

PARMESAN CREAM & PROSCIUTTO CHIPS
  2 tbsp mayonnaise + 2 tbsp sour cream
  ½ cup (100 ml) Parmesan cheese, finely grated
  salt and pepper
  PROSCIUTTO CHIPS *(see the recipe on page 286)*

With a spoon, remove the yolks, and mix them with
the other ingredients (except the prosciutto chips).
Pipe the filling into the yolk hole, and press a small
chip into the filling.

DEVILED EGGS
  4 tbsp mayonnaise + 1 tbsp sour cream
  1 tsp white wine vinegar + 1 tsp Dijon mustard
  1–2 drops Worcestershire sauce, optional
  paprika powder for garnish

Remove the yolks with a spoon and mix them with
the other ingredients. Pipe the filling into the yolk
hole, and sprinkle with paprika powder.

IN ADVANCE Eggs can be cooked and stored in the
refrigerator for 1 day. The fillings can also be stored
in the refrigerator for 1 day. The egg halves can be
prepared a few hours before serving.

SCRAMBLED EGGS WITH CAVIAR

MAKES approx. 12
TIME approx. 40 minutes

  12 eggs
  2 tbsp (25 g) butter, melted and cooled
  salt and pepper
  ½ cup (100 ml) heavy cream
  approx. 1 ¾ oz (50 g) fish roe/caviar

  fresh herbs for garnish

Carefully crack the top of the eggs and remove the
top third of the shell. Pour ten of the eggs in a bowl,
but save all twelve empty shells.

  Whisk the eggs lightly, and then mix with the
melted butter. Season with salt and pepper.

  Put the cleaned, empty shells back in the carton,
and fill the eggshells with the egg mixture. Place the
carton in a large pan. Fill the pan with water up to
just below the bottom of the eggs. Gently bring the
water to a boil and let it simmer for about 15 minutes
or until the eggs begin to set. While the water is
simmering, use a small spoon to stir the egg mixtures
gently. Let cool slightly. Whip the cream.

  Place the eggs in egg cups. Dollop cream and roe
on each egg, and garnish with fresh herbs.
Serve immediately.

  See photo on page 18.

TIP Cream (which will melt slightly) may be omitted
if the eggs are not to be served immediately, or if
many eggs are to be served at the same time.

IN ADVANCE The eggs taste best when served
immediately.

PÂTE À CHOUX PUFFS

MAKES 24–30
TIME approx. 1 hour

Pâte à choux puffs can either be flavored (see the recipe for GOUGÈRES*) or filled ready-baked with a variety of fillings. Cut off the top of a puff, then pipe or add a spoonful of the filling. Gently put the top back on.*

5 tbsp (75 g) unsalted butter
⅔ cup (150 ml) milk
⅔ cup (150 ml) all-purpose flour
2 eggs
1 egg white

Preheat the oven to 400°F (200°C).

Melt 1 tbsp of butter in a heavy-bottomed saucepan. Add the milk, and bring to a boil. Quickly whisk the flour into the mixture, and mix vigorously until the batter forms a ball.

Remove the saucepan from the heat.

Place the batter in a bowl and whisk with an electric beater until it has cooled slightly. Continue beating while adding the eggs, one at a time. Add the egg white and beat for another few minutes. Use a spoon or pipe the batter into small balls placed about 2 inches (5 cm) apart on a baking sheet—greased or lined with parchment paper.

Bake for 10 minutes. Reduce the heat to 350°F (175°C), and bake for another 20 minutes or until the puffs are golden brown.

See photo on page 20.

TIP Find fillings for the pâte à choux puffs in the index under dips.

IN ADVANCE The pâte à choux puffs can be baked up to 3 days in advance and stored in an air-tight container. Heat them in the oven at 400°F (200°C) for 3 minutes if they are to be served hot. They can be stored in the freezer for up to 1 month.

GOUGÈRES

MAKES 24–30
TIME approx. 1 hour

1 batch of PÂTE À CHOUX PUFF DOUGH (*see recipe on the left side of this page*)
4 oz (100 g) Gruyère, finely grated
a pinch of cayenne pepper
sea salt

Make the pâte à choux puff dough according to the recipe. Add the Gruyère cheese and cayenne pepper. Use a spoon or pipe the mixture into small balls, and place them about 1 ½ inches (4 cm) apart on a baking sheet, greased or lined with parchment paper. Sprinkle with a little sea salt.

Bake for 10 minutes at 400°F (200°C). Reduce heat to 350°F (175°C), and bake for another 20 minutes or until they are golden brown. Serve either hot or cold.

See photo on page 20.

WITH CHEDDAR & BACON Add 4 oz (100 g) of grated Cheddar and 4–5 slices of crispy, crumbled bacon to the dough. Omit the Gruyère and cayenne pepper.

WITH CHEDDAR & CARAWAY SEEDS Add 4 oz (100 g) of grated Cheddar cheese and 1 tbsp of caraway seeds to the dough. Omit the Gruyère and cayenne pepper.

WITH CURRY Add 1 tsp of curry powder and ½ tsp turmeric to the dough. Omit the Gruyère and cayenne pepper.

WITH CHORIZO Add 4 oz (100 g) chopped chorizo (without skin) to the dough.

WITH SALMON & DILL Add 4 oz (100 g) finely chopped smoked salmon and 1 tbsp finely chopped dill to the dough. Omit the Gruyère and cayenne pepper.

TIP Other aged hard cheeses can also be used in gougères.

IN ADVANCE *See* PÂTE À CHOUX PUFFS *on the left side of this page.*

VOL-AU-VENTS

MAKES approx. 28
TIME approx. 30 minutes + 1 hour in the refrigerator

approx. ¾ lb (350 g), puff pastry sheets
1 egg, lightly beaten

Cut circles, approx. 1 ½ inches (4 cm) in diameter from the puff pastry sheets. With a smaller ring, cut a hole in the middle without cutting completely through. Place the circles on a baking tray covered with parchment paper. Refrigerate for at least 1 hour.

Preheat the oven to 400°F (200°C).

Brush the circles with the egg, but be careful not to allow the egg to drip down the sides, which will prevent the pastry from rising. Bake for approx. 15 minutes, or until the pastry has risen and becomes golden brown. Remove from the oven. Carefully remove the small circle from the center with a sharp knife and save it as a lid.

See photo on page 23.

IN ADVANCE The vol-au-vents can be stored for about 2 days in open air. Heat at 400°F (200°C) for about 3 minutes just before serving. If they are to be filled with a cold dip, let cool first.

MUSHROOM & COGNAC FILLING

5 oz (150 g) chanterelles or other mushroom, coarsely chopped
2 oz (50 g) button mushrooms, coarsely chopped
1 shallot, finely chopped
1 small clove garlic, pressed
1 tbsp butter
¼ cup (50 ml) heavy cream
1 tbsp coarse-grained French mustard
1 tbsp cognac
salt and pepper

finely chopped parsley for garnish

Sauté the mushrooms, shallots, and garlic in butter for a few minutes. Add the cream, mustard, and cognac, and simmer for about 5 minutes while stirring. Season with salt and pepper.

Fill the holes in the vol-au-vents with the mushroom mixture. Sprinkle with parsley, and

carefully place the puff pastry lid on the vol-au-vents. Serve immediately.

BRIE & CRAB FILLING

approx. 5 oz (150 g) brie cheese
¼ cup (50 ml) finely chopped leeks
¼ cup (50 ml) finely chopped onion
1 clove garlic, pressed
1 tbsp olive oil
2 artichoke hearts, finely chopped
2 oz (50 g) fresh spinach, finely chopped
6 oz (170 g) crabmeat, drained
¼ cup (50 ml) heavy cream
1 tbsp finely chopped parsley
1 tsp finely chopped dill
1 tsp finely chopped fresh tarragon
1 tsp lemon zest
1 tsp Dijon mustard
a few drops of Tabasco
salt and pepper

Remove the rind from the brie and cut the cheese into smaller pieces. Sauté the leeks, onion, and garlic in oil for a few minutes. Add the artichoke hearts and spinach, and cook for another few minutes. Add the crabmeat, cream, brie cheese, herbs, lemon zest, and Dijon mustard, and simmer for another few minutes. Season with Tabasco, salt, and pepper.

Fill the vol-au-vents and serve immediately.

IN ADVANCE The fillings can be stored in the refrigerator for about 2 days.

FRENCH VOL-AU-VENT
A vol-au-vent—French for "fly in the wind"—is a feather-light puff pastry that can be filled with countless fillings. Our favorites are CREAMY "SKAGEN" SHRIMP (*see the recipe on page 80*), EGG & ANCHOVY SALAD (*see the recipe on page 90*), CHÈVRE SPREAD WITH FIGS & PECANS (*see the recipe on page 237*), or TURKEY & PEAR DIP WITH WALNUTS (*see the recipe on page 237*). Vol-au-vents are also delicious when filled with a tasty piece of aged cheese and some marmalade. Or, if you prefer a sweet vol-au-vent, whipped cream or ice cream with fresh berries is a perfect match!

PUFF PASTRY STICKS, WHEELS & PALMIERS

MAKES 24–30
TIME approx. 30 minutes

approx. 6 oz (170 g), puff pastry sheets
1 egg, lightly beaten

filling of your choice (see recipes below)

Preheat the oven to 400°F (200°C). Thinly roll out the puff pastry sheets.

Mix the ingredients for the filling of your choice.

Brush the pastry with egg, and sprinkle or cover with any of the fillings.

STICKS Cut the puff pastry into thin strips. Twist them and place on a baking tray with parchment paper. Bake in the middle of the oven for about 12 minutes or until golden brown.

WHEELS Place the puff pastry sheet with the long side facing you. Roll up the dough. Slice it, and place on a baking tray covered with parchment paper. Bake for about 12 minutes or until golden brown.

PALMIERS From both long sides, roll the puff pastry toward the middle. Cut the puff pastry into slices and place on a baking tray with parchment paper. Bake for about 12 minutes or until golden brown.

See photo on page 21.

TIP Can be served both hot and cold.

ANCHOVIES & PARMESAN
1 oz (35 g) anchovies, finely chopped
¼ cup (50 ml) Parmesan cheese, grated

EGG, DILL & ANCHOVIES
1 hard-boiled egg, finely chopped
⅓ oz (10 g) anchovies, finely chopped
1 tbsp finely chopped dill

SUN-DRIED TOMATOES & PECORINO
6 sun-dried tomatoes in oil, finely chopped
½ clove garlic, pressed
2 tsp olive oil
1 tbsp finely chopped basil
3 tbsp grated pecorino

MORE FILLINGS
→ 3–4 tsp of caraway seeds, poppy seeds, black and/or white sesame seeds

→ ½ cup (100 ml) crumbled feta, grated Parmesan, pecorino, manchego, or Cheddar

→ 4 tbsp pesto (see the recipe on page 178)

→ 4 tbsp fig tapenade (see the recipe on page 199)

TIP Try using phyllo pastry instead, which is crispier. Consider mixing different fillings, such as caraway seeds and Cheddar cheese or fig tapenade and crumbled feta cheese.

IN ADVANCE The puff pastries may be prepared the day before and stored unbaked in the refrigerator. Slice them just before baking.

CARPACCIO ROLL WITH PARMESAN & ARUGULA

MAKES approx. 24
TIME approx. 30 minutes + 30 minutes in the fridge

⅓ lb (150 g) beef tenderloin
½ cup (100 ml) grated Parmesan
1 oz (20 g) arugula
½ lemon
black pepper

Cut the fillet of beef into very thin slices. Lay out the slices of meat, slightly overlapping each other, on a cutting board covered with plastic. Cover the slices with plastic and gently pound with a meat mallet until thin.

Remove the top sheet of plastic and cover the meat with Parmesan, arugula, and some coarsely ground black pepper. Finish with freshly squeezed lemon juice.

Using the plastic wrap, roll into a tight roll. Refrigerate for at least 30 minutes. With a sharp knife, cut the roll into slices about ½-inch (1 cm) thick. Serve on round (possibly toasted) bread pieces.

See the photo on page 17.

IN ADVANCE The roll can be stored in the refrigerator for 1 day.

OMELET ROLLS

MAKES approx. 24
TIME approx. 45 min. + 30 min. in the refrigerator

4 eggs, of which 2 are separated
filling of your choice (*see the recipes below*)

Preheat the oven to 400°F (200°C). Grease a sheet of parchment paper and place on a baking sheet.

Beat the 2 eggs with the 2 yolks. Add any flavoring you like from below.

Beat the egg whites until stiff and fold gently into the egg mixture. Thinly spread the omelet batter into a rectangle on the parchment paper.

Bake in the oven for about 10 minutes or until firm. Turn it upside down onto a clean sheet of parchment paper. Let cool, and carefully remove the top sheet of parchment paper.

Prepare the filling of your choice and spread it on the omelet. Using the bottom paper, roll up the omelet, and refrigerate for at least 30 minutes. With a sharp knife, cut into slices about 1 inch (2 ½ cm) wide.

See the photo on page 17.

OMELET WITH SALMON & CHIVES
1 tbsp finely chopped chives
salt and pepper

4 oz (100 g) cream cheese
3 tbsp sour cream or crème fraîche
approx. ½ lb (250 g) sliced smoked salmon

Follow the basic recipe for the omelet rolls, but add the chives into the egg mixture, and season with salt and pepper. Mix cream cheese and sour cream to a smooth cream, and spread onto the omelet. Top with the salmon slices, and with the parchment paper, roll the omelet lengthwise into a tight roll. Slice and serve.

IN ADVANCE All omelet rolls except the beetroot omelet can be stored in the refrigerator for 1 day before being sliced and served. The beetroot omelet can be refrigerated for about 3 hours.

CARROT OMELET WITH FETA
4 oz (100 g) carrots, boiled and puréed
4 oz (100 g) carrots, finely grated
1 tsp lemon juice
salt and pepper

4 oz (100 g) cream cheese
4 oz (100 g) feta cheese
1 tbsp finely chopped chives

Follow the basic recipe for omelet rolls, but add puréed and grated carrots and lemon juice to the egg mixture before adding the egg whites. Season with salt and pepper. Add the egg whites and follow the rest of the recipe.

Mix the cream cheese, feta cheese, and chives to a smooth cream, and spread onto the omelet. Using the parchment paper, roll the omelet lengthwise into a tight roll. Slice and serve.

See the photo on page 17.

BEETROOT OMELET WITH CHÈVRE & WALNUTS
1 cooked beet (approx. 2 ½ oz [70 g]), peeled and puréed
1 tsp freshly squeezed lemon juice
salt and pepper

3 oz (75 g) cream cheese
3 oz (75 g) chèvre
¼ cup (50 ml) walnuts, toasted and finely chopped
1 bunch basil

Follow the recipe for the CARROT OMELETTE WITH FETA above, but replace the carrots with the beets. Mix the cream cheese and the chèvre, and spread it over the omelet. Sprinkle with the walnuts and basil leaves—pressing them down lightly—and roll the omelet.

See the photo on page 17.

SPINACH OMELET WITH CAVIAR
14 oz (400 g) fresh spinach
1 tsp finely chopped dill
a pinch of ground nutmeg
salt and pepper

4 oz (100 g) cream cheese
3 tbsp sour cream or crème fraîche
1 tsp freshly squeezed lemon juice
1 tsp lemon, zested
approx. 3 oz (75 g) caviar or fish roe

Boil water in a saucepan, and blanch the spinach for about 1 minute. Rinse in cold water, and squeeze out as much water as possible from the spinach. Follow the recipe for the CARROT OMELET WITH FETA, but mix the spinach with the egg yolks and the eggs. Add the dill and nutmeg, and season with salt and pepper. Fold in the stiff egg whites.

Mix the cream cheese, sour cream, lemon juice, and lemon zest. Spread it on the omelet and top with the caviar. Roll the omelet together lengthwise with parchment paper and cut into slices.

See the photo on page 17.

SALMON ROLLS

MAKES approx. 24
TIME approx. 15 min. + 30 min. in the refrigerator

approx. 14 oz (400 g) sliced smoked salmon filling of your choice *see below*

Cover a cutting board with plastic wrap, and lay out the salmon slices so they are slightly overlapping each other.

Mix the filling of your choice and spread it onto the salmon. Roll it with the plastic wrap into a tight roll. Refrigerate for at least 30 minutes.

Cut into slices with a sharp knife. Serve as is or on round (possibly toasted) pieces of bread.

See the photo on page 17.

CHIVE CREAM
5 oz (150 g) cream cheese
3 tbsp sour cream or crème fraîche
2 tbsp finely chopped chives

WASABI CREAM
5 oz (150 g) cream cheese
3 tbsp sour cream or crème fraîche
1–2 tsp wasabi paste

AVOCADO & LIME
1 avocado, mashed
1 tsp freshly squeezed lime juice
a pinch of salt

MUSTARD & DILL CREAM CHEESE
5 oz (150 g) cream cheese
2 tbsp mustard
1 tbsp chopped dill

IN ADVANCE The salmon rolls can be prepared and kept in the refrigerator for 1 day. All rolls except the one with avocado can be stored in the freezer for about 3 months. The rolls are easiest to cut when they are slightly thawed.

A VARIETY OF FILLINGS

We have given suggestions for various fillings for different types of rolls, but feel free to experiment with your favorite flavors.

A flatbread roll, for example, can be filled with the crêpe roll's MUSHROOM & BLUE CHEESE SPREAD (*see the recipe on page 32*), and the spinach omelet roll is both tasty and beautiful when filled with the flatbread's AJVAR RELISH & CREAM CHEESE or FETA, OLIVES & SUNDRIED TOMATOES (*see the recipe page 33*). Or, why not try the CRAB & APPLE DIP (*see the recipe page 81*), ROASTED BELL PEPPER & WALNUT DIP (*see the recipe page 118*), or FENNEL & ALMOND ANCHOÏADE (*see the recipe on page 200*).

All rolls benefit from resting in the refrigerator for about 30 minutes before slicing. Roll them tightly in plastic wrap so that they keep their shape and don't dry out. Rolls that have been frozen are easier to cut when slightly thawed.

ROAST BEEF ROLL WITH SWEET CHILI & AVOCADO

MAKES approx. 24
TIME approx. 20 min. + 30 min. in the refrigerator

approx. 5 oz (150 g) roast beef, sliced
4 oz (100 g) cream cheese
4 tsp sweet chili sauce
½ avocado, thinly sliced

6 slices of sandwich bread
cilantro for garnish

Cover a cutting board with plastic wrap, and lay out the roast beef slices so they are slightly overlapping each other.

Stir together the cream cheese and sweet chili sauce, and spread it over the roast beef. Top with the avocado slices. With the plastic wrap, shape into a roll. Refrigerate for at least 30 minutes.

With a sharp knife, cut the roast beef roll into slices about 1 inch (2 ½ cm) thick. Serve on round (possibly toasted) pieces of bread. Garnish with cilantro.

See the photo on page 17.

IN ADVANCE The roll can be stored in the refrigerator for 1 day.

PROSCIUTTO ROLL WITH ROASTED BELL PEPPERS & BASIL

MAKES approx. 24
TIME approx. 15 min. + 30 min. in the refrigerator

5 oz (140 g) prosciutto, sliced
4 oz (100 g) cream cheese
½ ROASTED BELL PEPPERS (*see the recipe on page 118*), finely chopped
1 tbsp chopped basil
salt and pepper

6 slices of sandwich bread

Cover a cutting board with plastic wrap, and lay out the slices of prosciutto so they are slightly overlapping each other.

Mix the cream cheese and roasted peppers, and season with salt and pepper. Spread the mixture onto the prosciutto, and top with basil.

Roll into a roll using the plastic wrap. Refrigerate for at least 30 minutes.

With a sharp knife, cut the roll into slices approx. ¾ inches (2 cm) thick. Serve as is or on round (possibly toasted) pieces of bread.

See the photo on page 17.

IN ADVANCE The roll can be stored in the refrigerator for 1 day or in the freezer for about 3 months. The roll is easier to slice when slightly thawed.

CRÊPE WITH MUSHROOM & BLUE CHEESE SPREAD

MAKES approx. 24
TIME approx. 45 minutes

⅔ cup (150 ml) milk
1 egg
½ cup (100 ml) all-purpose flour
1 tbsp butter, melted
1 tsp salt

MUSHROOM & BLUE CHEESE SPREAD
4 oz (100 g) mixed mushrooms, finely chopped
2 oz (50 g) blue cheese, crumbled
4 oz (100 g) cream cheese
1 tbsp chives, finely chopped

Whisk the milk, eggs, flour, and butter until smooth. Add the salt. Refrigerate for at least 30 minutes.

Pour 5 tbsp of the batter into the pan, tilting the pan to spread the batter evenly. Cook 3 crêpes until golden brown on both sides. Let cool.

Fry the mushrooms in a non-stick frying pan. Cool and mix with the other ingredients for the filling. Spread the filling over the crêpes and roll them up. With a sharp knife, cut them into slices about 1 inch (2 ½ cm) thick.

See the photo on page 17.

IN ADVANCE The roll can be stored in the refrigerator for 1 day or in the freezer for about 3 months.

FLATBREAD ROLLS

MAKES 24–30
TIME approx. 10–15 minutes

> 3 rectangular soft flatbreads
> **filling of your choice** (*see the recipes below*)

Spread the filling of your choice on the flatbreads. Roll them lengthwise, and cut into slices.
> *See the photo on page 17.*

HAM & SPINACH

> 5 oz (150 g) cream cheese
> 2 tsp Dijon mustard
> 3 tsp honey
> approx. 1 oz (30 g) fresh spinach
> 4 oz (100 g) smoked ham, sliced

Mix cream cheese, mustard, and honey, and spread on the flatbreads. Place the ham and spinach on top.

FETA, OLIVES & SUN-DRIED TOMATOES

> 4 oz (100 g) feta cheese
> 4 oz (100 g) cream cheese
> ¼ cup (50 ml) sun-dried tomatoes in oil, finely chopped
> 2 tbsp finely chopped fresh basil
> ¼ cup (50 ml) finely chopped black olives

Mix ingredients, and spread on the flatbreads.

SMOKED MEAT & HORSERADISH

> 4 oz (100 g) smoked meat, finely chopped
> 4 oz (100 g) cream cheese
> 1 tsp grated horseradish
> 1 tbsp finely chopped chives

Mix ingredients, and spread on the flatbreads.

AJVAR RELISH & CREAM CHEESE

> 5 oz (150 g) cream cheese
> 2 tbsp Ajvar relish

Mix ingredients, and spread on the flatbreads.

IN ADVANCE The rolls can be stored in the refrigerator, wrapped in plastic wrap, for 1 day or about 2 months in the freezer. Slice when slightly thawed.

BAKED NEW POTATOES

MAKES 24–30
TIME approx. 40 minutes

> 24 small new potatoes
> 1 tbsp olive oil + 1 tsp salt
> **optional toppings** (*see the recipes below*)
> **fresh herbs for garnish**

Preheat the oven to 400°F (200°C). Scrub the potatoes clean, and let dry. Pierce with a fork. Mix the potatoes with the oil and salt. Place the potatoes on a baking sheet, and bake in the oven for about 30 minutes or until tender inside and crispy outside. Let cool.

Cut a crisscross on top of each potato, and squeeze the sides gently so the center pops up and can be filled.
> *See the photo page 19.*

SOUR CREAM & CAVIAR

> approx. ½ cup (100 ml) sour cream
> approx. 3 oz (80 g) caviar or fish roe
> dill or chives for garnish

SOUR CREAM & PROSCIUTTO CHIPS

> approx. ½ cup (100 ml) sour cream
> PROSCIUTTO CHIPS, **crumbled** (*see the recipe on page 286*)

SOUR CREAM, MAYONNAISE & SHRIMP

> ¼ cup (50 ml) sour cream + ¼ cup (50 ml) mayonnaise
> 24 shrimp
> dill for garnish

SOUR CREAM & DEEP-FRIED CAPERS

> approx. ½ cup (100 ml) sour cream
> ¼ cup (50 ml) capers
> approx. ¼ cup (50 ml) oil

Dry the capers with a paper towel, and fry them in hot oil until crispy. Drain on paper towels.

TIP Try topping with FLAVORED CREAM CHEESE (*see the recipe on page 246*).

IN ADVANCE The potatoes taste best served warm. Top them just before serving. Capers can be fried 1 hour before serving and kept at room temperature.

PIES

CHEDDAR CHEESE
& WALNUTS

SWEET POTATO,
BACON & CHÈVRE

SALMON, LEEK
& FETA

QUICHE LORRAINE

The recipes are available on pages 40–41

RICOTTA, SPINACH &
SUN-DRIED TOMATOES

PROSCIUTTO,
PARMESAN & HERBS

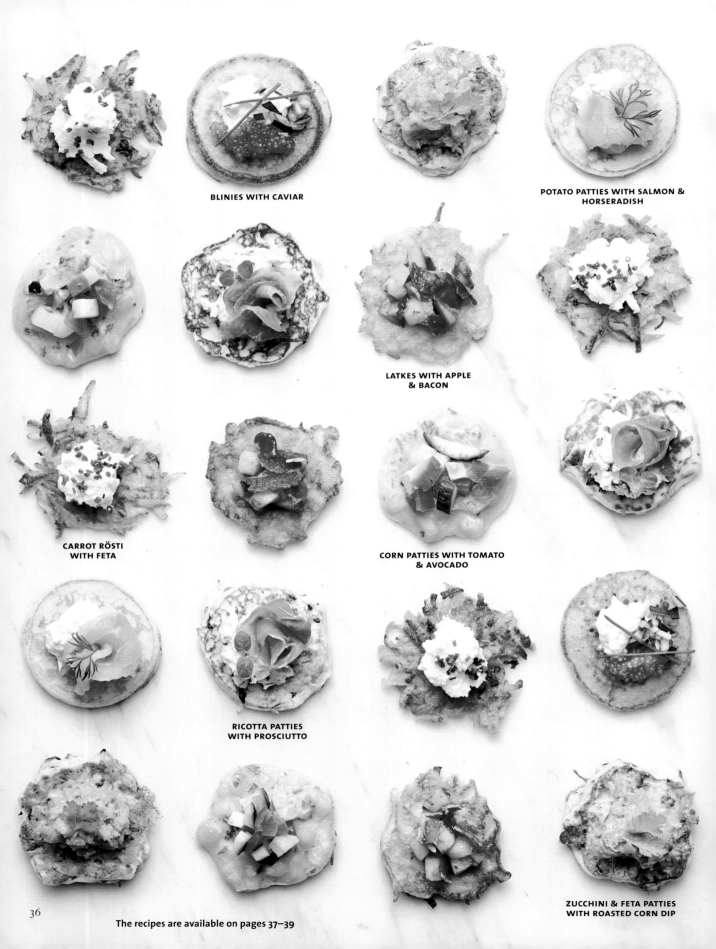

BLINIES WITH CAVIAR

POTATO PATTIES WITH SALMON & HORSERADISH

LATKES WITH APPLE & BACON

CARROT RÖSTI WITH FETA

CORN PATTIES WITH TOMATO & AVOCADO

RICOTTA PATTIES WITH PROSCIUTTO

ZUCCHINI & FETA PATTIES WITH ROASTED CORN DIP

The recipes are available on pages 37–39

PIES & PATTIES

Blinies, rösti, and latkes are all different types of patties, and can be topped with just about anything. Likewise, a pie can be stuffed with numerous fillings. Here we offer pies and patties with both classic and modern flavor combinations.

BLINIES WITH CAVIAR

MAKES approx. 36
TIME approx. 40 minutes + 1 hour to rise

½ oz (12 g) fresh yeast
1 ⅓ cups (300 ml) milk
2 eggs, separated
¾ cup (200 ml) buckwheat flour
½ cup (100 ml) all-purpose flour
½ tsp salt
3 ½ tbsp (50 g) butter, melted and cooled

½ cup (100 ml) sour cream
3 oz (80 g) fish roe or caviar
¼ cup (50 ml) finely chopped red onion
¼ cup (50 ml) finely chopped chives

Sprinkle the yeast into a bowl. Heat the milk to 100°F (37°C), and stir a part of it into the yeast. Add the remaining milk and egg yolks while whisking.

Mix the buckwheat flour, all-purpose flour, and salt. Add into the milk and egg mixture, and whisk until smooth. Cover the bowl and set in a warm place to rise for about 1 hour.

Beat the egg whites into a firm foam.

Mix the butter with the batter. Gently fold the egg whites into the batter. Melt a little butter in a frying pan. Add a few dollops of batter—about 1 tbsp per blini. Cook the blinies until golden brown on both sides.

Top each blini with a dollop of sour cream, caviar, red onion, and chives.

See the photo on page 36.

IN ADVANCE *See* RICOTTA PATTIES WITH PROSCIUTTO *on page 39.*

CORN PATTIES WITH TOMATO & AVOCADO

MAKES approx. 20
TIME approx. 40 minutes

⅓ cup (75 ml) all-purpose flour
½ tsp baking powder
a pinch of salt
1 small egg
⅓ cup (75 ml) milk
1 tbsp finely chopped shallots
½ tsp finely chopped and seeded red chili
2 tbsp chopped cilantro
approx. 7 oz (200 g) corn
1 tbsp butter
½ avocado, diced
3 oz (75 g) cucumber, seeded and diced
12 cherry tomatoes, cut into wedges
salt and pepper

Mix the avocado, cucumber, and cherry tomatoes. Season with salt and pepper.

Stir together the flour, baking powder, and salt. Whisk the eggs and the milk, and stir into the flour. Add shallots, chili, cilantro, and corn.

Melt the butter in a frying pan. Add a few dollops of the batter—about 1 tbsp per pancake. Cook the patties until golden brown on both sides.

Top each patty with some of the tomato mixture.
See the photo on page 36.

IN ADVANCE *See* RICOTTA PATTIES WITH PROSCIUTTO *on page 39.*

LATKES WITH APPLE &
BACON

MAKES approx. 20
TIME approx. 45 minutes

¼ cup (50 ml) all-purpose flour
a pinch of salt
¼ cup (50 ml) milk
1 small egg
7 oz (200 g) potatoes, grated
butter

2 slices of bacon
½ apple, cored and diced
1 tbsp butter
¼ cup (50 ml) cranberry sauce

Cook the bacon until crispy, and drain on paper
towels. Crumble it into pieces.

Clean the pan and sauté the apple pieces in
butter until tender. Add the cranberry sauce and
stir. Keep warm.

Whisk the flour, salt, milk, and egg to a smooth
batter. Stir in the potatoes. Melt the butter in a frying
pan. Add a few dollops of batter—about 1 tbsp per
potato patty. Cook the latkes until golden brown on
both sides.

Top each latke with the apples and bacon.
See the photo on page 36.

IN ADVANCE *See* RICOTTA PATTIES WITH
PROSCIUTTO *on page 39.*

POTATO PATTIES WITH
SALMON & HORSERADISH

MAKES approx. 30
TIME approx. 1 hour

⅔ lb (300 g) potatoes, boiled, peeled, and
    mashed
¼ cup (50 ml) all-purpose flour
3 eggs
¼ cup (50 ml) heavy cream
salt and white pepper
1 tbsp butter

HORSERADISH CREAM
½ cup (100 ml) sour cream
1 tsp grated horseradish

approx. 5 oz (150 g) smoked salmon, cut in
    fine strips
dill for garnish

Combine the horseradish with the sour cream.

Mix the mashed potato with the flour, and add
the eggs one at a time. Mix in the cream. Season
with salt and pepper. Melt the butter in a frying pan.
Add a few dollops of batter. Cook the patties until
golden brown on both sides.

Pipe or dollop the horseradish cream onto the
patties. Swirl the salmon strips to shape roses. Add a
rose to each patty, and garnish with dill.
See the photo on page 36.

IN ADVANCE *See* RICOTTA PATTIES WITH
PROSCIUTTO *on the next page.*

CARROT RÖSTI WITH FETA

MAKES approx. 30
TIME approx. 40 minutes

1 ¼ cups (300 ml) shredded carrots
¾ cup (200 ml) grated potatoes
2 scallions, chopped
1 tbsp all-purpose flour
1 egg, lightly beaten
salt and pepper
1 tbsp butter

FETA CHEESE CREAM
3 oz (75 g) feta cheese, crumbled
3 tbsp sour cream
finely chopped chives for garnish

Combine the feta cheese and sour cream. Mix
the carrots and potatoes with the scallions, flour,
and eggs. Add salt and pepper. Melt the butter
in a frying pan. Add a few dollops of batter—about
1 tbsp per rösti. Cook the rösti until golden brown
on both sides.

Top each rösti with feta. Garnish with chives.
See the photo on page 36.

RICOTTA PATTIES WITH PROSCIUTTO

MAKES approx. 24
TIME approx. 40 minutes

9 oz (250 g) ricotta
¼ cup (20 g) finely grated Parmesan
2 tbsp all-purpose flour
¼ cup (50 ml) finely chopped basil
1 egg
salt and pepper
1 egg white
1 tbsp butter

approx. 4 oz (100 g) mascarpone
1 tbsp finely chopped basil
salt and pepper

4 oz (100 g) prosciutto, cut in fine strips
fresh herbs for garnish

Mix the mascarpone and 1 tbsp of basil. Season with salt and pepper.

Mix ricotta, Parmesan, flour, remaining basil, and the whole egg. Season with salt and pepper. Beat the egg white until stiff, and fold it gently into the batter.

Melt the butter in a frying pan. Add a few dollops of the batter—about 1 tbsp per patty. Cook the patties until golden brown on both sides.

Swirl the prosciutto strips into roses. Pipe or dollop a little mascarpone on to each patty, and top with a rose of prosciutto. Garnish with fresh herbs.

See the photo on page 36.

IN ADVANCE The prepared patties can be stored in the refrigerator for 1 day or in the freezer for about 3 months. Warm them in the oven at 400˚F (200°C) for 3–4 minutes. Add the topping right before serving.

ZUCCHINI & FETA PATTIES WITH ROASTED CORN DIP

MAKES approx. 24
TIME approx. 40 minutes

7 oz (200 g) zucchini
2 scallions, sliced
2 tbsp chopped parsley
4 oz (100 g) feta cheese, crumbled
1 egg
½ cup (100 ml) all-purpose flour
1 tsp baking powder
salt and pepper
1 tbsp butter

ROASTED CORN DIP (*see the recipe on page 236*)
cilantro for garnish

Start by making the corn dip.

Grate the zucchini, and squeeze out as much liquid as possible. Mix it with the scallions, parsley, and feta. Stir in the egg.

Mix the flour and baking powder, and stir into the batter. Season with salt and pepper.

Melt the butter in a frying pan. Add a few dollops of the batter—about 1 tbsp per patty. Cook the patties until golden brown on both sides.

Top each patty with corn dip. Garnish with cilantro.

See the photo on page 36.

IN ADVANCE See RICOTTA PATTIES *to the left*.

VARY PATTIES & TOPPINGS
Try replacing the various toppings with one another on different patties. For example, caviar, crème fraîche, and red onion are also delicious on ricotta patties, and prosciutto and mascarpone pair well with blinies.

Feel free to experiment with other dips and fillings in the book (*see* DIPS *in the index*). Why not top carrot rösti with BACON & CHEDDAR SPREAD (*see the recipe on page 236*)?

PIE DOUGH

MAKES approx. 24
TIME approx. 1 hour and 15 minutes

> 6 oz (175 g) cold butter
> 1 ¾ cups (400 ml) all-purpose flour
> ice-cold water as needed
> ½ tsp salt

Mix together the butter, flour, and salt, either by hand or in a food processor. Do not overwork the dough. Add a few drops of water if the dough feels dry. Refrigerate for about 30 minutes.

Grease a mini muffin pan. Press the dough into the muffin pan to form pie shells. Refrigerate for 15 minutes more.

For fillings, follow any of the recipes below.

IN ADVANCE The pie dough can be stored in the refrigerator for about 2 days or in the freezer for about 2 months. All pies can be baked and stored in the refrigerator for about 2 days, or for about 2 months in the freezer. The pies can be served thawed to room temperature or re-heated at 300°F (150°C) for 5–10 minutes.

PROSCIUTTO & PARMESAN PIE WITH HERBS

MAKES approx. 24
TIME approx. 2 hours

> 1 batch PIE DOUGH (*see the recipe above*)
> 1 shallot, finely chopped
> 1 tsp olive oil
> 2 eggs
> ½ cup (100 ml) whole milk
> 2 tsp Dijon mustard
> 4 oz (100 g) prosciutto, finely chopped
> 3 oz (75 g) Parmesan, finely grated
> 2 tsp chopped fresh rosemary
> 1 tsp chopped fresh basil
> salt and pepper

Preheat the oven to 400°F (200°C). Prepare the dough according to the recipe.

Sauté the shallots in olive oil for a few minutes.

Beat the eggs. Stir in the milk, add the shallots and the remaining ingredients. Season with salt and pepper.

Fill the pie shells with mixture. Bake for about 20 minutes.

See the photo on page 35.

SALMON, LEEK & FETA PIE

MAKES approx. 24
TIME approx. 2 hours

> 1 batch PIE DOUGH (*see the recipe to the left*)
> ½ leek, finely chopped
> 1 tsp olive oil
> 2 eggs
> ½ cup (100 ml) whole milk
> 5 oz (125 g) smoked salmon, finely sliced
> 3 oz (75 g) feta, crumbled
> salt and pepper

Preheat the oven to 400°F (200°C). Prepare the dough according to the recipe. Sauté the leeks in olive oil for a few minutes.

Beat the eggs. Stir in the milk and add the leeks and the rest of the ingredients. Season with salt and pepper.

Fill the pie shells with the mixture. Bake for about 20 minutes.

See the photo on page 34.

MAKE A LARGE PIE INSTEAD
Although these recipes are intended as mini pies, they can, of course, be made into a large pie in a regular pie dish. You'll just need to increase the amounts to 4 eggs and ¾ cup of milk for the filling.

RICOTTA & SPINACH PIE
WITH SUN-DRIED TOMATOES

MAKES approx. 24
TIME approx. 2 hours

1 batch PIE DOUGH (*see the recipe on the left page*)
1 egg
½ cup (100 ml) whole milk
5 oz (125 g) ricotta
approx. 2 oz (40 g) fresh spinach, finely chopped
1 tbsp finely chopped fresh basil
2 tbsp pine nuts, toasted and finely chopped
4 sun-dried tomatoes in oil, finely chopped
salt and pepper

Preheat the oven to 400°F (200°C). Prepare the dough according to the recipe.

Beat the egg. Stir in the milk and add the remaining ingredients. Season with salt and pepper.

Fill the pie shells with the mixture. Bake for about 20 minutes.

See the photo on page 35.

QUICHE LORRAINE

MAKES approx. 24
TIME approx. 2 hours

1 batch PIE DOUGH (*see the recipe on the left page*)
2 eggs
½ cup (100 ml) whole milk
approx. 3 oz (75 g) smoked ham, finely chopped
3 oz (75 g) sharp cheese, grated
1 tsp Dijon mustard
salt and pepper

Preheat the oven to 400°F (200°C). Prepare the dough according to the recipe.

Whisk the eggs. Stir in the milk and add the remaining ingredients. Season with salt and pepper.

Distribute the filling into the molds. Bake for about 20 minutes.

See the photo on page 34.

CHEDDAR CHEESE &
WALNUT PIE

MAKES approx. 24
TIME approx. 2 hours

1 batch PIE DOUGH (*see the recipe on the left page*)
2 eggs
½ cup (100 ml) whole milk
5 oz (125 g) Cheddar, finely grated
½ cup (100 ml) walnuts, chopped
salt and pepper

Preheat the oven to 400°F (200°C). Prepare the dough according to the recipe.

Beat the eggs. Stir in the milk and add the cheese and walnuts. Season with salt and pepper.

Fill the pie shells with mixture. Bake for about 20 minutes.

See the photo on page 34.

SWEET POTATO & CHÈVRE
PIE WITH BACON

MAKES approx. 24
TIME approx. 2 hours

1 batch PIE DOUGH (*see the recipe on the left page*)
7 oz (200 g) sweet potatoes, peeled and diced
3 slices bacon
2 eggs
½ cup (100 ml) whole milk
4 oz (100 g) chèvre, crumbled
salt and pepper
24 sage leaves

Preheat the oven to 400°F (200°C). Prepare the dough according to the recipe.

Boil the sweet potatoes until soft—about 10 minutes. Cook the bacon until crispy and drain on paper towels. Let it cool, and crumble it into pieces.

Beat the eggs. Stir in the milk and add the bacon, chèvre, and sweet potatoes. Season with salt and pepper.

Fill the pie shells with the mixture, and garnish with sage leaves. Bake for about 20 minutes.

See the photo on page 34.

CHANTERELLE SOUP
WITH TRUFFLE OIL

CORN SOUP
WITH CHILI & CRAB

BEETROOT SOUP
WITH APPLE
& BLACKCURRANTS

CARROT SOUP WITH CURRY,
GINGER & CUMIN

CRÈME NINON
WITH SHRIMP

AJO BLANCO—
CHILLED GARLIC &
ALMOND SOUP

CHILLED TOMATO SOUP
WITH SMOKED PAPRIKA

CHILLED AVOCADO &
GRAPEFRUIT SOUP

CHILLED CUCUMBER SOUP
WITH SCALLOPS

PUMPKIN SOUP WITH CHILI &
COCONUT MILK

42

The recipes are available on pages 46–50

ASIAN POTATO SALAD WITH
BEEF & SWEET CHILI

WALDORF SALAD

LOBSTER, PINK GRAPEFRUIT &
AVOCADO SALAD

CAESAR SALAD

BEET, CHÈVRE &
PINE NUT SALAD

SALADE NIÇOISE

ORANGE, FENNEL &
OLIVE SALAD

The recipes are available on pages 51–53

ASIAN SHRIMP
CAKE SKEWERS

SWEET CHILI SAUCE

CHICKEN &
PROSCIUTTO
SKEWERS

CHICKEN, SAGE &
LEMON SKEWERS

PORK SKEWERS WITH
SATAY SAUCE

SATAY SAUCE

The recipes are available on pages 54–57

WASABI MAYO

BEEF & VEGETABLE SKEWERS

SKEWERS WITH BEETS &
HALLOUMI

LAMB SKEWERS

SESAME-CRUSTED
SALMON SKEWERS

MINT PESTO

45

SOUPS, SALADS & SKEWERS

*Soups, salads, and skewers are perfect for garden parties. Serve the soup
and salad in small glasses, bowls, or cups, and serve the skewers
either on beautiful plates or directly from the grill.*

CHILLED CUCUMBER SOUP WITH SCALLOPS

MAKES approx. 20
TIME approx. 30 minutes + 1 hour in the refrigerator

CUCUMBER SOUP
2 ¼ lbs (1 kg) cucumbers, peeled and seeded
1 ⅓ cups (300 ml) cold chicken or vegetable broth
2 tbsp white balsamic vinegar
2 cloves garlic, pressed
3 tbsp finely chopped parsley
2 tbsp finely chopped chives
1 ⅓ cups (300 ml) sour cream
salt and black pepper

10 scallops, divided
olive oil
salt and pepper

chives for garnish

Cut the cucumbers into pieces. Mix them with the broth, balsamic vinegar, garlic, parsley, and chives and blend into a smooth purée in a food processor or with a hand blender. Stir in the sour cream and season with salt and pepper. Refrigerate the soup for at least 1 hour, so that it is properly chilled before serving.

Brush the scallops with olive oil and season with salt and pepper. Heat up a grill or frying pan and sear the scallops for about 1 minute on each side. Pierce half a scallop on each toothpick.

Pour the soup into chilled tumblers, cups, or bowls, and adorn the edge with the toothpick with the half scallop. Garnish with strands of chives.

See the photo on page 42.

IN ADVANCE The soup can be stored in the refrigerator for 1 day. Scallops should be seared right before serving.

CRÈME NINON WITH SHRIMP

MAKES approx. 20
TIME approx. 40 minutes

3 shallots, finely chopped
2 tbsp olive oil
approx. 2 ½ cups (600 ml) chicken or vegetable broth
¼ cup (50 ml) dry white wine
14 oz (400 g) frozen green peas (2 ½ cups [600 ml])
salt and pepper
¾ cup (200 ml) heavy cream, whipped
20 peeled shrimp
champagne or dry sparkling white wine

Sauté the shallots in a saucepan with oil for a few minutes. Add the broth, wine, and peas. Bring to a boil. Simmer for about 3 minutes. Blend the soup in a food processor or with a hand blender. Season with salt and pepper. Keep it warm.

Skewer each shrimp with a toothpick.

Carefully fold the cream into the soup. Pour the soup into small glasses, cups, or bowls. Pour a little champagne or sparkling wine into the soup just before serving. Add a toothpick with a shrimp and serve immediately.

See the photo on page 42.

TIP The soup can also be served cold.

IN ADVANCE The soup without cream and champagne can be cooked a few hours in advance, cooled quickly in cold water, and refrigerated. Heat carefully, and add cream and champagne before serving.

CARROT SOUP WITH CURRY, GINGER & CUMIN

MAKES approx. 20
TIME approx. 40 minutes

1 onion, peeled and chopped
1 clove garlic, pressed
2 tbsp olive oil
1 ⅓ lbs (600 g) carrots, peeled and sliced
2 tbsp grated fresh ginger
2 tsp curry powder
½ tsp cumin
4 cups (1 liter) chicken or vegetable broth
salt and pepper

plain yogurt
cilantro for garnish

Sauté the onion and the garlic in olive oil for a few minutes. Add the carrots, ginger, curry powder, and cumin, and stir to combine. Pour in the broth, bring to a boil, and simmer for about 15 minutes or until the carrots are tender.

Blend the soup in a food processor or with a hand blender. Season with salt and pepper.

Pour the soup into small glasses, cups, or bowls. Top with yogurt and garnish with cilantro. Serve immediately.

See the photo on page 42.

TIP The soup can also be served cold.

IN ADVANCE The soup can be stored in the refrigerator for about 2 days or in the freezer for about 2 months.

CHILLED TOMATO SOUP WITH SMOKED PAPRIKA

MAKES approx. 20
TIME approx. 30 minutes + about 8 hours to drain

approx. 4 ½ lbs (2 kg) plum tomatoes, blanched and peeled
2 shallots, finely chopped
1 clove garlic, pressed
1 cup (250 ml) cold chicken or vegetable broth
salt and pepper
½–1 tsp paprika or Pimentón de la Vera

finely chopped basil for garnish

Mix the tomatoes, shallots, and garlic in a food processor or with a hand blender until it is a smooth purée. Let the tomato purée drain through a fine-mesh strainer (preferably overnight in the refrigerator).

Mix the drained tomato liquid with the cold broth, and season with salt, pepper, and paprika.

Pour the soup into small chilled glasses, mugs, or bowls, and garnish with basil.

See the photo on page 42.

IN ADVANCE The soup can be stored in the refrigerator for about 2 days or in the freezer for about 2 months.

PIMENTÓN DE LA VERA
Pimentón de la Vera is smoked paprika powder from Spain with a deep red color and rich aroma. The powder is traditionally used in Spanish charcuterie like chorizo, but is also used to flavor dishes with seafood, meat, chicken, and vegetables (*see* PATATAS BRAVAS *on page 103*).

BEETROOT SOUP WITH APPLE & BLACKCURRANTS

MAKES approx. 20
TIME approx. 40 minutes

- 1 onion, chopped
- 1 tbsp canola or sunflower oil
- 14 oz (400 g) fresh beets, peeled and diced
- 1 carrot, peeled and sliced
- 2 potatoes, peeled and sliced
- 1 small apple, peeled, cored, and chopped
- 2 ⅓ cups (550 ml) of chicken or vegetable broth
- 1 cup blackcurrant juice
- salt and pepper

- sour cream and chopped parsley for garnish

In a large pot, sauté the onion in oil in a large pot for a few minutes. Add the beets, carrots, potatoes, and apples, and cook for another few minutes. Pour in the broth and simmer for about 15 minutes until the vegetables are tender.

Add the blackcurrant juice and blend the soup in a food processor or with a hand blender. Add a little more broth if needed. Season with salt and pepper.

Pour the soup into small glasses, cups, or bowls. Top with sour cream just before serving, and garnish with parsley. Serve immediately.

See the photo on page 42.

TIP The soup can also be served cold.

IN ADVANCE The soup can be stored in the refrigerator for about 2 days or in the freezer for about 2 months.

CHILLED AVOCADO & GRAPEFRUIT SOUP

MAKES approx. 20
TIME approx. 30 minutes

- 1 grapefruit
- 6 avocados
- 2 tsp grated fresh ginger
- freshly squeezed juice from 2 limes
- 3 ⅓ cups (800 ml) of cold chicken or vegetable broth
- approx. ¾ cup (200 ml) ice cold water
- salt

With a sharp knife, peel the grapefruit over a bowl and catch the juice. Fillet the wedges and remove the pith. Put the pieces of grapefruit aside and squeeze the juice out of the remaining grapefruit.

Open the avocados and remove the pit. Scoop out the flesh, and mix it into a smooth paste in a food processor or hand mixer. Add the ginger, lime juice, grapefruit juice, and the cold broth, and blend a bit more. Mix in the cold water until you achieve the desired consistency. Season with salt.

Pour the soup into chilled tumblers, cups, or bowls. Garnish with grapefruit.

See the photo on page 42.

IN ADVANCE The grapefruit can be peeled and cut the day before, but the rest should be done about 1 hour before serving to avoid discoloration of the soup.

> **AVOCADO**
>
> If the avocado is not ripe, you can accelerate the ripening process by putting it in a paper bag with an apple or a tomato. Keep the bag at room temperature.
>
> To remove the pit, hold the avocado in one hand. Using a sharp knife, cut through the center of the avocado lengthwise until the knife comes in contact with the pit. Make a continuous slice around the pit until the knife meets the initial incision point. Separate the halves by carefully twisting them. Insert the knife blade into the pit, and turn it until the pit detaches from the flesh, but stays on the blade. Scoop out the flesh with a spoon.

CORN SOUP WITH CHILI & CRAB

MAKES approx. 20
TIME approx. 40 minutes

- 1 onion, chopped
- 2 cloves garlic, pressed
- 2 tbsp olive oil
- 1 tsp chopped and seeded red chili pepper
- 1 tsp chili powder
- 4 cups (1 liter) of corn, canned and drained
- 5 ¼ cups (1 ¼ liters) chicken or vegetable broth
- 6 oz (170 g) crabmeat drained
- 1 lime, zested
- 1 tsp freshly squeezed lime juice
- 2 tbsp chopped cilantro
- salt and pepper
- cilantro for garnish

In a saucepan, sauté the onion, garlic, chili, and chili powder in the oil for a few minutes. Add the corn and broth and bring to a boil. Let the soup simmer for 10–15 minutes.

Blend half of the soup in a food processor or with a hand blender. Mix it with the rest of the soup.

Let the crabmeat drain and mix it with the lime zest, lime juice, and cilantro. Add to the soup. Heat it up, and season with salt and pepper.

Pour the soup into small glasses, cups, or bowls. Garnish with cilantro. Serve immediately.

See the photo on page 42.

IN ADVANCE Without the cilantro, the soup can be stored in the refrigerator for about a day or in the freezer for about 1 month. Garnish with cilantro just before serving.

PUMPKIN SOUP WITH CHILI & COCONUT MILK

MAKES approx. 20
TIME approx. 40 minutes

- 1 onion, chopped
- 1 clove garlic, pressed
- 2 tsp chopped and seeded red chili peppers
- approx. 21 oz (600 g) pumpkin, peeled and diced
- 1 ⅓ cups (300 ml) milk
- 1 ⅓ cups (300 ml) coconut milk
- salt and pepper
- cilantro and chopped chili for garnish

Sauté the onion, garlic, and chili in oil in a saucepan for a few minutes. Add the pumpkin, milk, and coconut milk. Bring to a boil, and simmer for about 10 minutes or until the pumpkin is soft.

Blend the soup in a food processor or with a hand blender. Add more broth if needed. Season with salt and pepper.

Pour the soup into small glasses, cups, or bowls. Garnish with cilantro and some finely chopped chili.

See the photo on page 42.

TIP The soup can also be served cold.

IN ADVANCE The soup can be made and then stored in the refrigerator for about 2 days or in the freezer for about 2 months.

CHANTERELLE SOUP WITH TRUFFLE OIL

MAKES approx. 20
TIME approx. 1 hour

2 shallots, finely chopped
2 tbsp (25 g) butter
1 lb (500 g) fresh chanterelles or 11 oz (300 g)
    canned
2 cups (450 ml) chicken or vegetable broth
2 cups (450 ml) milk
⅔ cup (150 ml) dry white wine
½–¾ cup (100–200 ml) heavy cream
salt and pepper

truffle oil
fresh thyme for garnish

In a saucepan, sauté the shallots in the butter for
a few minutes. Add the mushrooms and sauté for
about 3 minutes. Pour in the broth, milk, and wine.
Simmer for about 20 minutes.

Blend everything to a smooth purée in a food
processor or with a hand blender. Pour the purée
through a fine mesh strainer. Be sure to squeeze out
all the liquid (it takes a little while). Pour the liquid
back into the saucepan, add the cream, and bring to a
boil. Season with salt and pepper.

Pour the soup into small glasses, cups, or bowls.
Drizzle a little truffle oil over the soup, and garnish
with thyme. Serve immediately.

See the photo on page 42.

IN ADVANCE The soup can be stored in the
refrigerator for about 2 days or in the freezer
for about 2 months. Drizzle with truffle oil, and
garnish with thyme before serving.

AJO BLANCO—CHILLED GARLIC & ALMOND SOUP

MAKES approx. 20
TIME approx. 1 hour + 1 hour cooling

2 tbsp olive oil
3 whole heads of garlic
1 onion, chopped
1 tbsp butter
⅔ cup (150 ml) bread crumbs (1–2 slices of
    white bread)
⅔ cup (150 ml) blanched and peeled almonds
approx. 5 ¼ cups (1 ¼ liters) chicken or
    vegetable broth
salt and pepper

10 seedless grapes, split
toasted slivered almonds for garnish

Preheat the oven to 350°F (175°C).

Grease an ovenproof dish with 1 tbsp of olive oil.

Slice ½ inch (1 cm) off the top of each garlic head,
and place them in the dish with the cut-side down.
Roast in the oven for about 30 minutes.

Sauté the onion in the remaining oil and butter
on low heat for about 20 minutes.

Remove the garlic from the oven and let it cool.

Toast the breadcrumbs and the almonds separately
in the oven or in a non-stick pan.

Carefully squeeze the garlic cloves out of their
skins. Mix them together with the onions, almonds,
and breadcrumbs in a food processor or with a hand
blender. Pour in a little of the broth and blend it
to a smooth paste. Mix with the rest of the broth.
Season with salt and pepper. Let the soup cool in the
refrigerator for at least 1 hour, so that it is properly
chilled before serving.

Pour the soup into chilled tumblers, mugs, or
bowls. Garnish with grapes and almonds.

See the photo on page 42.

CAESAR SALAD

MAKES approx. 20
TIME approx. 30 minutes

2 slices of white bread
2 tbsp olive oil
½ tsp herb salt

½ lb (250 g) chicken fillets
salt and pepper

CAESAR DRESSING
1 egg
1 clove garlic, pressed
1–2 anchovy fillets, finely chopped
1 tbsp freshly squeezed lemon juice
a few drops of Worcestershire sauce
¼–½ cup (50–100 ml) olive oil
⅔ cup (150 ml) grated Parmesan
salt and pepper

6 oz (175 g) romaine lettuce, chopped
2 oz (50 g) Parmesan for garnish

Preheat the oven to 350°F (175°C). Remove the crusts, and cut the bread into small cubes. Put the cubes in a roasting pan and toss with 1 tbsp of oil and herb salt. Toast the bread until it is golden brown. Stir occasionally.

Roast the chicken fillets in oil until cooked through. Add salt and pepper. Let cool, and cut into small pieces.

Whisk together the egg, garlic, anchovies, lemon juice, and Worcestershire sauce. Pour in the oil in a thin stream while whisking constantly. Stir in the Parmesan. Season with salt and pepper.

Mix the lettuce with croutons and chicken. Pour in the dressing a little at a time, and stir well. Divide into small glasses or bowls, and serve immediately.

See the photo on page 43.

IN ADVANCE Croutons, dressing, and chicken can be made the day before. Keep the croutons at room temperature and refrigerate the dressing and chicken. Mix the salad together right before serving.

SALADE NIÇOISE

MAKES approx. 20
TIME approx. 40 minutes

14 oz (400 g) potatoes, boiled and cooled
4 oz (100 g) green beans, lightly blanched
3–4 eggs, hard boiled
7 oz (200 g) lettuce of choice, chopped
4 oz (100 g) cherry tomatoes, cut into wedges
10 anchovies, sliced
3 oz (75 g) black olives, sliced
½ red onion, thinly sliced
6 oz (185 g) drained canned tuna

VINAIGRETTE
1 tbsp white wine vinegar
1 tbsp freshly squeezed lemon juice
2 tsp Dijon mustard
4 tbsp olive oil
salt and pepper

Peel the potatoes, and cut them and the green beans into smaller pieces. Peel the eggs and cut them into wedges.

Stir together the vinegar, lemon juice, mustard, and olive oil. Season with salt and pepper.

Mix all salad ingredients, except the eggs, with vinaigrette. Distribute the lettuce into small glasses or bowls, and top with the egg wedges.

See the photo on page 43.

IN ADVANCE The potatoes and green beans can be cooked the day before, cut into pieces, and stored in the refrigerator. The vinaigrette can also be prepared the day before. Mix the salad right before serving.

WALDORF SALAD

MAKES approx. 20
TIME approx. 30 minutes

¼ lb (120 g) bacon slices
7 oz (200 g) lettuce of choice, chopped
4 ½ oz (125 g) walnuts, roughly chopped

DRESSING
1 apple, diced
2 stalks of celery, sliced
3 tbsp sour cream
3 tbsp MAYONNAISE, store bought
 (or *see the recipe on page 74*)
2 tbsp freshly squeezed lemon juice
salt and pepper

Cook the bacon until crispy, drain on paper towels, and let cool. Crumble into small pieces.

Stir together the apple, celery, sour cream, mayonnaise, and lemon juice. Season with salt and pepper.

Layer the lettuce and the apple dressing in small glasses or bowls. Top with the bacon and walnuts.

See the photo on page 43.

IN ADVANCE The apple and celery can be cut and mixed with the sour cream, mayonnaise, and lemon, and refrigerated for a few hours. Mix the walnuts and bacon into the salad right before serving.

BEET, CHÈVRE & PINE NUT SALAD

MAKES approx. 20
TIME approx. 40 minutes

¾ lb (350 g) red, chioggia, and golden beets
approx. ⅔ lb (300 g) chèvre, crumbled
4 tbsp pine nuts, toasted
7 oz (200 g) mixed lettuce, chopped

HONEY DRESSING
4 tbsp olive oil
3 tbsp honey

sea salt

Boil each type of beet separately—otherwise they will stain each other—until they are soft (about 20–40 minutes). Let them cool, and rub or cut away the skin. Cut the beets into small wedges.

Mix the olive oil and honey.

Layer the beets, chèvre, pine nuts, and lettuce in small glasses or bowls. Drizzle with the dressing and sprinkle with a little sea salt.

See the photo on page 43.

IN ADVANCE Boil the beets the day before, and cut them into pieces. Store them separately in the refrigerator. The vinaigrette and the toasted pine nuts can be stored for several days. Mix the salad right before serving.

ASIAN POTATO SALAD WITH BEEF & SWEET CHILI

MAKES approx. 20
TIME approx. 30 minutes

1 ⅓ lbs (600 g) potatoes, boiled and cooled
⅓ lb (175 g) roast beef, shredded
10 radishes, sliced
5 oz (150 g) lettuce of choice, chopped

SWEET CHILI DRESSING
¼ cup sweet chili sauce
1 tbsp freshly squeezed lime juice
1 tsp water
2 tbsp sesame oil

toasted sesame seeds for garnish

Peel the potatoes and cut them into small pieces.

Prepare the dressing. Mix with the potatoes, beef, radishes, and lettuce. Divide into small glasses or bowls, and sprinkle with sesame seeds.

See the photo on page 43.

LOBSTER, PINK GRAPEFRUIT & AVOCADO SALAD

MAKES approx. 20
TIME approx. 25 minutes

1 pink grapefruit
⅔ lb (300 g) cooked lobster meat, lobster tail,
    or king crab
1 avocado pitted and peeled, cut
approx. 7 oz (200 g) lettuce of
    choice, chopped
½ red onion, sliced

LIME VINAIGRETTE
2 tbsp freshly squeezed lime juice
1 tbsp honey
4 tbsp olive oil
salt and pepper

Peel the grapefruit with a sharp knife. Fillet the wedges and remove the pith.

Cut the lobster meat into small pieces.

Whisk together the lime juice, honey, and olive oil. Season with salt and pepper.

Layer the ingredients for the salad in small glasses or bowls. Lightly drizzle with the vinaigrette.

See the photo on page 43.

IN ADVANCE One day in advance, you can pick the lobster meat from the shells, fillet the grapefruit, and whisk together the dressing. Refrigerate. Mix the salad just before serving.

ORANGE, FENNEL & OLIVE SALAD

MAKES approx. 20
TIME approx. 25 minutes

2 oranges (approx. 14 oz [400 g])
approx. 5 oz (150 g) fennel, finely shredded
3 oz (75 g) pitted black olives, sliced
7 oz (200 g) lettuce of choice, chopped

DRESSING
4 tbsp olive oil
2 tbsp red wine vinegar
salt and pepper

Peel the orange with a sharp knife. Fillet the wedges and remove the pith. Stir together the olive oil and vinegar. Season with salt and pepper.

Mix everything in a large bowl. Divide the salad among small glasses or bowls.

See the photo on page 43.

IN ADVANCE The fennel can be shredded and the oranges filleted the day before and stored in the refrigerator. The vinaigrette can also be mixed the day before. Mix together the salad right before serving.

LETTUCE & SPROUTS
For both flavor and aesthetics, mix different types of lettuce, and vary the flavor, color, and texture. In addition to the types of lettuce that come in different shades of green, there is the beautiful burgundy *lolla rosa* as well as *arugula*, which has a slightly bitter and peppery taste. *Romaine* and *iceberg* are a bit crispier, whereas *mache* and *boston* have softer leaves. Fresh *baby spinach* and *baby red swiss chard*, as well as sprouts such as *sunflower* and *pea sprouts*, are a beautiful and tasty addition to salads.

Lettuce regains its crispness when rinsed in cold water, then dried in a towel or salad spinner. Keep pre-washed and tossed salad in a plastic bag in the refrigerator.

LAMB SKEWERS WITH MINT PESTO

MAKES approx. 24
TIME approx. 40 minutes + 1 hour marinating

approx. 1 ⅓ lbs (600 g) lamb fillet

MARINADE
2 tbsp freshly squeezed lemon juice
3 cloves garlic, pressed
1 tsp salt
½ tsp black pepper
2 tbsp canola oil
2 tbsp chopped fresh mint

MINT PESTO
¾ cup (200 ml) fresh mint
¼ cup (50 ml) parsley
1 shallot, chopped
1 clove garlic, pressed
1 tsp lemon zest
¼–½ cup (50–100 ml) olive oil
salt and pepper

24 wooden skewers, soaked in water

Cut the lamb fillet into 1-inch (3 cm) cubes. Mix the ingredients for the marinade. Add the lamb to the marinade and refrigerate for at least 1 hour.

Mix the mint, parsley, shallot, garlic, and lemon zest in a food processor or with a hand blender. Pour in the oil in a thin stream while the machine is running. Season with salt and pepper.

Preheat the oven to 400°F (200°C). Brush an oven rack with a little oil.

Pierce the lamb on the skewers. Put directly on the oven rack and place over a baking sheet covered with foil to catch the drippings. Broil for about 10 minutes or until the meat has browned on the outside, but is still pink inside. Serve the skewers hot or cold with mint pesto.

See the photo on page 45.

IN ADVANCE The mint pesto can be prepared 2 days in advance and stored in the refrigerator. The skewers can be prepared and stored uncooked in the refrigerator for about 1 day. Cook the day they are to be served.

PORK SKEWERS WITH SATAY SAUCE

MAKES approx. 24
TIME approx. 45 minutes + at least 1 hour marinating

1 ⅓ lbs pork tenderloin (600 g), cut in strips

MARINADE
1 clove garlic, pressed
1 tbsp grated fresh ginger
½ tsp ground cumin
½ tsp ground coriander
1 tbsp brown sugar
1 tbsp canola oil
1 tsp turmeric
½ tsp salt

SATAY SAUCE
½ cup (100 ml) salted peanuts, finely chopped
¾ cup (200 ml) peanut butter
¾ cup (200 ml) coconut milk
2 tsp red curry paste
1 tsp grated fresh ginger
1 clove garlic, pressed
salt

24 wooden skewers, soaked in water

Mix the ingredients for the marinade. Place the meat in the marinade, and let it marinate in the refrigerator for at least 1 hour.

Preheat the oven to 400°F (200°C). Brush a baking rack with a little oil.

Mix all ingredients for the peanut sauce. Season with salt.

Pierce the meat on the skewers and place on a baking rack in the oven over a baking sheet covered in foil to catch the fat drippings. Broil for about 10 minutes or until the meat is cooked through. Serve the skewers either hot or cold with the sauce.

CHICKEN, SAGE & LEMON SKEWERS

MAKES approx. 24
TIME approx. 45 minutes + 1 hour marinating

approx. 1 ⅓ lbs (600 g) chicken
24 small lemon wedges
1–2 bunches sage

MARINADE
¼ cup (50 ml) olive oil
1 lemon, zested
freshly squeezed juice of ½ lemon
2 cloves garlic, pressed
2 tbsp finely chopped fresh sage
1 tsp salt
a pinch ground black pepper

24 wooden skewers, soaked in water

Cut the chicken into 1-inch (3 cm) cubes. Mix all the ingredients for the marinade. Place the chicken in the marinade, and let marinate in the refrigerator for at least 1 hour.

Preheat the oven to 400°F (200°C). Brush a baking rack with a little oil.

Start by piercing a lemon wedge on each skewer, and continue with 3 pieces of chicken and a sage leaf skewered between each piece. Place the skewers on the baking rack, and place in the oven over a baking sheet covered in foil to catch the drippings. Broil for 10–15 minutes or until the chicken is cooked through. Serve the chicken skewers hot or cold.

See the photo on page 44.

IN ADVANCE The chicken can be marinated and covered in the refrigerator for 1 day. Prepare the skewers on the day they are to be served. They can be grilled a few hours before serving if they are not to be served hot.

CHICKEN & PROSCIUTTO SKEWERS

MAKES approx. 24
TIME approx. 45 minutes

¾–1 lb (350–400 g) chicken fillets
1 tbsp olive oil
approx. 4 oz (100 g) sliced prosciutto
2 tbsp balsamic vinegar
½ tsp thyme
a pinch of ground black pepper
¼ cup (50 ml) olive oil

24 wooden skewers, soaked in water

Preheat the oven to 400°F (200°C). Brush a baking rack with a bit of oil.

Cut the chicken into strips. Cut the prosciutto lengthwise into approximately 1-inch (3 cm) thick strips.

Whisk together the balsamic vinegar, thyme, pepper, and olive oil. Combine with the chicken.

Wrap the prosciutto around the chicken and thread onto skewers. Place the skewers on the baking rack and place in the oven over a baking sheet covered with foil to catch the drippings. Broil for 10–15 minutes or until cooked through. Serve the chicken skewers hot or cold.

See the photo on page 44.

IN ADVANCE The chicken skewers can be made the same day if kept cold.

COOKING & SERVING SKEWERS
Skewers can be cooked either in the oven or on a grill. To keep wooden skewers from catching fire on the barbecue, it is important to first soak them in water for about 30 minutes.

A nice way to socialize at a garden party is to let the guests gather around the grill with a cool summer drink while grilling their own skewers.

BEEF & VEGETABLE SKEWERS

MAKES approx. 24
TIME approx. 45 minutes + 1 hour marinating

approx. 14 oz (400 g) beef tenderloin
2 bell peppers of any color, seeded
1 red onion, peeled
24 small, button mushrooms (approx. 8 ½ oz
   [240 g])

TERIYAKI MARINADE
½ cup (100 ml) teriyaki sauce
½ cup (100 ml) honey
1 clove garlic, pressed
1 tbsp grated fresh ginger

24 wooden skewers, soaked in water

Mix the ingredients for the marinade.

Cut the meat into 1-inch (3 cm) cubes. Cut the bell peppers into 1 ½-inch (4 cm) pieces and the onion into wedges.

Mix the meat, peppers, onion, and mushrooms with the marinade. Let it marinate in the refrigerator for at least 1 hour.

Preheat the oven to 400°F (200°C). Brush a baking rack with oil.

Pierce a piece of meat, pepper, onion, and mushroom on a wooden skewer. Leave a bit of room between the pieces. Place the skewers on the rack and put it in the oven over a baking sheet covered with foil to catch the drippings. Broil for about 10 minutes or until the meat is cooked through. Serve the skewers hot or cold.

See the photo on page 45.

TIP The skewers are also good to dip into a tasty sauce, such as CREAMY SWEET CHILI SAUCE (*see the recipe on page 169*).

IN ADVANCE The skewers can be prepared and stored uncooked in the refrigerator for about 1 day. Cook the same day they are to be served.

SKEWERS WITH BEETS & HALLOUMI

MAKES approx. 24
TIME approx. 1 hour

1 ½ lbs (700 g) red, chioggia, and golden beets
21 oz (600 g) halloumi
2 tbsp olive oil
2 tbsp honey
1 tbsp Dijon mustard
24 rosemary sprigs

24 wooden skewers, soaked in water

Preheat the oven to 400°F (200°C). Brush a baking rack with a bit of oil.

Boil each kind of beet separately until soft. Cool slightly. Peel and cut them into small wedges. Place the beets into three separate bowls, so that their colors do not mix. Cut the halloumi into 48 squares.

Mix the olive oil, honey, and Dijon mustard. Divide the oil mixture into the 3 bowls of beets and mix.

Pierce the beets on the skewers with a piece of halloumi in between. Stick the rosemary into the beet at the bottom end of the skewer (the end you hold). Put the skewers on the baking rack and place in the oven over a baking sheet covered with foil to catch the drippings. Broil for about 10 minutes or until the halloumi is golden brown. Serve the skewers hot or cold.

See the photo on page 45.

TIP Chioggia and golden beets can be difficult to find, in which case you can use red beets. These skewers are also great to dip into a tasty sauce, such as CHIVE DIP or CREAMY PESTO DIP (*see the recipe on page 198*).

IN ADVANCE The beets can be cooked and marinated in a separate dish a day in advance. The skewers can be prepared and left at room temperature for an hour before grilling or cooking.

SESAME-CRUSTED SALMON SKEWERS

MAKES approx. 24
TIME approx. 45 minutes

approx. 1 ½ lbs (700 g) salmon fillet
2 tbsp canola oil
a few drops of sesame oil
salt and pepper
½ cup (100 ml) sesame seeds, black and white
2 oz (50 g) nigiri (Japanese pickled ginger)

WASABI MAYO
½ cup (100 ml) MAYONNAISE, store bought
    (*or see the recipe on page 74*)
¼ cup (50 ml) sour cream
approx. 2 tsp wasabi paste

24 wooden skewers, soaked in water

Preheat the oven to 400°F (200°C). Cover a baking sheet with aluminum foil, and brush with a little oil.

Mix the ingredients for the wasabi dip.

Cut the salmon into 1-inch (3 cm) cubes. Combine the canola oil and sesame oil, and mix with the salmon. Season with salt and pepper. Mix the salmon and sesame seeds in a plastic bag, and shake until the salmon is completely covered with the seeds. Pierce 2-3 salmon pieces on each skewer with a slice of nigiri in between.

Place the skewers on the baking sheet and broil in the oven for about 10 minutes. Serve hot or cold with the wasabi dip.

See the photo on page 45.

IN ADVANCE If the salmon skewers are to be eaten hot, they taste best when freshly grilled. If they are to be eaten cold, grill them the same day. The wasabi dip can be prepared the day before serving and stored in the refrigerator.

ASIAN SHRIMP CAKE SKEWERS

MAKES approx. 24
TIME approx. 1 hour + thawing of frozen shrimp

approx. 1 ¾ lbs (800 g) raw shrimp, peeled
¼ cup (50 ml) brown sugar
2 cloves garlic, pressed
2 tbsp fish sauce
2 tbsp sweet chili sauce
2 stalks lemongrass (only the white part), finely grated
2 egg whites, lightly beaten

24 stalks lemongrass for skewers

If the shrimp are frozen, be sure to squeeze out excess liquid. Mix the shrimp with brown sugar, garlic, fish sauce, sweet chili sauce, and grated lemon-grass in a food processor. Blend to a smooth mixture. Mix the egg whites into the mixture and refrigerate for about 30 minutes.

Preheat the oven to 400°F (200°C). Cover a baking sheet with aluminum foil, and brush with a little oil.

Shape the shrimp mixture with wet hands around the white end of the lemongrass. Place the skewers on the baking sheet and broil in the oven for about 10 minutes or until cooked through. Turn after 5 minutes.

Serve immediately with sweet chili sauce or NUOC CHAM sauce (*see the recipe on page 167*).

See the photo on page 44.

IN ADVANCE Raw shrimp should be handled carefully to avoid food poisoning. The shrimp mixture can be made the day before and stored in the refrigerator, but should not be put on the lemongrass until 1 hour before cooking in the oven.

MORE SKEWERS

→ LAMB SHISH KEBABS (*see the recipe on page 121*)
→ SHISH KEBABS (*see the recipe on page 121*)
→ CORN DOGS (*see the recipe on page 133*)

CELERIAC PURÉE WITH BACON & APPLE

SCALLOPS IN CHAMPAGNE SAUCE

PARSNIP PURÉE WITH SALMON & CHEDDAR CRISPS

JERUSALEM ARTICHOKE GNOCCHI WITH MUSHROOM SAUCE

ZUCCHINI WITH SHRIMP & PROSCIUTTO

LAMB SAUSAGE WITH SWEET POTATO PURÉE & CHÉVRE

POTATO PURÉE WITH LOBSTER & HERB BUTTER

LAMB FILLET WITH CREAMY HERB POLENTA

58

The recipes are available on pages 60–63

ASPARAGUS MOUSSE WITH
PARMESAN CRISPS

CAULIFLOWER MOUSSE
WITH PROSCIUTTO CHIPS

SALMON MOUSSE WITH CUCUMBER &
CELERY SALAD

SPINACH PANNA COTTA WITH
CAVIAR & QUAIL EGGS

The recipes are available on pages 64–65

AMUSE-BOUCHE

*In French "amuse-bouche" literally means "mouth entertainer." Amuse-bouches are
simply small appetizers served before the first course at fancy restaurants.
What distinguishes an amuse-bouche from a starter is that it is smaller,
and you neither order nor pay for it. We find that they make an ideal
hors d'oeuvre at a posh cocktail party!*

CELERIAC PURÉE WITH BACON & APPLE

MAKES approx. 24
TIME approx. 45 minutes

⅔ lb (300 g) celeriac, peeled and diced
4 oz (100 g) mealy potatoes, peeled and diced
approx. 4 cups (1 liter) chicken broth
2 tbsp butter
salt and pepper

6 oz (175 g) bacon or pancetta, diced
1 small apple, cored and diced
1 tbsp butter

Boil the celeriac and potatoes in the broth until
tender. Strain and save the broth.

Mash the celeriac and potatoes with butter. Add
the broth a little at a time, and blend to a smooth
purée. Season with salt and pepper and keep warm.

Cook the bacon crispy, and place on paper towels
to drain.

Sauté the apple pieces in the butter for about
30 seconds.

Spoon the purée on small plates, decorative
spoons, or in small bowls. Top with bacon and apple.
Serve immediately.

See the photo on page 58.

IN ADVANCE Everything can be made the
day before and refrigerated. Heat up separately
before serving.

LAMB SAUSAGE WITH SWEET POTATO PURÉE & CHÈVRE

MAKES approx. 24
TIME approx. 45 minutes

14 oz (400 g) sweet potatoes, peeled and diced
2 tbsp butter
2 tbsp heavy cream
salt and pepper

4 oz (100 g) lamb sausage
1 tbsp olive oil
3 oz (75 g) chèvre, crumbled
4 tbsp crispy fried onions
fresh thyme for garnish

Boil the sweet potatoes in lightly salted water until
soft, about 10–15 minutes. Drain and add the butter
and cream. Blend to a smooth purée. Season with salt
and pepper and keep warm.

Cook the lamb sausage in oil. Cut it into slices.

Spoon some sweet potato purée on small plates,
decorative spoons, or small bowls. Add the sausage
and top with chèvre and fried onions. Garnish with
thyme. Serve immediately.

See the photo on page 58.

IN ADVANCE Everything can be prepared the day
before and kept in the refrigerator. Heat up the
purée and the sausage before serving.

JERUSALEM ARTICHOKE GNOCCHI WITH MUSHROOM SAUCE

MAKES approx. 24
TIME approx. 1 ½ hours

GNOCCHI

5 oz (150 g) Jerusalem artichokes, peeled
2 oz (50 g) mealy potatoes, peeled
approx. ¾ cup (200 ml) all-purpose flour
1 small egg
1 tsp olive oil
1 ¾ cups (50 g) grated Parmesan
1 tsp salt

MUSHROOM SAUCE

1 shallot, finely chopped
2 tsp butter
5 oz (150 g) mushrooms, chopped
½ apple, cored and diced
½ cup heavy cream
1 tbsp sherry
1 tsp beef or mushroom broth
1 tbsp chopped chives
salt and pepper

Boil the artichokes and potatoes in lightly salted water until soft. Drain and mash the vegetables. Mix the vegetables with most of the flour, and add the eggs, olive oil, Parmesan, and salt. Blend to a smooth dough. Add more flour if needed.

Put the dough on a floured surface. Shape the dough into a long roll 1 inch in diameter (2 ½ cm) and cut approx. 1-inch (2 ½ cm) long pieces. Press the gnocchi lightly with a fork, so that a striped pattern is formed on one side. Place on a baking sheet and sprinkle a little flour on top.

Sauté the shallot for the mushroom sauce in butter until soft. Add the mushrooms and cook for a couple of minutes. Stir in the apple, cream, sherry, and broth. Bring to a boil and simmer for a few minutes. Season with salt and pepper, and keep it warm.

Cook the gnocchi a few at a time in boiling salted water. When they float to the surface (after about 3 minutes), they are cooked. Retrieve with a slotted spoon and drain.

Place the gnocchi on small plates, spoons, or in small bowls, and top with the mushroom sauce. Serve immediately.

See the photo on page 58.

IN ADVANCE Gnocchi can be prepared and refrigerated uncooked for 1 day. Even the mushroom sauce can be made the day before and stored in the refrigerator. Cook the gnocchi and heat up the mushroom sauce before serving.

PARSNIP PURÉE WITH SALMON & CHEDDAR CRISPS

MAKES approx. 24
TIME approx. 40 minutes

PARSNIP PURÉE

1 shallot, finely chopped
1 tbsp butter
14 oz (400 g) parsnips, peeled and diced
2 cups (500 ml) chicken broth
2 tbsp heavy cream
salt and pepper

approx. 5 oz (150 g) smoked salmon, sliced
⅓ batch CHEDDAR & CARAWAY CRISPS (*see the recipe on page 286*)

Sauté the shallot in butter in a saucepan for a few minutes. Add the parsnips and cook for another few minutes.

Pour in the chicken broth, and cook until the parsnips are soft, about 10 minutes. Strain and mix the parsnips and cream into a smooth purée. Season with salt and pepper. Keep warm.

Cut the salmon into strips, and swirl together into small salmon roses. Crumble the cheese crisps.

Spoon the parsnip purée on small plates, spoons, or in small bowls. Top with a salmon rose, and sprinkle the cheese crumbles. Serve immediately.

See the photo on page 58.

IN ADVANCE The purée can be prepared and stored in the refrigerator for 1 day. Heat up before serving.

LAMB FILLET WITH CREAMY HERB POLENTA

MAKES approx. 24
TIME approx. 45 minutes

approx. 4 oz (100 g) lamb tenderloin
1 tbsp butter
salt and pepper

HERB POLENTA
1 cup (250 ml) chicken broth
⅓ cup (75 ml) polenta
1 tsp finely chopped fresh thyme
1 tsp finely chopped fresh sage
½ tsp finely chopped fresh rosemary
2 tbsp grated Parmesan
1 tbsp butter
½ cup (100 ml) heavy cream
salt and pepper

fresh herbs for garnish

Brown the lamb tenderloin in butter and cook until medium-rare. Season with salt and pepper. Let rest in foil for about 10 minutes.

Boil the broth. Add the polenta, cook, and stir for about 10 minutes or until the polenta is soft. Add herbs, Parmesan, butter, cream, and stir. Season with salt and pepper.

Cut the meat into thin slices.

Serve the creamy polenta on small plates, spoons, or in small bowls. Top with a slice of lamb and garnish with fresh herbs. Serve immediately.

See the photo on page 58.

IN ADVANCE This amuse-bouche tastes best when served freshly prepared.

POTATO PURÉE WITH LOBSTER & HERB BUTTER

MAKES approx. 24
TIME approx. 40 min. + time to make flavored butter

POTATO PURÉE
½ lb (250 g) mealy potatoes, peeled
1 tbsp butter
½ cup (100 ml) heavy cream
salt and white pepper

4 oz (100 g) cooked lobster, cut into small pieces
4 tbsp melted FLAVORED BUTTER
LEMON & CHIVE (*see the recipe page 246*)

Boil the potatoes in lightly salted water. Drain and mash the potatoes. Mix in the butter and cream, and beat into a fluffy purée. Season with salt and white pepper.

Spoon the potato purée on small plates, spoons, or small bowls. Add the pieces of lobster and drizzle with herb butter. Serve immediately.

See the photo on page 58.

IN ADVANCE The purée and herb butter can be prepared the day before and kept in the refrigerator. Heat up the purée and the melted herb butter before serving.

SERVING LARGER PORTIONS
Although the focus of this book is finger food—food in miniature—many of the recipes can also be served as a main course—especially these amuse-bouche recipes.

For example, each dish in the page 58 photo is enough to serve as two main courses.

The dishes that are served in small glasses on page 59 can also be offered as 8–12 starters.

ZUCCHINI WITH SHRIMP & PROSCIUTTO

MAKES approx. 24
TIME approx. 45 minutes

approx. 1 oz (30 g) prosciutto
24 fresh shrimp, peeled (approx. ¾ lb [350 g])
zest from ½–1 lemon
2 tbsp finely chopped parsley

ZUCCHINI DIP
¼ cup (50 ml) finely chopped leeks
1 small clove garlic, pressed

2 tbsp olive oil
7 oz (200 g) zucchini, diced
2 tbsp chopped basil
salt and pepper

Preheat the oven to 440°F (225°C).

Grill the prosciutto slices in the oven for about 5 minutes.

Be sure to watch them, so they don't burn. Let cool, and crumble into small pieces.

Stir together the lemon zest and parsley.

Sauté the leeks and the garlic in 1 tbsp of the olive oil for a few minutes. Add the zucchini, and cook for another few minutes. Stir in the basil, and season with salt and pepper. Keep warm.

Sauté the shrimp on high heat in the remaining oil until they are cooked through.

Add the zucchini and stir. Spoon the zucchini and shrimp mixture on small plates, spoons, or in small bowls. Top with prosciutto crumbs and lemon zest and parsley. Serve immediately.

See the photo on page 58.

IN ADVANCE The prosciutto and zucchini dip can be prepared the day before. Keep the zucchini cold, and heat it up before serving. Sauté the prawns right before serving.

SCALLOPS IN CHAMPAGNE SAUCE

MAKES approx. 24
TIME approx. 45 minutes

24 scallops (approx. ¾ lb [350 g])
salt and pepper
1 tbsp olive oil

CHAMPAGNE SAUCE
1 shallot, finely chopped
1 tbsp butter
½ cup (100 ml) white wine
1 ¾ cups (400 ml) fish stock
1 ⅓ cups (300 ml) heavy cream
1 tbsp cornstarch
1 tsp freshly squeezed lemon juice
½ cup (100 ml) Champagne or sparkling
   white wine
salt and white pepper

Sauté the shallot in the butter until it softens without browning. Pour in the wine and stock, and simmer until the liquid has reduced by half. Strain the onion, add ¾ cup (200 ml) cream, and cook for about 10 minutes. Thicken the sauce with cornstarch. Add the lemon juice, and season with salt and pepper. Keep the sauce warm.

Whip the remaining cream.

Season the scallops with salt and pepper. Heat up the oil in a frying pan, and sauté the scallops for about 1 minute on each side.

Fold the whipped cream into the sauce, and stir in the Champagne. Pour the sauce into spoons or small bowls. Place a scallop in the sauce. Serve immediately.

See the photo on page 58.

IN ADVANCE This amuse-bouche tastes best when served freshly prepared.

SPINACH PANNA COTTA
WITH CAVIAR & QUAIL EGGS

MAKES approx. 20
TIME approx. 15 min. + 3 hrs. in the refrigerator

SPINACH PANNA COTTA

1 tsp unflavored gelatin powder
2 tbsp water
7 oz (200 g) baby spinach
1 ¾ cups (400 ml) heavy cream
½ cup (100 ml) chicken broth

10 quail or small eggs, boiled and peeled
approx. 2 oz (50 g) caviar or fish roe

dill for garnish

Soften the gelatin in a bowl with 2 tbsp cold water.

Blanch the spinach for about 1 minute and drain.

Boil the cream and the broth. Dissolve the gelatin in the warm cream and add spinach. Mix to a smooth cream in a food processor or with a hand blender.

Pour into small glasses or bowls. Refrigerate for at least 3 hours or until the panna cotta is set.

Cut the eggs in half.

Top the panna cotta with a dollop of caviar, one egg half, and a sprig of dill.

See the photo on page 59.

IN ADVANCE The panna cotta and the cooked eggs can be stored in the refrigerator for 1 day.

CAULIFLOWER MOUSSE WITH
PROSCIUTTO CHIPS

MAKES approx. 20
TIME approx. 25 min. + 2 hrs. in the refrigerator

CAULIFLOWER MOUSSE

½ tsp unflavored gelatin powder
1 tbsp water
2 shallots, finely chopped
3 tbsp butter
14 oz (400 g) cauliflower, in small florets
4 cups (1 liter) chicken broth
2 cups (500 ml) heavy cream
salt and pepper

2 oz (50 g) prosciutto
1 slice of day-old white bread
2 tbsp finely chopped chives

Soften the gelatin in a bowl with 1 tbsp cold water.

Sauté the shallots in 1 tbsp of butter for a few minutes, then add the cauliflower and the broth. Bring to a boil, and simmer until the cauliflower is soft. Strain the broth, and mix the cauliflower with 2 tbsp butter into a purée.

Heat the cream and stir in the gelatin. Mix the cream with the cauliflower purée until smooth. Season with salt and pepper.

Divide into small glasses or bowls. Refrigerate for about 2 hours or until set.

Preheat the oven to 440°F (225°C). Roast the prosciutto slices in the oven for about 5 minutes. Keep an eye on them, so they do not burn. Let cool and break into smaller pieces.

Cut the bread into pieces, and roast it in the oven until golden brown. Let cool and crumble.

Mix the breadcrumbs and chives and sprinkle over the cauliflower mousse. Press a prosciutto chip down into each glass.

See the photo on page 59.

IN ADVANCE The mousse can be prepared the day before and stored in the refrigerator. The prosciutto and the breadcrumbs can be stored at room temperature for 1 day. Garnish just before serving.

SALMON MOUSSE WITH
CUCUMBER & CELERY SALAD

MAKES approx. 20
TIME approx. 40 min. + 2 hrs. in the refrigerator

SALMON MOUSSE
½ tsp unflavored gelatin powder
1 tbsp water
1 ⅓ cups (300 ml) fish stock
14 oz (400 g) smoked salmon
¾ cup (200 ml) heavy cream, whipped
salt and white pepper

CUCUMBER & CELERY SALAD
¾ cup (200 ml) finely diced cucumber
½ cup (100 ml) finely diced celery
1 tsp olive oil
1 tsp lemon zest
1 tsp freshly squeezed lemon juice
1 tbsp finely chopped dill
salt and pepper
dill for garnish

Combine the ingredients for the cucumber and
celery salad. Soften the gelatin in a bowl with 1 tbsp
cold water.

Boil the broth and stir in the gelatin. Allow to
slightly cool.

Mix the salmon to a smooth consistency in a
food processor or with a hand blender. Add the stock
and blend for another minute. Fold in the whipped
cream. Season with salt and pepper.

Spoon the cucumber salad into the bottom
of small glasses. Pipe the salmon mousse on
top. Refrigerate for at least 2 hours until the
mousse is set.

Garnish with dill.

See the photo on page 59.

IN ADVANCE The dish without the dill garnish
can be prepared and kept in the refrigerator
for 4–5 hours before serving.

ASPARAGUS MOUSSE WITH
PARMESAN CRISPS

MAKES approx. 20
TIME approx. 45 min. + 2 hrs. in the refrigerator

ASPARAGUS MOUSSE
1 tsp of unflavored gelatin powder
3 tbsp water
14 oz (400 g) green asparagus
½ cup (100 ml) chicken broth
½ cup (100 ml) heavy cream
3 oz (75 g) Parmesan, grated
20 asparagus tips for garnish

Soften the gelatin in a bowl with 3 tbsp cold water.

Blanch the asparagus in salted water for 3–5
minutes or until soft. Rinse in cold water, and purée
in a food processor or with a hand blender.

Heat the broth and add the gelatin. Remove
from the heat and let cool slightly. Mix the broth
with the asparagus purée. Let cool completely, but
don't let it set.

Whip the cream, and fold into the asparagus
purée. Season with salt and pepper.

Pipe the asparagus mousse into small glasses.
Refrigerate for at least 2 hours or until set.

Preheat the oven to 440°F (225°C). Sprinkle
the cheese in a thin layer on a baking tray lined
with parchment paper. Bake in the oven until the
cheese has melted—3–5 minutes. Watch that it
does not burn. Allow to cool, and then break it into
smaller pieces.

Blanch the asparagus buds for about 1 minute in
salted water, and rinse in cold water. Press down an
asparagus tip and a piece of Parmesan into each glass
of mousse.

See the photo on page 59.

IN ADVANCE The mousse and the cooked
asparagus tips can be kept cold for one day. The
Parmesan crisps can be made the day before.

BAKED CHILI &
LEMONGRASS MUSSELS

BAKED LEMON &
GARLIC MUSSELS

OYSTERS ROCKEFELLER

The recipes are available on pages 82–83

GRILLED SHRIMP WITH CHILI & CHÈVRE

SCALLOPS WITH
BAKED TOMATOES

GRILLED SESAME-CRUSTED TUNA

FINN CRISP BREAD WITH COTTAGE
CHEESE & MUSSELS

KIPPER & CREAM CHEESE BALLS

BACON-WRAPPED SCALLOPS

CRAB CAKES

ARTICHOKE WITH
CRAYFISH & FENNEL

GRILLED SESAME-CRUSTED
SALMON

The recipes are available on pages 76–78

CEVICHE

The recipe is available on page 75

SHRIMP WITH DIPPING SAUCES

RHODE ISLAND

TARTAR SAUCE

GINGER &
LIME SAUCE

COCKTAIL SAUCE

DILL & LEMON AIOLI

The recipes are available on page 74

69

CAJUN-FRIED OYSTERS

The recipe is available on page 82

CANAPÉS

CRAYFISH & SWEET CHILI

CREAMY "SKAGEN" SHRIMP

EGG & MACKEREL

CAVIAR, SOUR CREAM &
RED ONION

CRAB & APPLE

HORSERADISH CREAM &
SALMON

SMOKED SALMON SPREAD

CAVIAR SPREAD

SALMON TARTAR

The recipes are available on pages 79–81

MIGNONETTE

OYSTERS WITH
LEMON GRANITÉ

TARRAGON &
MUSTARD SAUCE

GINGER SAUCE

CHILI &
SESAME SAUCE

The recipes are are available on page 73

FISH & SEAFOOD

Shrimp, oysters, crab, scallops, salmon, tuna . . . Given the bounty of our oceans and lakes, we could write a whole book on this theme. Here, however, we have chosen to share with you our absolute favorite recipes—with influences from all around the world.

OYSTERS

MAKES approx. 12
TIME approx. 30 min. + 5 min. for the sauce of your choice

Oysters should be opened carefully. It is said that the most common injury in French emergency rooms are men who come in with cuts on their hands after opening oysters!

> 12 oysters
> sauces and sides of your choice, *see recipes below*

Use an oyster knife or a knife with a short blade. With a kitchen towel, grip the oyster firmly, with the flat side facing up. Carefully insert the knife near the hinge—remember to keep the knife away from your body—and twist the knife until the shell opens up. Slide the knife along the shell opening to sever the muscle from the top shell. Be careful—it's easy to cut yourself on the sharp edges. Lift the lid and gently loosen the oyster meat without letting the juice run out.

Serve oysters on a bed of ice with one or more sauces.

See the photo on page 72.

IN ADVANCE The oysters can be opened and placed on ice 1 hour in advance before serving.

MIGNONETTE (approx. ½ cup [100 ml])
> ½ cup (100 ml) red wine vinegar
> 1 shallot, finely chopped
> salt and black pepper
> lemon wedges

Stir together the vinegar and shallot, and season with salt and pepper. Serve with lemon wedges to squeeze on the oysters.

CHILI & SESAME SAUCE (approx. ½ cup [100 ml])
> ¼ cup (50 ml) sweet chili sauce
> 2 tsp sesame oil
> 1 tbsp freshly squeezed lime juice
> 1 tsp water

Stir together all ingredients.

GINGER SAUCE (approx. ½ cup [100 ml])
> 3 tbsp rice vinegar
> 2 tsp finely grated fresh ginger
> 2 tsp finely chopped scallions
> 2 tsp light soy sauce

Stir together all ingredients.

TARRAGON & MUSTARD SAUCE (approx. ⅔ cup [150 ml])
> ½ cup (100 ml) MAYONNAISE, store bought
> (or *see the recipe on page 74*)
> 1 tbsp Dijon mustard
> ½ tbsp mustard
> 1 tbsp chopped tarragon
> salt and pepper

Mix the mayonnaise, mustard, and tarragon. Season with salt and pepper.

LEMON GRANITÉ
> 1 ⅓ cups (300 ml) freshly squeezed lemon juice
> ½ cup (100 ml) red wine vinegar

Mix the lemon juice and vinegar, and freeze it. Shave the frozen liquid with a fork and layer the granité on the oysters. Serve immediately.

IN ADVANCE The sauces can be stored in the refrigerator for about 2 days before serving. The granité can be stored in the freezer for several months.

SHRIMP WITH DIPPING SAUCES

MAKES approx. 1 lb (600 g)
TIME approx. 20 min. + 5 min. for the sauce of
   your choice

approx. 1 lb (600 g) cooked shrimp
optional sauce (*see the recipe below*)

Peel the shrimp and put them in a bowl. Serve with
a few different sauces for dipping.
   See the photo on page 69.

HOME-MADE MAYONNAISE (approx. ¾ cup
[200 ml])
   1 egg yolk
   1 tsp white wine vinegar
   ½ tsp Dijon mustard
   2 pinches of salt
   ½ pinch of freshly ground white pepper
   ⅔ cup (150 ml) canola oil, or half canola oil
      and half olive oil

Whisk the egg yolk, vinegar, mustard, salt, and pepper
in a bowl. Add the oil in a thin stream, a little at a
time, while beating continuously—either by hand,
using an electric mixer, or a hand blender.
   Is not pictured.

TIP Mayonnaise can split when adding the oil too
quickly or if the ingredients are not at the same
temperature. In order to save the split mayonnaise's
consistency, start with one egg yolk and one
teaspoon of mustard in a bowl, and while slowly and
constantly whipping, add the split mayonnaise a little
at a time.

RHODE ISLAND (approx. 1 ⅓ cups [300 ml])
   ½ cup (100 ml) mayonnaise, store bought
      (or *see the recipe above*)
   ½ cup (100 ml) sour cream
   2–3 tbsp ketchup
   1 tbsp chopped parsley
   1 tbsp sweet relish
   salt and pepper

Stir together the mayonnaise, sour cream, ketchup,
parsley, and relish. Season with salt and pepper.

TARTAR SAUCE (approx. 1 ⅓ cups [300 ml])
   ¾ cup (200 ml) **MAYONNAISE, store bought**
      (or *see the recipe to the left*)
   3 tbsp sweet relish
   1 tbsp freshly squeezed lemon juice
   1 ½ tsp Dijon mustard
   2 tsp chopped parsley
   salt and pepper

Mix the mayonnaise, relish, lemon juice, mustard, and
parsley. Season with salt and pepper.

COCKTAIL SAUCE (approx. 1 ⅓ cups [300 ml])
   ¾ cup (200 ml) ketchup
   3 tbsp grated horseradish
   2 tbsp freshly squeezed lemon juice
   3–4 drops of Tabasco sauce
   salt and pepper

Mix the ketchup, horseradish, lemon juice, and
Tabasco sauce. Season with salt and pepper.

DILL & LEMON AIOLI (approx. 1 ⅓ cups [300 ml])
   1 ⅓ cups (300 ml) **MAYONNAISE, store bought**
      (or *see the recipe to the left*)
   1 clove garlic, pressed
   2 tbsp chopped dill
   1 tbsp freshly squeezed lemon juice
   ½ lemon, zested
   salt and lemon pepper

Mix the mayonnaise, garlic, dill, lemon juice, and
peel. Season with salt and lemon pepper.

GINGER & LIME SAUCE (about 1 ⅓ cups [300 ml])
   1 ⅓ cups (300 ml) plain low-fat yogurt
   1 tbsp honey
   1 tsp grated fresh ginger
   1 tbsp freshly squeezed lime juice

Mix all ingredients.

IN ADVANCE The sauces can be stored in the
refrigerator for about 2 days. The shrimp should be
peeled on the same day and stored in the refrigerator.

CEVICHE

MAKES approx. 24

TIME approx. 20 minutes + 2 hours marinating

7 oz (200 g) calamari, cut into rings
7 oz (200 g) fresh salmon, diced
11 oz (300 g) fresh cod fillets, diced
2 cloves garlic, pressed
1 tbsp finely chopped red chili, seeded
3 tbsp chopped cilantro
4 ½ oz (125 g) mango, diced
freshly squeezed juice from 2 limes
salt and pepper

cilantro leaves for garnish

Mix the calamari, salmon, cod, garlic, chili, cilantro, mango, and lime juice. Stir gently, and let marinate in the refrigerator for a few hours. Season with salt and pepper.

Spoon the cold ceviche into glasses or small bowls. Garnish with cilantro.

See the photo on page 68.

IN ADVANCE The ceviche should be made the same day and stored in the refrigerator. To avoid any possible parasites in raw fish, *see* RAW FISH in the text box to the right.

CEVICHE

Ceviche is a Peruvian dish in which raw fish is marinated in the juice of lime or lemon. Before the Spanish conquistadors introduced lime, it is said that the Incas used chicha, a local fermented corn drink. Today, ceviche is prepared in many different ways with different ingredients, but the basic ingredients are always fish, chili, and lime or lemon juice.

RAW FISH

Harmful parasites that may be present in raw fish are killed when the fish is either frozen or heated to 160°F (70°C). Therefore, fish that is to be eaten raw (e.g., ceviche or as sushi), or is to be cured or lightly marinated, must be first frozen for 3 days at 0°F (−18°C). Ask your fishmonger how fresh the fish is and what he or she recommends. Remember to always keep seafood cold.

✦

KALIX BLEAK ROE

The Swedish delicacy "löjrom"—Kalix caviar—comes from the roe of whitefish Coregonus albula. Since 2010, this has the status of Protected Designation of Origin (PDO) issued by the European Union, giving the producer the exclusive right to use the name "Kalix bleak roe."

✦

MUSSELS & OYSTERS

Only use live mussels, which you can easily check by tapping the mussel shells with your finger. Those that close shut are alive; those that don't should be discarded, as well as any with broken shells. When the mussels are fully cooked, the shell opens. Those that do not open should be discarded.

Raw oysters and mussels that are not completely cooked can contain bacteria and viruses that cause food poisoning.

Oysters are extremely sensitive and should be kept for as short a time as possible after purchasing. Put them in the refrigerator on a hard surface, and cover them with damp newspaper. Place something heavy on top of them so that the shells don't open and the liquid doesn't flow out.

CRAB CAKES

MAKES approx. 24
TIME approx. 40 minutes

6 oz (170 g) cooked crabmeat
¼ cup (50 ml) mayonnaise
1 tbsp Dijon mustard
a few drops of Tabasco sauce
1 tbsp Worcestershire sauce
½ tsp dried thyme
½ tsp ground ginger
1 tsp paprika

crumbs from approx. 10 saltine crackers

½ cup (100 ml) all-purpose flour
1 egg, lightly beaten
½ cup (100 ml) breadcrumbs

oil

Drain all the liquid from the crabmeat.

Mix the mayonnaise, mustard, Tabasco sauce, Worcestershire sauce, and the spices.

Combine the crabmeat with the cracker crumbs and the mayonnaise mixture. Shape into small patties. Dip first in the flour, then in the egg, and finally in the breadcrumbs.

Heat a little oil in a frying pan. Cook the crab cakes for a few minutes per side until golden brown color. Serve hot or cold.

See the photo on page 67.

TIP The crab cakes are also good to dip in a sauce, such as TARRAGON & MUSTARD SAUCE (*see the recipe on page 73*).

IN ADVANCE The cooked crab cakes can be stored in the refrigerator for 1 day or in the freezer for about 2 months. If serving them hot, heat them in the oven at 300°F (150°C) for 5–6 minutes right before serving.

BACON-WRAPPED SCALLOPS

MAKES approx. 24
TIME approx. 30 minutes

24 scallops
24 fresh sage leaves
12 slices of bacon
freshly grounded black pepper

Place a sage leaf on each scallop.

Cut the bacon slices in half lengthwise, and wrap a slice around each scallop.

Cook the scallops in a hot frying pan until the bacon is crispy. Season the scallops with black ground pepper, and serve immediately.

See the photo on page 67.

IN ADVANCE The scallops can be prepared and stored in the refrigerator for a few hours, and fried right before serving.

SCALLOPS WITH BAKED TOMATOES

MAKES approx. 24
TIME approx. 10 minutes + 3 hours in the oven

24 scallops
salt and pepper
olive oil for brushing

BAKED TOMATOES
24 cherry tomatoes
2 tbsp olive oil
1 small clove garlic, pressed
1 tsp sugar
1 tsp balsamic vinegar
1 tsp herbs de Provence

salt and pepper
¼ cup (50 ml) crispy fried onions (optional)

Preheat the oven to 210°F (100°C).

Place the tomatoes in an ovenproof dish. Mix the olive oil, garlic, sugar, balsamic vinegar, herbs de Provence, salt, and pepper. Drizzle the marinade over the tomatoes, and bake them for about 3 hours. Stir occasionally.

Season the scallops with salt and pepper, and brush them with olive oil. Sauté them in a frying pan for about 1 minute on each side.

Place a tomato on each scallop. Garnish with fried onions, and fasten with a toothpick. Serve immediately.

See the photo on page 67.

IN ADVANCE The tomatoes can be baked the day before and kept in the refrigerator. Heat in the oven at 300°F (150°C) for a few minutes right before serving.

KIPPER & CREAM CHEESE BALLS

MAKES approx. 30
TIME approx. 40 minutes

11 oz (300 g) kipper or other smoked fish
2 eggs, hard boiled
2 tbsp (25 g) butter, unsalted
2 oz (50 g) cream cheese
salt and pepper
¾ cup (200 ml) finely chopped chives

Remove the skin and bones from the fish. Finely chop the eggs.

Mash together all the ingredients. Season with salt and pepper. Refrigerate until paste is firm.

Shape the mixture into balls, and roll in the chives.

See the photo on page 67.

TIP The chives can be replaced with dill or parsley.

IN ADVANCE The kipper balls without chives can be stored in the refrigerator for 1 day or in the freezer for about 2 months. Roll them in the chives before serving.

GRILLED SHRIMP WITH CHILI & CHÈVRE

MAKES approx. 24
TIME approx. 40 minutes

24 raw king prawns, peeled
2 cloves garlic, finely chopped
2 tsp seeded and finely chopped red chili pepper
3 tbsp olive oil
approx. 5 oz (150 g) chèvre, crumbled
2 tbsp chopped parsley
salt and pepper

chopped parsley for garnish

Preheat the oven to 440°F (225°C).

Carefully cut a small incision in each shrimp from tail to the head without cutting through. Sauté the garlic and the chili in 1 tbsp of olive oil for 1 minute. Combine the chili mixture with the chèvre and the parsley, and season with salt and pepper. Stuff the shrimp with the mixture.

Grease an ovenproof dish with the rest of the oil. Place the shrimp in the dish and broil in the oven for 10–15 minutes or until the shrimp are cooked through. Plate them, and top with the hot oil from the dish. Sprinkle with parsley and serve immediately.

See the photo on page 67.

IN ADVANCE The filling can be stored in the refrigerator for about 2 days. Stuff the shrimp and grill them right before serving.

FINN CRISP BREAD WITH COTTAGE CHEESE & MUSSELS

MAKES approx. 24
TIME approx. 10 minutes

9 oz (250 g) cottage cheese
2 tbsp finely chopped red onion
2 tbsp finely chopped chives
12 Finn crisp bread pieces
24 mussels, in brine (4 oz [100 g]), drained

Mix the cottage cheese, red onion, and chives. Break the Finn crisp breads in half. Spread the cottage cheese dip on the bread, and top with the mussels.
See the photo on page 67.

IN ADVANCE The cottage cheese dip can be stored in the refrigerator for a few hours before putting it on the bread.

GRILLED SESAME-CRUSTED TUNA & SALMON

MAKES approx. 24
TIME approx. 25 minutes

½ lb (250 g) fresh tuna or salmon *see text box* RAW FISH *on page 75*
½ cup (100 ml) sesame seeds, black and/or white
olive oil

Cut the fish into cubes. Dip the top and bottom of the cubes in sesame seeds.

Heat the oil in a frying pan until very hot. Cook the fish cubes top and bottom, about 30 seconds per side. The fish should still be pink inside. Skewer each piece of salmon or tuna on a toothpick, and serve with WASABI MAYONNAISE *(see the recipe on page 57)* or sweet chili sauce.
See the photo on page 67.

IN ADVANCE The fish cubes can be dipped in sesame seeds and prepared a few hours before cooking.

ARTICHOKE WITH CRAYFISH & FENNEL

MAKES approx. 24
TIME approx. 1 hour and 15 minutes

1 cooked ARTICHOKE *(see the recipe on page 198)*

CRAYFISH & FENNEL
7 oz (200 g) cooked crayfish meat, chopped
¾ cup (200 ml) finely chopped fennel
2 oz (50 g) feta, crumbled
½ red onion, finely chopped
freshly squeezed juice from 1 lime
2 tbsp chopped parsley

Let the cooked artichoke cool. Stir together all the ingredients for the crayfish and fennel topping.

Pull all the leaves off of the artichoke. Place them on a plate, and spoon on the topping.
See the photo on page 67.

IN ADVANCE The cooked artichoke and the filling can be stored separately in the refrigerator for 1 day. Complete before serving.

ARTICHOKE LEAVES
The artichoke's leaves are perfect as "bowls" for tasty fillings and dips. We like to use GRILLED SHRIMP WITH CHILI & CHÈVRE *(see the recipe on page 77)*.

Or why not TABBOULEH *(see the recipe on page 123)*, PANZANELLA *(see the recipe on page 180)*, BRIE & CRAB FILLING *(see the recipe on page 28)*, or SPICY PORK FILLING *(see the recipe on page 165)*?

You can also simply dip the leaves in butter or a sauce, *(see the recipes on page 198)*.

CANAPÉ WITH SMOKED
SALMON SPREAD

MAKES approx. 24
TIME approx. 20 minutes

11 oz (300 g) smoked salmon
4 oz (100 g) cream cheese
3 tbsp mayonnaise
1 tbsp finely chopped dill
2 tsp lemon zest
salt and pepper

6 slices white or whole-wheat bread
dill for garnish

Mix the salmon, cream cheese, mayonnaise, dill, and lemon zest. Season with salt and pepper.

Toast the bread, if you like. Press down a round cutter into one of the bread slices, fill with approx. 1 tbsp of the salmon spread and remove the cutter. Proceed in the same way to make 4 canapés from each bread slice. It is also possible to punch out circles or cut bread into squares, and then dollop on the spread. Garnish with dill.

See the photo on page 71.

IN ADVANCE The salmon spread can be stored in the refrigerator for 1 day. The canapés can be prepared a few hours in advance.

CANAPÉ WITH SALMON
TARTAR

MAKES approx. 24
TIME approx. 25 minutes

14 oz (400 g) fresh salmon, finely chopped
 (see text box RAW FISH *on page 75)*
2 tbsp red onion, finely chopped
4 tbsp caviar or fish roe
2 tbsp dill, finely chopped
salt and pepper

6 slices white or whole-wheat bread
dill for garnish

Mix the salmon, red onion, caviar, and dill. Season with salt and pepper.

Toast the bread, if you like. Press down a round cutter into one of the bread slices, fill with approx. 1 tbsp of the salmon tartar and remove the cutter. Proceed in the same way to make 4 canapés from each bread slice. It is also possible to punch out circles or cut bread into squares, and then dollop on the spread. Garnish with dill.

See the photo on page 71.

IN ADVANCE The canapés can be prepared a few hours in advance.

CANAPÉ WITH HORSERADISH
CREAM & SALMON

MAKES approx. 24
TIME approx. 20 minutes

4 oz (100 g) cream cheese
2 tsp grated horseradish
2 tbsp milk

6 slices white or whole-wheat bread

7 oz (200 g) smoked salmon, thinly sliced
fresh herbs for garnish

Mix together the cream cheese, horseradish, and milk. Toast the bread, if you like. Punch out circles or cut the bread into squares. Pipe a bit of horseradish cream on each piece of bread.

Slice the salmon pieces lengthwise, and roll them up into small roses. Place a rose on each piece of bread. Garnish with fresh herbs.

See the photo on page 71.

IN ADVANCE The canapés can be prepared a few hours in advance.

CANAPÉ WITH CREAMY "SKAGEN" SHRIMP

MAKES approx. 24
TIME approx. 20 minutes

7 oz (200 g) cooked shrimp, peeled and
    chopped
4 tbsp mayonnaise
2 tbsp sour cream or crème fraîche
3 tbsp chopped dill
1 tbsp freshly squeezed lemon juice
salt and white pepper

approx. 6 slices white or whole-wheat bread
dill for garnish

Mix the shrimp, mayonnaise, sour cream, dill, and
lemon juice. Season with salt and white pepper.

Toast the bread, if you like. Press down a round
cutter into one of the bread slices, fill with approx.
1 tbsp of the shrimp filling and remove the cutter.
Proceed in the same way to make 4 canapés from
each bread slice. It is also possible to punch out
circles or cut bread into squares, and then dollop on
the filling. Garnish with dill.

See the photo on page 71.

IN ADVANCE The shrimp mixture can be stored
in the refrigerator for 1 day. The canapés can be
prepared a few hours in advance.

CANAPÉ WITH CAVIAR, SOUR CREAM & RED ONION

MAKES approx. 24
TIME approx. 15 minutes

3 oz (75 g) caviar or fish roe
½ cup (100 ml) sour cream
⅓ cup (75 ml) red onion, finely chopped

6 slices white or whole-wheat bread,
dill or chives for garnish

Toast the bread, if you like. Punch out circles or cut
the bread into squares.

Add a little caviar and a dollop of sour cream to
each bread slice. Top with red onion and garnish
with dill or chives.

See the photo on page 71.

IN ADVANCE The canapés can be prepared a few
hours in advance.

CANAPÉ WITH CRAYFISH & SWEET CHILI

MAKES approx 24
TIME approx. 20 minutes

14 oz (400 g) cooked crayfish meat, chopped
4 oz (100 g) cream cheese
approx. ½ cup (100 ml) sweet chili sauce
2 tbsp cilantro, finely chopped
salt and pepper

6 slices white or whole-wheat bread
cilantro for garnish

Mix the crayfish meat, cream cheese, sweet chili sauce,
and cilantro. Season with salt and pepper.

Toast the bread, if you like. Press down a round
cutter into one of the bread slices, fill with approx.
1 tbsp of the crayfish spread and remove the cutter.
Proceed in the same way to make 4 canapés from
each bread slice. It is also possible to punch out
circles or cut bread into squares, and then dollop on
the spread.

Garnish with a little cilantro.

See the photo on page 71.

IN ADVANCE The spread can be stored in the
refrigerator for 1 day. The canapés can be prepared a
few hours in advance.

CANAPÉ WITH CRAB & APPLE

MAKES approx. 24
TIME approx. 20 minutes

1–2 legs of Kamchatka crab (King crab)
    or 11 oz (300 g) canned crabmeat, drained
3 ½ cups (100 g) cream cheese
2 tbsp mayonnaise
1 small apple, grated
1 tsp freshly squeezed lemon juice
salt and pepper

6 slices white or whole-wheat bread
fresh herbs for garnish

Mix the crabmeat, cream cheese, mayonnaise, apple, and lemon juice. Season with salt and pepper.

Toast the bread, if you like. Press down a round cutter into one of the bread slices, fill with approx. 1 tbsp of the crab and apple spread and remove the cutter. Proceed in the same way to make 4 canapés from each bread slice. It is also possible to punch out circles or cut bread into squares, and then dollop on the spread.

Garnish with fresh herbs.

See the photo on page 71.

IN ADVANCE The crab spread can be stored in the refrigerator for 1 day. The canapés can be prepared a few hours in advance.

CANAPÉ WITH EGG & MACKEREL

MAKES approx. 24
TIME approx. 25 minutes

11 oz (300 g) smoked mackerel, cleaned and
    finely chopped
2 tbsp red onion, finely chopped
2 tbsp chives, finely chopped
2 hard-boiled eggs, finely chopped

approx. 6 slices white or whole-wheat bread
chives for garnish

Mix the mackerel, red onion, and chives. Stir in the chopped eggs.

Toast the bread, if you like. Press down a round cutter into one of the bread slices, fill with approx. 1 tbsp of the mackerel spread and remove the cutter. Proceed in the same way to make 4 canapés from each bread slice. It is also possible to punch out circles or cut bread into squares, and then dollop on the spread.

Garnish with chives.

See the photo on page 71.

IN ADVANCE The spread can be stored in the refrigerator for 1 day. The canapés can be prepared a few hours in advance.

CANAPÉ WITH CAVIAR SPREAD

MAKES approx. 24
TIME approx. 10 min. + 30 min. in the refrigerator

⅔ cup (150 ml) heavy cream
4 tbsp of Swedish "kaviar" in a tube, fish roe,
    or caviar
2 tbsp chives, finely chopped

approx. 6 slices white or whole-wheat bread
dill or parsley for garnish

Whip the cream. Mix the caviar and the chives. Let chill for about 30 minutes.

Toast the bread, if you like. Punch out small circles or cut bread into squares. Pipe or dollop the spread onto each piece of bread. Garnish with dill or parsley.

See the photo on page 71.

IN ADVANCE The canapés can be prepared a few hours in advance.

CAJUN FRIED OYSTERS

MAKES approx. 24
TIME approx. 45 minutes

24 oysters
4 cups (1 liter) oil for deep frying

CAJUN SEASONING
1 ⅓ cups (300 ml) corn flour
1 tsp paprika
1 tsp garlic salt
1 tsp onion powder
1 tsp salt
½ tsp cayenne pepper
½ tsp chili powder
½ tsp dried thyme
½ tsp dried oregano
½ tsp black pepper
½ tsp white pepper

Open the oysters as directed on page 73. Carefully remove the oysters from the shells.

Mix the corn flour with the spices, and pour the mixture into a small plastic bag. Add the oysters and shake thoroughly to cover them.

In a heavy-bottomed saucepan, heat the oil to 355°F (180°C). Fry a few oysters at a time, for about 1 minute or until golden brown. Drain on paper towels.

Serve with TARTAR SAUCE and/or COCKTAIL SAUCE (see the recipe on page 74).

See the photo on page 70.

IN ADVANCE The spice mixture can be pre-mixed in a plastic bag several days in advance. Dip the oysters in the corn flour mixture and fry them right before serving.

OYSTERS ROCKEFELLER

MAKES approx. 12
TIME approx. 40 minutes

12 oysters
coarse grained salt for the baking tray

4 slices bacon
7 oz (200 g) fresh spinach
3 scallions, finely chopped
¼ cup (50 ml) breadcrumbs
1 tbsp chopped parsley
2 tbsp olive oil
1–2 tsp Pernod or Ricard
1–2 tsp Tabasco sauce
salt and pepper

Preheat the oven to 440°F (225°C).

Cook the bacon until crispy, drain, and cool on paper towels. Sauté the spinach in the bacon fat for about 1 minute. Crumble the bacon.

Stir together the bacon crumbs, spinach, scallions, breadcrumbs, parsley, olive oil, and liquor. Season with Tabasco, salt, and pepper.

Open the oysters as directed on page 73. Spread spinach mixture on top of the oysters in their shells.

Cover a baking tray with coarse salt, and place the shells on the salt. Place the tray in the upper part of the oven and bake for about 5 minutes or until the oysters are slightly golden brown. Make sure that they do not burn. Serve immediately.

See the photo on page 66.

IN ADVANCE The spinach mixture can be prepared the day before. Bake the oysters just before serving.

BAKED CHILI & LEMONGRASS MUSSELS

MAKES approx. 24
TIME approx. 40 minutes

24 mussels (approx. 14 oz [400 g])
1 lemongrass
¾ cup (200 ml) water
2 shallots, finely chopped
coarse salt

CHILI & LEMONGRASS FILLING

5 tbsp (75 g) butter, unsalted
1 clove garlic, pressed
1 tsp finely grated lemongrass (only the white part)
1–2 tsp seeded and finely chopped red chili pepper
salt and white pepper

freshly squeezed juice from 1–2 limes
chopped fresh cilantro for garnish

Preheat the oven to 440°F (225°C).

Scrub and debeard the mussels. Discard any mussels that have cracked shells and do not open when tapped with a finger.

Crush the lemongrass and cut it into pieces about 2 inches (5 cm) long.

Boil the water. Add the mussels, shallots, and lemongrass. Cover and bring to a boil. Simmer until mussels open, about 3 minutes. Discard any that have not opened. Remove the top shell of the mussels.

Sprinkle coarse salt in a baking tray. Place the mussels on the salt bed.

Mix the ingredients for the filling. Season with salt and pepper. Spread the filling over the mussels. Drizzle lime juice over each mussel, and bake in the top part of the oven for 3–5 minutes.

Garnish with cilantro and serve immediately.
See the photo on page 66.

IN ADVANCE Both the mussels and the filling can be prepared the day before and refrigerated separately. Put together and bake right before serving.

BAKED LEMON & GARLIC MUSSELS

MAKES approx. 24
TIME approx. 40 minutes

24 mussels (approx. 14 oz [400 g])
½ cup (100 ml) dry white wine
½ cup (100 ml) water
2 shallots, finely chopped
coarse salt

LEMON & GARLIC FILLING

5 tbsp (75 g) butter, unsalted
2 tbsp breadcrumbs
1 tbsp freshly squeezed lemon juice
1 tsp lemon zest
1 clove garlic, pressed
2 tbsp finely chopped parsley
salt and white pepper

finely chopped parsley for garnish

Preheat the oven to 440°F (225°C).

Scrub and debeard the mussels. Discard any mussels that have cracked shells and do not open when tapped with a finger.

Bring the wine, water, and shallots to a boil. Add the mussels, cover and simmer until the mussels open, about 3 minutes. Discard any that have not opened. Remove the top shell of the mussels.

Sprinkle coarse salt in a roasting pan. Place the mussels on the salt bed.

Mix the ingredients for the filling. Season with salt and pepper. Spread the filling over the mussels, and bake in the top of the oven for 3–5 minutes. Garnish with parsley. Serve immediately.
See the photo on page 66.

IN ADVANCE see BAKED CHILI & LEMONGRASS MUSSELS *to the left.*

**CAVIAR CHEESECAKE
WITH SHRIMP**

The recipe is available on page 94

BACON & APPLE

ROAST BEEF & REMOULADE

PÂTÉ & CORNICHONS

SMOKED KIPPER & CAPERS

GRAVLAX WITH MUSTARD SAUCE

CURRIED HERRING, EGGS, APPLE & CAPERS

The recipes are available on pages 92–93

HAM WITH MUSTARD & BUTTER-SAUTÉED APPLE

PICKLED HERRING DIP ON CRISP BREAD

SHRIMP & EGG ON SOFT FLATBREAD

SOFT GINGERBREAD WITH BLUE CHEESE CREAM

CRISP BREAD WITH HERRING

SOFT GINGERBREAD WITH MAPLE SYRUP CREAM

EGG & ANCHOVY SALAD ON CRISP BREAD

CRAYFISH WITH DILL CREAM ON SOFT FLATBREAD

VENISON & MUSHROOM ON CRISPY FLATBREAD

PUMPERNICKEL WITH CLOUDBERRY & CHEDDAR CHEESE

FRIED SMELTS & JARLSBERG CREAM ON CRISPY FLATBREAD

HERRING ROLL WITH ROE ON RYE BREAD

The recipes are available on pages 88–91

PICKLED CHANTERELLES

CHANTERELLE PESTO

BUTTER-SAUTÉED
CHANTERELLES

BUTTER-SAUTÉED CHANTERELLES
WITH PARMESAN & PINE NUTS

BUTTER-SAUTÉED
CHANTERELLES
WITH CRANBERRIES &
MASCARPONE

BUTTER-SAUTÉED
CHANTERELLES
WITH CREAM

The recipes are available on pages 94–95

SCANDINAVIA

The cold climate of Nordic countries does not allow for the same variety of fresh produce as places in warmer climates. However, native delicacies such as herring, salmon, wild game, cloudberries, lingonberries, and mushrooms give Scandinavian cuisine a distinct and appealing character.

VENISON & MUSHROOM ON CRISPY FLATBREAD

MAKES approx. 24
TIME approx. 40 minutes

SAUTÉED VENISON & MUSHROOM
5 oz (150 g) fresh or canned chanterelles
8 ½ oz (240 g) venison meat, finely chopped
3 tbsp butter
1 shallot, finely chopped
¼ cup (50 ml) crème fraîche or heavy cream
2 tbsp lingonberries or cranberry sauce
salt and pepper
4 oz (100 g) crispy flatbread
chopped parsley for garnish

Brush the fresh mushrooms until clean, and sauté them in a dry frying pan until the liquid has evaporated. Add 2 tbsp of butter and cook for a while longer. Set them aside.

Cook the meat until it is cooked through. Set aside.

Melt 1 tbsp of butter in the frying pan and sauté the onion for a few minutes. Add the meat, crème fraîche, and mushrooms. Simmer for a few minutes. Stir in the lingonberries or cranberry sauce, and season with salt and pepper.

Break the crispy flatbread into bite-size pieces. Spread mixture on the bread and garnish with parsley. Serve immediately.

See the photo on page 86.

IN ADVANCE The mixture can be done the day before, refrigerated, and then heated up just before serving.

PICKLED HERRING DIP ON CRISP BREAD

MAKES approx. 24
TIME approx. 30 minutes

PICKLED HERRING DIP
7 oz (200 g) of pickled herring
7 oz (200 g) cooked potatoes, cooled
½ cup (100 ml) sour cream
¼ cup (50 ml) cream cheese
¼ cup (50 ml) finely chopped leeks
¼ cup (50 ml) finely chopped dill
1 oz (30 g) Cheddar cheese, grated
salt and white pepper

5 oz (150 g) crisp bread
1 boiled egg, chopped
½ cup (100 ml) crispy fried onions (optional)

Drain the pickled herring and chop into pieces. Peel and dice the potatoes. Mix the herring and potatoes with the sour cream, cream cheese, leeks, dill, and cheese. Season with salt and pepper.

Break the bread into small pieces. Top each piece with the pickled herring dip, egg, and fried onions.

See the photo on page 86.

IN ADVANCE The pickled herring dip and the boiled egg can be stored in the refrigerator for 1–2 days. Prepare the canapés just before serving.

CRISP BREAD WITH HERRING

MAKES approx. 24
TIME approx. 40 minutes

½ lb (250 g) boiled potatoes, cooled
4 oz (100 g) pickled herring
2 oz (50 g) aged cheese, finely grated
½ cup (100 ml) crème fraîche or sour cream
¼ cup (50 ml) red onion, chopped

chives for garnish
5 oz crisp bread
butter

Break the bread into small pieces. Peel the potatoes, and cut them into cubes. Halve the pieces of herring. Combine the crème fraîche and the cheese.

Spread some butter on each piece of bread. Top with the potatoes, herring, and a dollop of cheese crème. Garnish with red onions, and chives.

See the photo on page 86.

IN ADVANCE Boil the potatoes and prepare the cheese mixture the day before. Prepare the canapés just before serving.

HERRING ROLL WITH ROE ON RYE BREAD

MAKES approx. 24
TIME approx. 30 minutes

½–⅔ lb (250–300 g) pickled herring
2 tbsp mayonnaise
2 tbsp sour cream
½ tsp Dijon mustard
1 tsp finely chopped chives
1 tbsp + ½ cup (100 ml) fish roe or caviar

salt and pepper
7–8 slices rye bread

Cut the herring into smaller pieces.

Mix the mayonnaise, sour cream, mustard, chives, 1 tbsp of caviar with the herring. Season with salt and pepper.

Trim the edges of the bread, and punch out little circles—about 1 inch (2 ½ cm) in diameter. Place some herring on a piece of bread and top with caviar.

See the photo on page 86.

IN ADVANCE The herring mixture can be prepared a few days in advance. Keep refrigerated and prepare the canapés just before serving.

HAM WITH MUSTARD & BUTTER-SAUTÉED APPLE

MAKES approx. 24
TIME approx. 25 minutes

1 apple, peeled and cored
2 tbsp butter
1 tbsp sugar
4 oz (100 g) deli ham sliced
¼ cup (50 ml) sweet and hot mustard
lettuce
6 slices bread

chervil for garnish

Cut the apple into small pieces. Sauté in butter together with the sugar for a few minutes until the pieces begin to soften. Allow to cool.

Cut the ham into strips. Cut the bread into squares. Spread the mustard on the bread, add some lettuce, ham, and top with the apple pieces. Garnish with chervil.

See the photo on page 86.

IN ADVANCE The canapés can be prepared a few hours before serving.

FRIED SMELTS & JARLSBERG CREAM ON CRISPY FLATBREAD

MAKES approx. 24
TIME approx. 25 minutes

approx. 5 oz (150 g) smelt fillets
¼ cup (50 ml) Jarlsberg cheese, finely grated
¼ cup (50 ml) cream cheese
1 tsp salt
1 tsp white vinegar
4 oz (100 g) crispy flatbread

dill for garnish

Rinse the smelt fillets and dry them with paper towels. Mix the Jarlsberg and cream cheese.

Heat a frying pan, and when very hot, sprinkle with salt and add the smelt fillets. Fry for a few minutes on each side until blackened. Sprinkle with a bit of vinegar. Let cool, and cut into pieces.

Break the bread into small pieces. Spread with the cheese mixture and top with a piece of fried smelt.

See the photo on page 86.

IN ADVANCE The canapés taste best if prepared at the last possible moment. However, if you prefer to avoid cooking odors before the guests arrive, the smelt can be fried a few hours before serving.

EGG & ANCHOVY SALAD ON CRISP BREAD

MAKES approx. 24
TIME approx. 30 minutes

EGG & ANCHOVY SALAD
5 oz (150 g) boiled potatoes, cooled
5 eggs, hard boiled
2 tbsp finely chopped onion
2 tbsp finely chopped chives
2 tbsp finely chopped dill
5 anchovy fillets, finely chopped
½ cup (100 ml) sour cream
white pepper

4 oz (100 g) crisp bread
dill and chives for garnish

Peel and dice the potatoes. Mix all ingredients for the egg and anchovy salad, and season with white pepper. Break the bread into small pieces. Spread the mixture on the bread and garnish with dill and chives.

See the photo on page 86.

IN ADVANCE The egg and anchovy salad can be stored in the refrigerator for about 2 days. Put it on the crisp bread just before serving.

CRAYFISH WITH DILL CREAM ON SOFT FLATBREAD

MAKES approx. 24
TIME approx. 15 minutes

approx. 7 oz (200 g) soft flatbread
butter
4 oz (100 g) cooked crayfish meat, or cooked shrimp

dill for garnish

DILL CREAM
2 tbsp chopped dill
⅔ cup (150 ml) sour cream
¼ cup (50 ml) mayonnaise
salt and pepper

Whisk the dill, sour cream, and mayonnaise. Season with salt and pepper.

Punch out circles about 1 ½ inches (4 cm) in diameter from the flatbread and butter.

Pipe or dollop a bit of dill cream on each bread circle. Top with crayfish and garnish with dill.

See the photo on page 86.

IN ADVANCE The dill cream can be made the day before and stored in the refrigerator.

PUMPERNICKEL WITH CLOUDBERRIES & CHEDDAR CHEESE

MAKES approx. 24
TIME approx. 15 minutes

9 oz (250 g) Cheddar
7 oz (200 g) pumpernickel bread
butter
approx. 5 oz (150 g) cloudberry jam

Cut the cheese into slices, about ¼-inch (⅔ cm) thick. Punch out circles, about 1 ½ inches (4 cm) in diameter.

Spread butter on the bread, and cut it into squares of about 1 ½ inches (4 cm). Add the cheese and top with cloudberries.

See the photo on page 86.

IN ADVANCE You can slice the bread and cheese the day before. Keep the cheese refrigerated. The canapés can be prepared a few hours before serving.

SHRIMP & EGG ON SOFT FLATBREAD

MAKES approx. 24
TIME approx. 30 minutes

24 cooked and peeled shrimp
4 hard-boiled eggs, peeled and sliced
½ cup (100 ml) mayonnaise
approx. 7 oz (200 g) soft flatbread
butter
dill for garnish

Cut the flatbread into squares and spread with butter. Add the sliced eggs, a shrimp, and a small dollop of mayonnaise per bread square. Garnish with dill.

See the photo on page 86.

IN ADVANCE The eggs can be boiled the day before and stored in the refrigerator. The canapés can be made a few hours before serving.

SOFT GINGERBREAD WITH BLUE CHEESE CREAM OR MAPLE SYRUP CREAM

MAKES approx. 24
TIME approx. 10 minutes

approx. 7 oz (200 g) soft gingerbread cake
cheese cream of your choice *(see the recipes below)*

MAPLE SYRUP CREAM (for 24 pieces)
¾ cup (200 ml) mascarpone
2 tbsp maple syrup
a pinch of salt

BLUE CHEESE CREAM (for 24 pieces)
4 oz (100 g) blue cheese
½ cup (100 ml) mascarpone

Cut the gingerbread into slices, and punch out circles of about 1 ½ inches (4 cm) in diameter, or cut out small squares.

Prepare the toppings, and pipe on the cake.
See the photo on page 86.

TIP If you like the combination of blue cheese and gingerbread, another suggestion is to serve ginger snaps with crumbled blue cheese. See also the recipe for the GINGERBREAD COVERED BLUE CHEESE on page 271.

IN ADVANCE The toppings can be stored in the refrigerator for about 2 days.

CRISP BREAD, FLATBREAD, OR PUMPERNICKEL?
The different breads used in this chapter can, of course, be replaced with one another. Crispy flatbread can be substituted with Matzo bread.

SMØRREBRØD WITH SMOKED KIPPER & CAPERS

MAKES approx. 24
TIME approx. 25 minutes

CAPERS DIP
4 tbsp finely chopped red onion
2 tbsp finely chopped chives
½ cup (100 ml) capers
1 tbsp Dijon mustard
1 egg yolk
salt and black pepper

14 oz (400 g) smoked kipper or other
   smoked fish
20 cherry tomatoes
chopped chives for garnish

20 slices rye bread or pumpernickel
butter

Mix the ingredients for the dip. Season with salt and pepper.

Cut the crusts off of the bread and slice it in half. Remove the skin and bones from the fish.

Spread butter across each piece of bread, and divide the fish and tomatoes on top. Top with dip, and garnish with chives.

See the photo on page 85.

IN ADVANCE The dip can be mixed the day before and stored in the refrigerator.

SMØRREBRØD WITH PÂTÉ & CORNICHONS

MAKES approx. 24
TIME approx. 20 minutes

½ cucumber, sliced
11 oz (300 g) pâté
½ cup (100 ml) Cumberland sauce
12 cornichons (extra fine gherkins), sliced
fresh herbs for garnish
12 slices of rye bread or pumpernickel
butter

Cut the crusts off of the bread and slice it in half. Butter the bread, and add a few cucumber slices and a bit of pâté. Top with Cumberland sauce, and garnish with cornichons and fresh herbs.

See the photo on page 85.

IN ADVANCE The smørrebrød can be prepared an hour before serving.

SMØRREBRØD WITH ROAST BEEF & REMOULADE

MAKES approx. 24
TIME approx. 20 minutes

REMOULADE SAUCE
⅔ cup (150 ml) mayonnaise
2 tbsp gherkins, finely chopped
1 tsp freshly squeezed lemon juice
½ tsp curry powder
1 tsp chopped parsley
salt and pepper
12 slices roast beef, halved
24 radishes, sliced
½ cup (100 ml) crispy fried onion
chives for garnish

12 slices of rye bread or pumpernickel
butter

Mix the ingredients for the remoulade sauce. Season with salt and pepper.

Cut the crusts off of the bread, and slice it in half. Spread with a little butter, and add the roast beef and radishes. Top with a dollop of remoulade sauce and sprinkle with fried onions. Garnish with chives.

See the photo on page 85.

IN ADVANCE The remoulade sauce can be prepared about 2 days in advance and stored in the refrigerator.

SMØRREBRØD WITH
BACON & APPLE

MAKES approx. 24
TIME approx. 40 minutes

  7 oz (200 g) bacon, diced
  1 apple, peeled and cored
  1 shallot, finely chopped
  1 tsp dried rosemary
  1 small head of lettuce
  12 radishes, halved for garnish
  fresh rosemary for garnish
  12 slices of rye bread or pumpernickel
  butter

Sauté the bacon until crispy. Do not rinse the frying pan. Drain the bacon on a paper towel.

Cut the apple into small cubes. Sauté the shallot and the rosemary in the bacon fat. Add the apple and cook for a few more minutes.

Cut the crusts off of the bread. Slice the bread in half, and spread with butter. Top with lettuce, apple, and bacon. Garnish with radishes and fresh rosemary.

See the photo on page 85.

IN ADVANCE Everything can be prepared separately a few hours in advance.

SMØRREBRØD WITH CURRIED
HERRING, EGGS, APPLE & CAPERS

MAKES approx. 24
TIME approx. 20 minutes

  4 oz (100 g) herring in sour cream
  ½ apple, peeled and cored
  1 tbsp mayonnaise
  1 tsp curry powder
  2 tbsp capers
  a few leaves of lettuce
  4 hard-boiled eggs, peeled and sliced
  ½ red onion, chopped
  chives for garnish
  12 slices of rye bread or pumpernickel
  butter

Cut the herring and the apple into small pieces. Mix the herring with its sour cream sauce and the apples, mayonnaise, curry, and capers.

Cut the crusts off of the bread. Slice the bread in half, and spread with butter. Add lettuce and a few slices of egg. Divide the curry herring mixture on the bread slices, and top with red onion. Garnish with chives.

See the photo on page 85.

IN ADVANCE The herring mixture can be prepared, and the eggs can be boiled the day before. Store in the refrigerator.

SMØRREBRØD WITH GRAVLAX
WITH MUSTARD SAUCE

MAKES approx. 24
TIME approx. 10 minutes

  ½ lb (250 g) gravlax salmon, thinly sliced
  1 bunch dill, finely chopped

  MUSTARD SAUCE
  3 tbsp mustard
  1 tbsp sugar
  1 tbsp white wine vinegar
  ½ cup (100 ml) canola oil
  ½ cup (100 ml) chopped dill
  salt and white pepper

  12 slices of rye bread or pumpernickel
  butter

Whisk the mustard, sugar, and vinegar. Add the oil in a fine steady stream while whisking. Mix in the dill and season with salt and pepper.

Cut the crusts off of the bread. Slice the bread in half, and spread with butter. Top with the salmon, dill, and a dollop of mustard sauce.

See the photo on page 85.

IN ADVANCE The mustard sauce can be prepared a couple of days in advance. The smørrebrød can be prepared an hour before serving.

CAVIAR CHEESECAKE WITH SHRIMP

MAKES approx. 32
TIME approx. 30 minutes + 3 hours cooling

7 oz (200 g) dark rye bread
5 tbsp (75 g) butter, melted
2 tsp unflavored gelatin powder
3 + 3 tbsp water
½ cup (100 ml) crème fraîche or sour cream
11 oz (300 g) cream cheese
½ red onion, finely chopped
2 ¾ oz (80 g) fish roe or caviar
1 tsp lemon zest + 1 tsp freshly squeezed
    lemon juice
salt and white pepper

32 cooked and peeled shrimp
½ cup (100 ml) finely chopped chives
sliced radishes for garnish

Line 4 small pie pans (approx. 4 inches (10 cm) in diameter) with plastic wrap. Soften the gelatin in a bowl with 3 tbsp cold water.

Blend the dark rye bread in a food processor, and add the butter. Press the breadcrumbs into the bottom of the pans.

Stir together sour cream, cream cheese, red onion, fish roe, lemon zest, and lemon juice. Season with salt and pepper.

Place the bowl with the gelatin in a pan with simmering water until the gelatin melts. Mix well with the filling and spread evenly in the pan. Refrigerate for at least 3 hours or until the filling has set.

When the filling is firm, gently lift the cheesecake out of the pan using the plastic wrap. Sprinkle chives over the pies, and press gently so they stick. Wet a knife in hot water and cut small pie pieces. Garnish with shrimp and radishes.

See the photo on page 84.

TIP You can also make the cheesecake in a rectangular pan lined with plastic wrap. Cut the cheesecake into squares.

IN ADVANCE The cheesecake can be prepared the day before and refrigerated. Garnish with shrimp and radishes a few hours before serving.

BUTTER-SAUTÉED CHANTERELLES

MAKES approx. 24
TIME approx. 20 minutes

1 lb (500 g) fresh chanterelles or other
    mushroom
½ onion, finely chopped
1 clove garlic, pressed
3 tbsp + 3 tbsp butter
3 tbsp chopped parsley
salt and pepper
6 slices of white bread

Sauté the onion and garlic in 3 tbsp butter for a few minutes. Add the chanterelles and cook for a couple more minutes. Stir in the parsley, and season with salt and pepper.

Remove the crust from the bread, and cut each slice into 4 triangles.

Heat the remaining butter in a clean frying pan. Fry the bread pieces on both sides until golden brown.

Spread the mushroom mixture on the bread pieces. Serve immediately.

See the photo on page 87.

BUTTER-SAUTÉED CHANTERELLES WITH CRANBERRIES & MASCARPONE
Add ¼ cup (50 ml) cranberry sauce to the chanterelles. Spread some mascarpone cheese on each piece of bread.

BUTTER-SAUTÉED CHANTERELLES WITH PARMESAN & PINE NUTS
Add ¼ cup (50 ml) grated Parmesan cheese and ¼ cup (50 ml) toasted pine nuts. Substitute the parsley for chopped basil.

BUTTER-SAUTÉED CHANTERELLES WITH CREAM
Add ½ cup (100 ml) heavy cream to the chanterelles, and simmer for a few minutes.

IN ADVANCE The toasts taste best when freshly made.

CHANTERELLE PESTO

MAKES approx. 2 cups (500 ml)
TIME approx. 20 minutes

1 lb (500 g) fresh chanterelles or
    other mushroom
3 tbsp olive oil
½ onion, finely chopped
¾ cup (200 ml) grated Parmesan
½ cup (100 ml) pine nuts, toasted
½ bunch fresh basil
salt and pepper

Sauté the onion in 1 tbsp olive oil for a few minutes.
Add the chanterelles and cook for a couple more
minutes. Let cool.

With a food processor or hand blender, mix the
chanterelles with the cheese, pine nuts, and basil.
Gradually pour in the remaining oil in a thin
stream. Season with salt and pepper. Serve with
toasted bread.

See the photo on page 87.

IN ADVANCE The pesto can be made the day
before and stored in the refrigerator.

PICKLED CHANTERELLES

MAKES approx. 4 cups (1 liter)
TIME approx. 20 minutes + 2 days in the refrigerator

1 lb (500 g) fresh chanterelles or other
mushroom

PICKLING LIQUID
⅔ cup (150 ml) water
⅔ cup (150 ml) white vinegar
½ cup (100 ml) sugar
3 slices fresh ginger
1 bay leaf
1 cinnamon stick
½ tbsp yellow mustard seeds
2 black peppercorns

Boil lightly salted water in a large saucepan. Add the
chanterelles and cook for 10 minutes. Drain, and
quickly cool down the mushrooms by rinsing in
cold water.
Mix the ingredients for the pickling liquid in a
saucepan. Simmer for about 8 minutes. Strain
the spices.

Add the chanterelles to hot, sterilized glass jars.
Pour the pickling liquid over the mushrooms so they
are completely covered, and seal immediately. Let
cool, and refrigerate for at least 2 days.

See the photo on page 87.

IN ADVANCE The pickled chanterelles last about
2 weeks in the refrigerator.

**ANCHOVIES & ROASTED
BELL PEPPERS**

TUNA SPREAD & GREEN OLIVES

PAN CON TOMATE

**SWEET & SPICY CHORIZO &
FIGS**

**MANCHEGO &
FIG JAM**

**SHERRY MUSHROOMS &
AIOLI**

SALSICCIA & MANCHEGO

CHICKPEA & SPINACH DIP

**CRAB DIP AND ROASTED
BELL PEPEPRS**

The recipes are available on pages 105–108

GAZPACHO
WITH OYSTERS

GOLDEN GAZPACHO
WITH MELON & LIME

The recipes are available on page 109

GRILLED SHRIMP WITH GARLIC & CHILI

GILDAS—SKEWERS WITH ANCHOVIES, CHILI & OLIVES

CROQUETAS DE JAMON Y MANCHEGO

TORTILLA DE PATATA

DEEP-FRIED DATES WITH CHÈVRE & BACON

The recipes are available on pages 100—104

STUFFED
MUSHROOMS

MUSSELS WITH
TOMATO, LEMON &
PARSLEY

MARINATED
MUSHROOMS

DEEP-FRIED
CALAMARI

PATATAS BRAVAS

TAPAS

Tapas are Spanish appetizers that are often eaten standing by a bar counter. The word comes from the verb "tapar," which means "to cover." There are as many theories about the word's origin as there are different types of tapas. One theory says that it comes from back in the days when people covered their sherry glass with a small piece of bread, cheese, or ham to protect against flies.

TORTILLA DE PATATA

MAKES approx. 16
TIME approx. 45 minutes

approx. 1 ½ lbs (650 g) potatoes, peeled and thinly sliced
½–⅔ cup (100–150 ml) olive oil
5 eggs
2 shallots, finely chopped
1–2 tsp salt

Heat the olive oil in a nonstick pan, and add the potatoes—they should almost be covered in oil. Fry on low heat for 15–20 minutes or until potatoes are soft, but not browned. Stir often. Add the onions when there are about 5 minutes left of cooking time. Drain the potatoes and onions in a colander, but save the oil.

Beat the eggs until fluffy. Mix with the potatoes, shallots, and salt.

Pour back about 2 tbsp of the oil into the frying pan. Pour in the potato and egg mixture, and fry the tortilla without stirring until it begins to set. Loosen the edges with a soft spatula, and tilt the pan so that the egg mixture flows down the edges.

When the top of the tortilla has set, place a plate over the pan. Turn the pan upside down, so that the tortilla is on top of the plate, and then let it slide back in the pan to cook the other side. Cook for a few minutes until the tortilla is firm.

Transfer the tortilla to a plate, and let it cool slightly. Cut into triangles. Serve hot or cold.

See the photo on page 98.

IN ADVANCE *See* TORTILLA DE PATATA CON CHORIZO *to the right.*

TORTILLA DE PATATA CON CHORIZO

MAKES approx. 16
TIME approx. 45 minutes

7 oz (200 g) chorizo, sliced
½–⅔ cup (100–150 ml) olive oil
1 lb (500 g) potatoes, peeled and thinly sliced
2 shallots, finely chopped
5 eggs
2 oz (50 g) Manchego cheese, grated
1–2 tsp salt

Heat 1 tbsp of olive oil in a nonstick frying pan, and fry the sliced chorizo for a few minutes. Set it aside.

Heat the rest of the olive oil in a nonstick pan, and add the potatoes—they should almost be covered by oil. Fry on low heat for 15–20 minutes or until the potatoes are soft, but not browned. Stir frequently.

Add the shallots when about 5 minutes of cooking time are left. Drain the potatoes and shallots in a colander, but save the oil.

Whisk the eggs until fluffy, and add the potatoes, shallots, chorizo, cheese, and salt. Follow the recipe for TORTILLA DE PATATA.

See the photo on page 98.

IN ADVANCE The tortilla can be stored for about 2 days in the refrigerator or in the freezer for about 3 months. Heat them in the oven at 300°F (150°C) for 5–10 minutes right before serving.

TORTILLA DE PATATA CON ZUCCHINI

MAKES approx. 16
TIME approx. 45 minutes

5 oz (150 g) zucchini, grated
1 lb (500 g) potatoes, peeled and thinly sliced
½–⅔ cup (100–150 ml) olive oil
5 eggs
2 shallots, finely chopped
1–2 tsp salt

Place the zucchini in a sieve with a bit of salt. Let it drain for about 20 minutes.

Heat the olive oil in a nonstick pan, and add the potatoes—they should almost be covered in oil. Fry on low heat for 15–20 minutes or until potatoes are soft, but not browned. Stir often.

Add the shallots, zucchini, and salt when about 5 minutes of cooking time are left. Follow the recipe for TORTILLA DE PATATA.

See the photo on page 98.

IN ADVANCE *See* TORTILLA DE PATATA CON CHORIZO *on the opposite page.*

GILDAS—SKEWERS WITH ANCHOVIES, CHILI & OLIVES

MAKES approx. 20
TIME approx. 10 minutes

approx. 2 oz (53 g) anchovies
10 Spanish Guindilla chilies
    or whole jalapeños, canned
20 green olives, pitted

Halve the anchovies and the chilies. Put an olive, an anchovy half, a chili, and another olive on a toothpick.

See the photo on page 98.

IN ADVANCE The gildas can be stored in the refrigerator for 1 day.

DEEP-FRIED CALAMARI

MAKES approx. 20
TIME approx. 40 minutes

7 oz (200 g) calamari, cut in rings
½ cup (100 ml) rye flour
½ cup (100 ml) all-purpose flour
1 tbsp olive oil
1 egg yolk
¾ cup (200 ml) beer
salt
1 egg white

approx. 4 cups (1 liter) of oil for
    deep frying

Whisk together the flour, oil, egg yolk, and half a cup of beer into the batter. Add the rest of the beer little by little. Season with salt.

Beat the egg whites firm in a clean bowl. Fold it gently into the batter.

Heat the oil to 320°F (160°C) in a heavy-bottomed saucepan. Dip the calamari in the batter. Place a few at a time in the hot oil, and fry until golden brown. Drain on paper towels.

Serve with lemon wedges.

See the photo on page 99.

TIP Dipping sauces which taste good with the calamari are TARRAGON & MUSTARD SAUCE (*see the recipe on page 73*), TARTAR SAUCE, COCKTAIL SAUCE, or DILL & LEMON AIOLI (*see the recipe on page 74*), HOLLANDAISE SAUCE, CREAMY PESTO DIP, or CHIVE DIP (*see the recipe on page 198*).

IN ADVANCE The calamari tastes best if served right away.

DEEP-FRIED DATES WITH CHÈVRE & BACON

MAKES approx. 24
TIME approx. 30 minutes

¼ lb (120 g) bacon slices
approx. 3 oz (75 g) chèvre
6 small dates, pitted and halved
4 cups (1 liter) of oil for deep frying

Cut the bacon in half widthwise and then lengthwise into 4 strips.

Place a piece of chèvre inside a date. Wrap a strip of bacon around the date, and secure with a toothpick.

Heat the oil to 320°F (160°C). Fry the dates until the bacon is cooked through. Drain on paper towels. Serve warm.

See the photo on page 98.

IN ADVANCE The dates can be filled with chèvre and wrapped with bacon a few hours before frying.

GRILLED SHRIMP WITH GARLIC & CHILI

MAKES approx. 30
TIME approx. 25 minutes

14 oz (400 g) raw shrimp, peeled
4 tbsp olive oil
1 clove garlic, finely chopped
1 tsp dried chili flakes

Preheat the oven to 480°F (250°C). Set an ovenproof serving dish in the oven for serving the shrimp.

Heat the olive oil on medium heat in a frying pan. Sauté the garlic and the chili flakes for about 20 seconds without browning. Add the shrimp, and cook on medium heat for 3–4 minutes or until the shrimp are golden brown. Plate the shrimp with garlic oil on the heated dish and serve immediately.

See the photo on page 98.

TIP Don't let the tasty oil go to waste—enjoy it by dipping bread in it!

IN ADVANCE The shrimp taste best if served right away.

CROQUETAS DE JAMON Y MANCHEGO

MAKES approx. 30
TIME approx. 1 hour and 15 minutes

7 tbsp (100 g) butter or margarine
½ cup (100 ml) all-purpose flour
1¾ cups (400 ml) milk
4 oz (100 g) Serrano ham, finely chopped
¾ cup (200 ml) Manchego cheese, grated
a pinch grated nutmeg
salt and pepper

½ cup (100 ml) all-purpose flour
1 egg, beaten
¾ cup (200 ml) breadcrumbs

approx. 4 cups (1 liter) of oil for deep frying

Melt the butter in a saucepan, and whisk in the flour. Add the milk little by little while whisking. Simmer and stir for about 5 minutes or until the sauce thickens.

Stir in the ham, cheese, and nutmeg, and season with salt and pepper. Let it cool in the refrigerator for at least 30 minutes or until the batter is firm and can be rolled by hand.

Shape the dough into oblong rolls, about 1 inch (2 ½ cm) thick. Roll them first in the flour, then in the beaten egg, and lastly in the breadcrumbs.

Heat the oil in a heavy saucepan to 320°F (160°C). Fry the croquettes until they are golden brown. Place onto a paper towel and let drain. Serve warm.

See the photo on page 98.

TIP The ham can be replaced with other fillings such as chicken, shrimp, or tuna.

IN ADVANCE When covered with breadcrumbs, the croquettes can be stored in the refrigerator for 1 day. Fry them just before serving.

PATATAS BRAVAS

MAKES approx. 60
TIME approx. 45 minutes

1 ¾ lbs (800 g) potatoes, peeled
3 tbsp olive oil
2 tsp paprika or Pimentón de la Vera
a pinch of chili powder

SPICY TOMATO SAUCE
1 small onion, finely chopped
2 cloves garlic, pressed
2 tbsp olive oil
14 oz (400 g) chopped tomatoes, fresh
    or canned
1 tbsp tomato paste
2 tsp red wine vinegar
1 tsp paprika or Pimentón de la Vera
1 tsp sugar
a pinch of cayenne pepper
salt and pepper

CHILI AIOLI
¾ cup (200 ml) MAYONNAISE, store bought (or
    see the recipe on page 74)
1 clove garlic, pressed
1 tbsp tomato paste
a few drops of Tabasco sauce
salt and pepper

Boil the potatoes in salted water until they are
almost soft. Allow them to cool slightly, and cut
into pieces.

For the tomato sauce, sauté the onion and garlic
in olive oil for a few minutes. Add the chopped
tomatoes, tomato paste, vinegar, paprika, sugar, and
cayenne pepper. Simmer for 10 minutes. Mix the
sauce, and season with salt and pepper. Stir together
the mayonnaise, garlic, and tomato paste for the chili
aioli. Season with Tabasco sauce, salt, and pepper.

Heat the olive oil in a frying pan. Fry the potatoes
quickly on high heat until golden brown and slightly
crispy. Sprinkle with paprika and chili powder, and
stir. Season with salt and pepper. Serve the potatoes
hot with tomato sauce and/or chili aioli.

See the photo on page 99.

IN ADVANCE The tomato sauce and the aioli can
be stored in the refrigerator for about 2 days. The
potatoes should be cooked right before serving.

MUSSELS WITH TOMATO, LEMON & PARSLEY

MAKES approx. 24
TIME approx. 30 minutes

24 mussels (approx. 14 oz [400 g])
½ cup (100 ml) dry white wine
½ cup (100 ml) water
2 shallots, finely chopped

TOMATO TOPPING
½ cup (100 ml) seeded and chopped fresh
    tomatoes
1 ½ tbsp finely chopped shallots
1 tbsp finely chopped parsley
2 tbsp olive oil
a few drops of Tabasco sauce
salt and pepper
½ of a lemon, freshly squeezed juice

Scrub and de beard the mussels. Discard any mussels
that have cracked shells and do not open when
tapped with a finger.

Boil the wine, water, and shallots. Add the mussels
and stir. Cook, covered, for 5 minutes. Remove the
mussels and discard those that have not opened.
Discard the empty shells. Allow the mussels to cool.

Stir together the tomatoes, shallots, parsley, and
olive oil. Season with Tabasco sauce, salt, and pepper.
Spread the tomato mixture on the mussels, and
sprinkle with lemon juice.

See the photo on page 99.

IN ADVANCE Mussels can be cooked the day before
and kept in the refrigerator. The tomato topping can
be made several hours in advance.

STUFFED MUSHROOMS

MAKES approx. 24
TIME approx. 30–45 minutes

**24 large button mushrooms with filling of
your choice** (*see the recipes below*)

Preheat the oven to 400°F (200°C).
 Remove the mushroom stems and brush the
caps clean.
 Prepare the filling of your choice. Fill the
mushroom caps, and put them in an ovenproof dish.
Roast in the oven for about 15 minutes or until the
filling is golden brown. Serve warm.

PARMESAN & CHORIZO
 1 shallot, chopped
 1 clove garlic, pressed
 1 tbsp olive oil
 4 oz (100 g) chorizo, finely chopped
 ½ cup (100 ml) grated Parmesan
 2 tbsp chopped parsley
 ½ tsp Italian salad seasoning
 salt and pepper

Sauté the shallot and the garlic in oil for a few
minutes, add the chorizo, and cook for another
few minutes.
 Mix chorizo mixture with Parmesan, parsley,
and Italian salad seasoning. Season with salt
and pepper.
 See the photo on page 99.

RICOTTA, PECORINO & SUN-DRIED TOMATO
 4 oz (100 g) ricotta
 ½ cup (100 ml) grated pecorino
 3 tbsp chopped fresh basil
 2 oz (50 g) sun-dried tomatoes in oil,
  finely chopped
 salt and pepper

Stir together all the ingredients for the filling. Season
with salt and pepper.
 See the photo on page 99.

CRAB & HORSERADISH
 ½ can of crab (3 oz [85 g])
 1 ¾ oz (50 g) cream cheese
 1 tbsp mayonnaise
 1 tsp grated horseradish
 ½ tsp Worcestershire sauce
 salt and white pepper

Stir together all the ingredients for the filling. Season
with salt and white pepper.
 See the photo on page 99.

SPINACH, WALNUTS & FETA
 1 shallot, finely chopped
 1 tbsp butter
 3 oz (75 g) spinach, chopped
 3 tbsp walnuts, chopped
 3 oz (75 g) feta cheese, crumbled
 salt and pepper

Melt the butter in a frying pan. Fry the shallot for
a few minutes. Add the spinach, and cook it for
another minute. Let it cool slightly, and then mix in
the walnuts and cheese. Season with salt and pepper.
 See the photo on page 99.

IN ADVANCE All the fillings can be made a day in
advance and kept cold. Mushrooms can be filled a
few hours before being grilled.

MARINATED MUSHROOMS

MAKES approx. 24
TIME approx. 20 minutes

 ½ lb (250 g) small button mushrooms
 3 cloves garlic, finely chopped
 ¾ cup (200 ml) white wine vinegar
 ½ cup (100 ml) olive oil
 1 bay leaf
 3 tbsp water
 3 tbsp honey
 ½ tsp dried chili flakes
 a few sprigs of basil, thyme, and parsley

Mix the mushrooms with the rest of the ingredients in a saucepan. (Save some of the fresh herbs for garnish.) Bring to a boil, and simmer for about 8 minutes. Allow to cool. Strain the liquid, and remove the herbs. Garnish with the rest of the herbs.

See the photo on page 99.

IN ADVANCE The mushroom can be stored in the refrigerator for about 2 days.

PAN TOSTADO WITH SWEET & SPICY CHORIZO & FIGS

MAKES approx. 20
TIME approx. 40 minutes

1 shallot, finely chopped
1 tbsp olive oil
5 oz (150 g) chorizo, thinly sliced
3 tbsp sherry
3 tbsp red wine vinegar
3 tbsp sugar
1 cinnamon stick
a pinch of nutmeg
3 fresh figs, cut in wedges
salt
rustic-style bread
approx. 3 tbsp olive oil

Preheat the oven to 440°F (225°C).

Sauté the shallot in olive oil for a few minutes. Add the chorizo and sauté for a few minutes more. Stir in the sherry, vinegar, sugar, cinnamon stick, and nutmeg. Simmer for about 20 minutes. Add the figs, and heat them for approximately 30 seconds. Remove the cinnamon stick. Season with salt.

Cut the bread into thin slices and then into rectangular pieces of about 1 ½ × 3 inches (4 × 8 cm). Brush the bread with oil and bake it in the oven for a few minutes or until golden brown. Top with the chorizo and fig mixture.

See the photo on page 96.

IN ADVANCE The bread pieces can be toasted the day before and kept at room temperature. The rest should be done right before serving.

PAN TOSTADO WITH ANCHOVIES & ROASTED BELL PEPPERS

MAKES approx. 20
TIME approx. 20 minutes

10 canned anchovies
a few drops of freshly squeezed lemon juice
black pepper
2 oz (50 g) ROASTED BELL PEPPERS
    (see the recipe on page 118)
20 large capers
rustic-style bread
approx. 3 tbsp olive oil

Preheat the oven to 440°F (225°C).

Mix the anchovies with the lemon juice to form a paste.

Season with black pepper. Cut the roasted bell peppers into strips.

Cut the bread into thin slices and then into pieces of about 1 ½ × 3 inches (4 × 8 cm). Brush the bread with oil and bake it in the oven for a few minutes or until golden brown.

Spread a little anchovy paste on each bread slice. Top with a strip of pepper and a caper.

See the photo on page 96.

IN ADVANCE The bell peppers and purée can be stored in the refrigerator for 1 day. The bread can be toasted the day before and kept at room temperature.

TAPAS IN BASQUE COUNTRY
In the Basque Country of northern Spain, tapas are called "pinxtos." Old Town San Sebastian is known for its narrow streets and alleys featuring an endless array of tapas bars—each one boasting its own signature tapa.

PAN TOSTADO WITH CHICKPEA & SPINACH DIP

MAKES approx. 30
TIME approx. 30 minutes

CHICKPEA & SPINACH DIP
1 shallot, finely chopped
1 clove garlic, pressed
2 tbsp olive oil
7 oz (200 g) cooked chickpeas, drained
2 oz (50 g) fresh spinach
a pinch of ground cumin
1 tbsp freshly squeezed lemon juice
1 tbsp chopped parsley
salt and pepper
rutic-style bread
3 tbsp olive oil

Preheat the oven to 440°F (225°C).

Sauté the shallot and the garlic in 1 tbsp of olive oil for a few minutes in a frying pan. Add the chickpeas and cook for another few minutes. Add the spinach and cumin, and cook until the spinach has softened. Place the mixture into a bowl, add 1 tbsp olive oil, and mash gently. Add the lemon juice and parsley. Season with salt and pepper.

Cut the bread first into thin slices and then into rectangular pieces of about 1 ½ × 3 inches (4 × 8 cm). Brush with oil and bake in the oven for a few minutes or until golden brown. Spread the mixture on the bread slices, and serve hot or cold.

See the photo on page 96.

IN ADVANCE The dip can be stored in the refrigerator for about 2 days. If served warm, heat it up slightly right before serving. The bread can be roasted the day before and kept at room temperature.

PAN TOSTADO WITH SHERRY MUSHROOMS & AIOLI

MAKES approx. 20
TIME approx. 30 minutes

4 oz (100 g) button mushrooms, sliced
2 tbsp olive oil
2 tbsp sherry
salt and pepper

AIOLI
2 cloves garlic, pressed
2 egg yolks, at room temperature
¾ cup (200 ml) olive oil, at room temperature

rustic-style bread
approx. 3 tbsp olive oil
chopped parsley for garnish

Preheat the oven to 440°F (225°C).

Whisk together the garlic and the egg yolks for the aioli.

Add the olive oil a drop at a time while whisking constantly—toward the end, pour in a fine stream while continuing to whisk. Season with salt and pepper

Cut the bread first into thin slices and then into rectangular pieces of about 1 ½ × 3 inches (4 × 8 cm). Brush with oil and bake in the oven for a few minutes or until golden brown.

Heat the oil in a frying pan. Add the mushrooms and sherry, and simmer, covered, for about 5 minutes. Season with salt and pepper.

Spread a little aioli on the bread, and top with the mushrooms. Garnish with parsley.

See the photo on page 96.

IN ADVANCE The aioli can be stored in the refrigerator for about 2 days. The bread can be roasted the day before and kept at room temperature. The mushrooms will taste best if they are cooked at the last minute.

PAN TOSTADO WITH CRAB DIP & ROASTED BELL PEPPERS

MAKES approx. 20
TIME approx. 45 minutes

CRAB DIP

2 eggs, hard boiled and peeled
6 oz (170 g) cooked crab meat
1 shallot, finely chopped
3 tbsp mayonnaise
1 tbsp lemon juice
1 tsp freshly squeezed lemon zest
1 tsp finely chopped parsley
a pinch of cayenne pepper
salt and pepper

rustic-style bread
approx. 3 tbsp olive oil
3 ½ cups (100 g) ROASTED BELL PEPPERS
   (see the recipe on page 118)

Preheat the oven to 440°F (225°C).

Cut the bread first into thin slices and then into rectangular pieces of about 1 ½ × 3 inches (4 × 8 cm). Brush with oil and bake in the oven for a few minutes or until golden brown.

Gently halve the eggs. Divide the egg yolks and whites into separate bowls. Into the egg yolks, mix the crab meat, shallot, mayonnaise, lemon juice, lemon zest, and parsley. Season with cayenne pepper, salt, and pepper.

Cut the bell peppers similarly to the bread. Place them on the bread, and top with the crab dip. Grate the egg whites and sprinkle over crab dip.

See photo page 96.

IN ADVANCE The bell peppers and the crab mix can be stored in the refrigerator for 1 day. The bread can be roasted the day before and kept at room temperature.

PAN TOSTADO WITH TUNA SPREAD & GREEN OLIVES

MAKES approx. 20
TIME approx. 30 minutes

TUNA SPREAD

3 eggs, hard boiled and chopped
7 oz (185 g) canned tuna, drained
4 tbsp mayonnaise
1 onion, sliced
1 small tomato, seeded and finely chopped
a few drops of Tabasco sauce
salt and pepper

SAUCE

½ cup (100 ml) Greek yogurt
2 tbsp mayonnaise
rustic-style bread
approx. 3 tbsp olive oil

4 oz (100 g) pitted green olives, sliced,
   for garnish

Preheat the oven to 440°F (225°C).

Cut the bread first into thin slices and then into rectangular pieces of about 1 ½ × 3 inches (4 × 8 cm). Brush with oil and bake in the oven for a few minutes or until golden brown.

Mix the ingredients for the tuna spread. Season with Tabasco, salt, and pepper.

Mix the yogurt with the mayonnaise.

Spread the tuna on the bread slices, and top with the sauce. Garnish with olives.

See the photo on page 96.

IN ADVANCE The tuna dip can be stored in the refrigerator for about 2 days. The bread can be roasted the day before and kept at room temperature.

PAN CON TOMATE

MAKES approx. 20
TIME approx. 20 minutes

11 oz (300 g) plum tomatoes, halved
½ cup (100 ml) olive oil
rustic-style bread
course-ground sea salt

Preheat the oven to 440°F (225°C). Grate the tomatoes on the coarsest side of a cheese grater. Drain in a fine mesh strainer. Stir in 2 tbsp of olive oil.

Cut the bread first into thin slices and then into rectangular pieces of about 1 ½ × 3 inches (4 × 8 cm). Brush with the remaining oil and bake in the oven for a few minutes or until golden brown.

Spread a thin layer of tomato on the bread, and sprinkle with sea salt.

See the photo on page 96.

TIP Top with salsiccia, pata negra, Serrano ham, Manchego cheese, or anchovies.

IN ADVANCE Pan con tomate tastes best served right away.

PAN TOSTADO WITH SALSICCIA & MANCHEGO

MAKES approx. 20
TIME approx. 15 minutes

2 oz (50 g) salsiccia salami, sliced
2 oz (50 g) Manchego, sliced
rustic-style bread
approx. 3 tbsp olive oil

Preheat the oven to 440°F (225°C). Cut the bread first into thin slices and then into rectangular pieces of about 1 ½ × 3 inches (4 × 8 cm). Brush with oil and bake in the oven for a few minutes or golden brown.

Top with the salami and cheese, and cook for another minute until the cheese melts.

See the photo on page 96.

IN ADVANCE These taste best served right away.

PAN TOSTADO WITH MANCHEGO & FIG JAM

MAKES approx. 20
TIME approx. 15 minutes

4 oz (100 g) Manchego, sliced
½ cup (100 ml) fig jam
rustic-style bread
approx. 3 tbsp olive oil

Preheat the oven to 440°F (225°C). Cut the bread first into thin slices and then into rectangular pieces of about 1 ½ × 3 inches (4 × 8 cm). Brush with oil and bake in the oven for a few minutes or until golden brown.

Add a slice of cheese to each bread slice, and top with fig jam.

See the photo on page 96.

IN ADVANCE These taste best served right away.

WHAT TO DRINK WITH TAPAS
Drinks of choice when serving tapas are, of course, the Spanish classics. On a hot summer day, serve SANGRIA (*see the recipe on page 278*), beer, dry cider, or chilled cava. A glass of red Rioja is excellent year round, and if you want to keep it really traditional, consider serving dry sherry. *Salud!*

GAZPACHO WITH OYSTERS

MAKES approx. 15
TIME approx. 25 min. + 1 hrs. in the refrigerator

½ lb (250 g) tomatoes, blanched and peeled
2 tbsp finely chopped onion
1 clove garlic, pressed
½ red bell pepper, seeded
1 ⅓ cups (300 ml) cold chicken broth
½ cup (100 ml) tomato juice
1 tbsp sherry or white wine vinegar
½ cup (100 ml) finely diced cucumber
1 tbsp finely chopped cilantro
salt and black pepper
Tabasco sauce (optional)

20 small oysters, for example, Fine de Claire

Combine the tomatoes, onion, garlic, and bell pepper in a food processor or with a hand blender. Mix with the broth, tomato juice, vinegar, cucumber, and cilantro. Season with salt, pepper, and Tabasco sauce.

Refrigerate the gazpacho until ready to be served—at least one hour.

Open the oysters (*see page 73*). Let them remain in the shell.

Pour the gazpacho in chilled shot glasses and place an oyster on each glass. Serve immediately.

See the photo on page 87.

TIP If you are not an oyster lover, the gazpacho tastes just as good without them. The bell pepper can also be replaced with about 5 oz (150 g) of watermelon.

IN ADVANCE The gazpacho can be stored in the refrigerator for 1 day.

GOLDEN GAZPACHO WITH MELON & LIME

MAKES approx. 15
TIME approx. 25 minutes + 1 hour in the refrigerator

7 oz (200 g) yellow tomatoes, blanched and peeled
2 tbsp finely chopped red onion
1 clove garlic, pressed
½ of a yellow bell pepper, seeded
¼ of a honeydew melon, cut it into cubes
½ of a red chili pepper, seeded and finely chopped
3 tbsp diced cucumber
freshly squeezed juice from 1–2 limes
1 tbsp finely chopped cilantro
approx. 1 ¾ cups (400 ml) cold chicken broth
salt and pepper

Mix the tomatoes, onion, garlic, bell pepper, melon, and chili in a food processor or with a hand blender. Add the cucumber, lime juice, cilantro, and broth. Season with salt and pepper. Refrigerate the gazpacho until ready to be served—at least 1 hour.

Pour into chilled shot glasses. Serve immediately.
See the photo on page 87.

IN ADVANCE The gazpacho can be stored in the refrigerator for 1 day.

GAZPACHO

Gazpacho is a chilled Spanish soup made with tomatoes and raw vegetables. It originated in Andalusia, however, there are those who claim its origin as Arabic. A traditional gazpacho is made from tomato, dry bread, garlic, olive oil, salt, and vinegar. Nowadays, there are many varieties consisting of different ingredients, including the two unconventional recipes we've offered above.

Spain also offers a "white" gazpacho—which consists of garlic, bread, and almonds—called AJO BLANCO (*see the recipe on page 50*).

ROASTED BELL PEPPER & WALNUT DIP

BEETROOT HUMMUS

BABA GHANOUSH

TZATZIKI

DUKKAH

TARAMASALATA

HUMMUS

BEAN DIP WITH SAFFRON & AJVAR RELISH

110

The recipes are available on pages 118–120 and 227 (pita)

STUFFED PITA BREAD

The recipe is available on page 120

FETA CHEESE STICKS

**PHYLLO TRIANGLES
WITH SPINACH & FETA**

**PHYLLO TRIANGLES
WITH SPICY BEEF**

SHISH KEBABS

LAMB SHISH KEBABS

The recipes are available on pages 121–123

113

GRILLED HALLOUMI WITH CAPERS

TABBOULEH IN LETTUCE LEAVES

GRILLED HALLOUMI WITH NECTARINE & MINT

COUSCOUS-STUFFED TOMATOES

GRILLED HALLOUMI WITH CHILI & HONEY

The recipes are available on pages 123–124

DOLMADES—STUFFED GRAPE LEAVES

DOLMADES—BEEF WRAPPED GRAPE LEAVES

The recipes are available on page 125

115

FALAFEL

The recipe is available on page 117

MEZE

*Meze are small dishes served throughout the Mediterranean and Middle East.
When it comes to food in this region, generosity has no limits and guests are lavished
with an abundance of sumptuous treats. Sometimes meze is served as a snack before a
meal and other times as a meal in itself. While traveling through Turkey, we were
invited into the home of a hospitable family who served no less than nineteen
different dishes! When we serve meze, we are not quite as ambitious,
settling for five or six instead.*

FALAFEL

MAKES approx. 24
TIME approx. 30 min. + 8 hrs. soaking and 1 hour
    in the refrigerator

7 oz (200 g) dry chickpeas
2 cloves garlic, chopped
1 small onion, chopped
3 tbsp chopped parsley
a pinch cayenne pepper
1 tsp ground cumin
½ tsp ground coriander
2 pinches of cinnamon
1 tbsp all-purpose flour
½ tsp baking powder
1 tsp salt

½ cup (100 ml) sesame seeds (optional)
4 cups (1 liter) of oil for frying

Soak the chickpeas in water for at least 8 hours.
Drain and combine the chickpeas in a food processor
with everything except the flour, baking powder, and
salt. Process into a coarse mixture. Pour into a bowl
and stir in the flour, baking powder, and salt. Mix
well. Refrigerate for about 1 hour.

    Roll the mixture into small balls. If you like, roll
them in sesame seeds.

Heat the oil in a heavy-bottomed saucepan to
340°F (170°C). Add a few balls at a time and fry
for about 1 minute or until the balls are golden
brown and baked through. Drain on paper towels.
Serve immediately.

    See the photo on page 116.

FALAFEL WITH MINT
Add 3 tbsp chopped fresh mint.

FALAFEL WITH CHILI PEPPERS
Add one seeded and finely chopped red chili pepper.

TIP Flatten falafel balls slightly before they are fried.
The fried falafel can be topped with ROASTED BELL
PEPPER & WALNUT DIP (*see the recipe on page 118*),
BEAN DIP WITH SAFFRON & AJVAR RELISH (*see the
recipe on page 119*), or any other dip in this chapter.
Feel free to add some feta cheese and garnish with
cilantro or parsley.

IN ADVANCE Falafel taste best right after they have
been fried. They can also be stored in the refrigerator
for about 2 days or in the freezer for about 3 months,
but they will lose their crispiness. Heat in the oven at
300°F (150°C) for about 10 minutes.

HUMMUS

MAKES approx. 2 cups
TIME approx. 10 minutes

28 oz (800 g) cooked chickpeas, drained
1–2 cloves of garlic
2 tbsp tahini (sesame paste)
1 tbsp freshly squeezed lemon juice
¼–½ cup (50–100 ml) olive oil
salt and black pepper
olive oil
pomegranate seeds, finely chopped parsley,
    or paprika for garnish

Blend the chickpeas, garlic, tahini, and lemon juice in a food processor or with a hand blender. Pour in 3 tbsp oil in a thin stream while blending. Mix until smooth (add more oil if needed). Season with salt and black pepper. Drizzle with olive oil and garnish with the seasoning of your choice.

See the photo on page 110.

IN ADVANCE Hummus can be stored in the refrigerator for 2 days.

BEETROOT HUMMUS

MAKES approx. 2 cups
TIME approx. 30 minutes

1–2 cloves garlic
14 oz (400 g) cooked chickpeas, drained
7–9 oz (200–250 g) beets, cooked and peeled
1 tbsp tahini (sesame paste)
approx. 3 tbsp olive oil
salt and pepper
olive oil and finely chopped parsley
    for garnish

Mix garlic, chickpeas, beets, and tahini in a food processor or with a hand blender. Pour in the oil in a thin stream while blending. Mix until smooth. Season with salt and pepper.

See the photo on page 110.

IN ADVANCE Hummus can be stored in the refrigerator for 2 days.

ROASTED BELL PEPPER & WALNUT DIP

MAKES approx. 2 cups
TIME approx. 1 hour

5 red bell peppers
1 clove garlic, pressed
3 tbsp Ajvar relish
1–2 slices of day-old bread
1 tbsp pomegranate syrup (or grenadine) or
    1 tsp sugar
1 ⅓ cups (300 ml) walnuts, finely chopped
salt and pepper

Preheat the oven to 480°F (250°C).

Slice each bell pepper, and remove the seeds. Place the bell peppers skin side up on a baking sheet lined with foil or parchment paper. Broil until the skin blackens (20–25 minutes). Place the peppers in a plastic bag, tie, and let cool slightly. Then remove the skin.

Blend all ingredients except the walnuts into a thick mixture in a food processor. Season with salt and pepper, and stir in the walnuts.

See the photo on page 110.

IN ADVANCE The roasted bell peppers dip can be stored for about 2 days in the refrigerator. Mix in the walnuts just before serving.

BEANS AND CHICKPEAS
Although we suggest canned beans and chickpeas in the recipes, it is cheaper, healthier, and tastier to soak and boil dried beans and chickpeas oneself. Although it can take some time, it is straightforward.

Soak the beans or chickpeas for 12–24 hours. Follow the instructions on the package for boiling. Cool them quickly in cold water. Boiled beans and chickpeas can be frozen.

BABA GHANOUSH

MAKES approx. 2 cups
TIME approx. 45 minutes

2 eggplants
approx. 1 tbsp olive oil
2 tbsp tahini (sesame paste)
2 cloves garlic
1 tbsp freshly squeezed lemon juice
salt and pepper

Preheat the oven to 440°F (225°C). Pierce the
eggplants with a fork, brush them with olive oil,
and broil for 25–30 minutes. Take them out and let
cool slightly.

Halve the eggplants and scoop out the flesh.
Put it in a food processor along with the rest of the
ingredients, and blend to a smooth paste. Season with
salt and pepper.

See the photo on page 110.

IN ADVANCE The baba ghanoush can be stored in
the refrigerator for about 2 days.

BEAN DIP WITH SAFFRON & AJVAR RELISH

MAKES approx. 2 cups
TIME approx. 5 minutes

28 oz (800 g), cooked white beans, drained
1 clove garlic
a pinch of saffron
2–3 tbsp Ajvar relish
¼–½ cup (50–100 ml) olive oil
salt and black pepper

Mix all the ingredients except the oil, salt, and pepper
in a food processor or with a hand blender. Continue
to mix and pour the oil in a thin stream while blending.
Blend until the mixture is smooth, and add more oil if
needed. Season with salt and pepper.

See the photo on page 110.

IN ADVANCE The bean dip can be stored in the
refrigerator for about 2 days.

TARAMASALATA

MAKES approx. 2 cups
TIME approx. 15 minutes

7 slices white sandwich bread (approx. 5 oz
[120 g])
½ cup (100 ml) milk
7 oz (200 g) caviar or fish roe
1 egg yolk
1 clove garlic
½ cup (100 ml) olive oil
2 tbsp freshly squeezed lemon juice
1 tbsp finely chopped parsley

Remove the edges of the bread and soak the bread
in milk for 5 minutes.

Mix the bread, caviar, egg yolk, and garlic to
a smooth purée. Continue to mix and pour the oil
in a thin stream while blending. Add the lemon juice
and parsley.

See the photo on page 110.

IN ADVANCE The taramasalata can be stored in the
refrigerator for 1 day.

DIPS

Serve dips from this chapter in the traditional
way—in small bowls with PITA BREAD on the
side, (*see the recipe on page 227*). This way, guests
can serve themselves.

If you want to serve the dips more like
a canapé, consider topping small rounds or
triangles of pita bread with a dip or spread of
choice. Garnish with fresh herbs like cilantro
or parsley, and crumbled feta.

DUKKAH

MAKES approx. 1 ⅓ cups (300 ml)
TIME approx. 20 minutes

    3 tbsp ground caraway seeds
    3 tbsp sesame seeds
    1 tsp coarsely ground black pepper
    1 tsp fennel seeds
    ½ cup (100 ml) almonds, blanched
      and peeled
    2 tbsp ground cumin
    1 tsp fresh thyme leaves
    2 tsp salt flakes
    olive oil and pita bread for serving

Heat the coriander, sesame seeds, pepper, fennel, and almonds in a dry skillet over medium-high heat until the almonds begin to brown. Allow to cool completely before adding the ground caraway seeds, thyme, and salt. The mixture should be crumbly.

    Serve with olive oil and pita bread.

    See the photo on page 110.

IN ADVANCE Dukkah can be stored in the refrigerator for about 1 week.

SPICES, NUTS & SEEDS

Dukkah is an Egyptian spice mixture of ground nuts, seeds, and spices, the exact ingredients of which vary from kitchen to kitchen. *Dukkah* is eaten by first dipping a piece of bread in a fine extra virgin olive oil and then in the spice mixture.

    Almonds can be substituted with other nuts such as pistachios or cashews.

TZATZIKI

MAKES approx. 2 cups (500 ml)
TIME approx. 10 minutes + 1 hour salting

    2 cucumbers
    1 tsp salt
    2 cups (500 ml) Greek yogurt
    2 cloves garlic, pressed
    freshly squeezed juice from ½ lemon
    2 tsp olive oil

Halve, core, and grate the cucumber coarsely. Mix it with salt in a bowl, and let sit for 1 hour.

    Drain the cucumber with a fine mesh strainer, and press out all the liquid.

    Mix the cucumber with yogurt, garlic, lemon juice, and olive oil.

    See the photo on page 110.

TIP Mix in 2 tbsp chopped fresh mint.

IN ADVANCE Tzatziki tastes best if it stands for at least 1 hour before serving. The dip can be stored in the refrigerator for 2 days.

STUFFED PITA BREAD

MAKES approx. 24
TIME approx. 15 minutes

    24 small pitas *(see the recipe on page 227)*

    FALAFEL *(see page 117)*, lamb patties
      (see page 130) or SHISH KEBAB patties
      (see page 121)
    dips of your choice *(see the index)*
    ½ red onion, thinly sliced
    6 cherry tomatoes, cut in wedges
    lettuce

    MINT YOGURT
    ½ cup (100 ml) Greek yogurt
    1 tbsp finely chopped fresh mint

Open up the pita carefully so that they are pocket-shaped.

Fill the pita with lettuce, warm falafel or meat patties, dip, red onion, tomato, and a dollop of mint yogurt.

See the photo on page 111.

IN ADVANCE Stuffed pita tastes best served right away.

LAMB SHISH KEBABS

MAKES approx. 24
TIME approx. 1 hour

    1 lb (500 g) ground lamb
    1 clove garlic, pressed
    1 egg
    4 oz (100 g) halloumi, grated
    3 tbsp chopped parsley
    ½ tsp salt
    ½ tsp black pepper
    butter for frying

    24 soaked wooden skewers

Mix the ground lamb, garlic, egg, halloumi, parsley, salt, and pepper. Mix well. Let cool for 30 minutes.

Preheat the oven to 400°F (200°C). Place aluminum foil on a baking sheet, and brush with oil.

Shape the meat with wet hands around the skewers. Place the skewers on the baking sheet and cook for about 10 minutes or until cooked through. Flip the skewers halfway through. You can also cook the skewers in a grill pan if you want grill marks.

See the photo on page 113.

TIP Shape the meat into mini patties instead, and put them into MINI PITA BREADS (*see the recipe on page 227*).

IN ADVANCE See SHISH KEBABS to the right.

SHISH KEBABS

MAKES approx. 24
TIME approx. 1 hour

    7 oz (200 g) ground beef
    7 oz (200 g) ground pork
    1 shallot, chopped
    1 clove garlic, pressed
    1 egg
    2 tbsp chopped parsley
    1 tsp dried mint
    1 tbsp dried oregano
    ½ tsp salt
    ½ tsp black pepper
    1 tbsp red wine vinegar
    ½ cup (100 ml) chopped tomatoes
    3 tbsp breadcrumbs
    butter for frying

    24 wooden skewers, soaked in water

Mix the ground beef, pork, shallot, garlic, egg, and the spices. Add the vinegar, tomatoes, and breadcrumbs. Mix well. Refrigerate for 30 minutes.

Preheat the oven to 400°F (200°C). Place aluminum foil on a baking sheet, and brush with oil.

Shape the meat with wet hands around the skewers. Place the skewers on the baking sheet, and cook for about 10 minutes or until cooked through. Flip the skewers halfway through. You can also cook the skewers in a grill pan if you want grill marks.

See the photo on page 113.

TIP Shape the meat into small patties instead, and put in MINI PITA BREADS (*see the recipe on page 227*).

IN ADVANCE The cooked skewers can be stored for about 2 days in the refrigerator and for about 3 months in the freezer. Reheat them at 300°F (150°C) until heated through. Avoid cooking for too long as the skewers may become dry.

PHYLLO TRIANGLES WITH SPINACH & FETA

MAKES approx. 24
TIME approx. 45 minutes

 1 shallot, finely chopped
 1 clove garlic, pressed
 1 tbsp olive oil
 ½ lb (250 g) spinach
 7 oz (200 g) feta, crumbled
 salt and pepper
 5 oz (150 g) phyllo dough
 approx. 3 ½ tbsp (50 g) butter, melted

Preheat the oven to 440°F (225°C).

Sauté the shallot and the garlic in oil for a minute. Stir in the spinach (if it has been frozen, squeeze out all the liquid first) and sauté it for a few minutes. Let cool, and add the crumbled feta. Season with salt and pepper. Remember that feta is already salty.

Cut the phyllo dough sheets lengthwise into strips of about 3 inches × 14 inches (8 × 35 cm). Cover with a damp towel to prevent them from drying. Lay the strips of pastry out with their shorter ends parallel to the edge of the work surface. Brush the strips with melted butter. Place a dollop of filling on the short end of each strip. Fold one corner of phyllo over filling, forming a small triangle. Repeat folding down length of strip (as when folding a flag) brushing twice with butter and to form a single, larger triangle. Brush both sides with butter. Place on a greased or parchment paper-lined baking sheet. Bake in the oven for about 5 minutes or until the triangles become golden brown.

See the photo on page 112.

TIP The phyllo dough can also be formed into cigars! Place the filling on the short side, roll the phyllo dough halfway, fold in the edges, and continue rolling. It can also be filled with the empanada fillings.

See the recipe on pages 140–141.

IN ADVANCE The filling can be stored in the refrigerator for about 2 days. The actual triangles can be prepared an hour before baking. They are crispiest when freshly baked, but can also be baked a few hours before serving.

PHYLLO TRIANGLES WITH SPICY BEEF

MAKES approx. 24
TIME approx. 1 hour

 1 small onion, finely chopped
 1 clove garlic, pressed
 1 tbsp olive oil
 ⅔ lb (300 g) ground beef
 ½ tsp ground cardamom
 ½ tsp ground cinnamon
 ½ tsp ground nutmeg
 ½ tsp ground ginger
 ½ tsp paprika
 a pinch ground cloves
 salt and pepper
 5 oz (150 g) phyllo dough
 approx. 3 ½ tbsp (50 g) butter, melted

Preheat the oven to 440°F (225°C).

Sauté the onion and garlic in olive oil for a few minutes. Stir in the meat, and cook until it is cooked through. Stir together all dry spices and add to the meat. Season with salt and pepper. Let the filling cool.

Follow the recipe for PHYLLO TRIANGLES WITH SPINACH & FETA (*see the recipe on page 122*).

See the photo on page 112.

TIP The phyllo dough triangles can also be filled with the empanada fillings.

See the recipe on pages 140–141.

IN ADVANCE The filling can be stored in the refrigerator for about 2 days. The triangles can be prepared an hour before baking. They are crispiest when freshly baked, but can also be baked a few hours before serving.

FETA CHEESE STICKS

MAKES approx. 12 large/24 small cheese sticks
TIME approx. 20 minutes

approx. 11 oz (300 g) feta
½ cup (100 ml) all-purpose flour
1 egg, lightly beaten
¾ cup (200 ml) breadcrumbs
oil for frying

Cut the feta cheese into bars about ½-inch (1cm) thick.

Pour the flour, the lightly beaten egg, and breadcrumbs into 3 separate bowls. Dip the bars first in the flour, then in the egg, and finally in the breadcrumbs. Cook the bars in a frying pan with a bit of oil until they are golden-brown on all sides. Serve immediately.

See the photo on page 112.

TIP You can use other firm and flavorful cheeses such as halloumi.

IN ADVANCE The cheese sticks taste best when served right away.

COUSCOUS-STUFFED TOMATOES

MAKES approx. 24
TIME approx. 30 minutes

½ batch couscous filling
  (*see the recipe on page 125*)
24 cherry tomatoes

Cut off the top of the cherry tomatoes, and scoop out the seeds. Fill the tomatoes with the couscous and gently replace the lids.

See the photo on page 114.

TIP Try filling the tomatoes with the lamb filling from the DOLMADES—STUFFED GRAPE LEAVES (*see the recipe on page 125*).

IN ADVANCE The couscous stuffing can be done the day before and kept in the refrigerator. The tomatoes can be stuffed a few hours before serving.

TABBOULEH IN LETTUCE LEAVES

MAKES approx. 24
TIME approx. 30 minutes

¾ cup (200 ml) cooked bulgur
2 tomatoes, finely chopped
2 tbsp finely chopped flat-leaf parsley
2 tbsp finely chopped fresh mint
2 tbsp cucumber, seeded and finely diced
1 ½ tbsp freshly squeezed lemon juice
1 ½ tbsp olive oil
salt and pepper

24 little gem lettuce leaves or other small
  lettuce leaves
fresh mint for garnish

Stir together the bulgur, tomatoes, parsley, mint, and cucumber. Mix the lemon juice and olive oil. Pour the mix over the bulgur salad, and season with salt and pepper.

Distribute the tabbouleh on salad leaves. Garnish with mint.

See the photo on page 114.

IN ADVANCE The tabbouleh can be stored in the refrigerator for 1 day. The salad leaves can be filled a few hours before serving.

> **LETTUCE CUPS**
> Small lettuce leaves such as *little gem*, *bibb*, and *endive* can be used as small bowls or cups for fillings. Try, for example, the recipe ARTICHOKE WITH CRAYFISH & FENNEL (*see the recipe on page 78*) or PANZANELLA (*see the recipe on page 180*).
>
> TACO FILLINGS (*see recipes on pages 144–145*) or SESAME SOBA NOODLES (*see the recipe on page 168*) are also great to serve on lettuce leaves. Just make sure to avoid a filling that is too runny.

GRILLED HALLOUMI
WITH CAPERS

MAKES approx. 12
TIME approx. 20 minutes

7 oz (200 g) halloumi
approx. 1 tbsp olive oil

CAPER TOPPING
3 tbsp finely chopped capers
2 tbsp finely chopped parsley
1 tsp Dijon mustard
1 tbsp freshly squeezed lemon juice
1 tsp lemon zest
3 tbsp olive oil
salt and pepper

Mix the ingredients for the caper topping. Season with salt and pepper.

Cut the halloumi first into slices and then into squares. Brush with oil and fry in a frying pan or in a grill pan until golden brown on both sides. Plate it, and spread the caper topping on the halloumi. Serve with toothpicks on the side.

See the photo on page 114.

IN ADVANCE   The dip can be stored in the refrigerator for 2 days.

GRILLED HALLOUMI
WITH CHILI & HONEY

MAKES approx. 12
TIME approx. 15 minutes

7 oz (200 g) halloumi
approx. 1 tbsp olive oil
1 red chili, seeded and finely chopped
1–2 tbsp honey

Cut the halloumi first into slices and then into squares. Brush both sides with oil and fry in a frying pan or in a grill pan until golden brown on both sides. Plate the halloumi. Sprinkle with chili and drizzle with honey. Serve with toothpicks on the side.

See the photo on page 114.

IN ADVANCE   The halloumi tastes best served right away.

GRILLED HALLOUMI
WITH NECTARINE & MINT

MAKES approx. 12
TIME approx. 15 minutes

7 oz (200 g) halloumi
approx. 1 tbsp olive oil
1–2 nectarines
12 fresh mint leaves

Cut the halloumi first into slices and then into squares. Brush it with oil and fry in a frying pan or grill pan until golden brown on both sides. Plate the halloumi.

Cut the nectarines into small wedges. Place a nectarine wedge and a mint leaf on each piece of halloumi. Serve with toothpicks on the side.

See the photo on page 114.

TIP   When fresh apricots are in season, try using them instead.

IN ADVANCE   The halloumi tastes best served right away.

HALLOUMI

Halloumi is a cheese from Cyprus traditionally made from sheep's milk. However, one can also find halloumi made from goat's milk and cow's milk. This salty, firm cheese has a slightly rubbery texture, and it is well suited to frying or grilling because it does not melt in the heat.

The cheese is salted and then either preserved or eaten fresh. In Cyprus, it is often served with watermelon; the sweetness of the watermelon compliments the saltiness of the cheese.

DOLMADES—STUFFED GRAPE LEAVES

MAKES approx. 30
TIME approx. 1 ½ hours

There are different schools of thought on how to make authentic stuffed grape leaves. We have chosen the faster method, in which you do not need to cook the rolls.

30 pickled grape leaves
2 lemons
½ cup (100 ml) olive oil

LAMB FILLING
2 shallots, finely chopped
1 clove garlic, finely chopped
1 tbsp olive oil
7 oz (200 g) ground lamb
¾ cup (200 ml) cooked rice
1 tsp ground cinnamon
1 tsp ground cumin
3 tbsp golden raisins, roughly chopped
3 tbsp pine nuts, toasted
2 tbsp parsley finely chopped
salt and pepper

Sauté the shallots and the garlic in oil for a few minutes. Add the ground lamb and cook until it is cooked through. Add rice, cinnamon, cumin, and raisins. Stir and add the pine nuts and parsley. Season with salt and pepper.

Rinse the grape leaves in running water, and separate them gently. Remove any thick center veins from the leaves. Place one grape leaf with the glossy side down. Place about 1 tbsp of the lamb and rice mixture on the leaf. Roll while tucking in the edges, until the leaf forms a firm cylindrical shape. Do the same with the remaining grape leaves. Plate the roll "seam" side down.

Squeeze some lemon juice over the rolls and drizzle with olive oil.

See the photo on page 115.

IN ADVANCE The stuffed grape leaves can be stored in the refrigerator for 1 day.

DOLMADES—BEEF WRAPPED GRAPE LEAVES

MAKES approx. 30
TIME approx. 1½ hours

30 pickled grape leaves
14 oz (400 g) beef tenderloin, in thin slices
3 tbsp olive oil
½ tsp ground cumin

COUSCOUS FILLING
1 tbsp red onion, finely chopped
⅔ cup (150 ml) cooked couscous
2 oz feta, crumbled
3 tbsp finely chopped orange bell peppers
1 tsp lemon zest
½ cup (100 ml) tomato, finely chopped
1 tbsp fresh mint, finely chopped
¼ tsp ground cumin
3 tbsp finely chopped pistachios

Preheat the oven to 400°F (200°C). Rinse the grape leaves in running water. Mix all ingredients for the filling.

Dry the grape leaves and roll them following the instructions in the recipe to the right.

Place a slice of beef on a cutting board and cover with plastic wrap. Gently pound the meat with a meat mallet into a thin rectangular shape. Cut the meat into long strips, the width of a dolma. Wrap a strip of meat around each dolma. Fasten with a toothpick and cut off excess meat. Mix the oil with the cumin, and brush onto the rolls. Season with salt and pepper.

Brush an oven rack with oil, and place the rolls on the rack. Place the rack on a baking sheet covered with foil. Cook in the oven for 10–15 minutes or until the meat has browned. Let cool for a few minutes. Cut each roll crosswise with a diagonal cut.
Serve either warm or cold.

See the photo on page 115.

TIP If you leave out the beef, these rolls are a great vegetarian dish.

IN ADVANCE The rolls can be stored uncooked in the refrigerator for 1 day. Cook right before serving. If they are to be served cold, then they can be stored already cooked in the refrigerator for 1 day.

PIGS IN A BLANKET

HUSH PUPPIES

BBQ BABY BACK
RIBS

FRIED CHICKEN

BUFFALO
CHICKEN WINGS

BLUE CHEESE DIP

The recipes are available on pages 131–133

COLESLAW

CORN ON THE COB

ZUCCHINI CORN BREAD

CORN DOGS

CLASSIC HAMBURGER
SLIDERS

TUNA SLIDERS WITH MANGO
SALSA & WASABI MAYO

SLIDERS DELUXE WITH
FOIE GRAS & TRUFFLE

LAMB SLIDERS WITH
CHÈVRE & BEETS

The recipes are available on pages 129–130

USA

*Defining "typical" American food can be tricky, as it is literally a melting
pot of the world's culinary traditions. However, here we hope
to capture a few dishes that can boast the label
"Made in the USA."*

CLASSIC HAMBURGER SLIDERS

MAKES approx. 24
TIME approx. 1 hour

1 ¾ lbs (800 g) ground beef
2 eggs
½ tsp salt
½–1 tsp freshly ground black pepper
butter for frying

8 hamburger buns
1 head of lettuce
4 small tomatoes, sliced
1 small red onion, sliced
ketchup and mustard

DRESSING
½ cup MAYONNAISE, store bought
(or *see the recipe on page 74*)
3 tbsp ketchup
2 tbsp sweet relish
salt and pepper

Punch out 3 mini hamburger buns from each
hamburger bun.

Mix the ground beef with the eggs, salt, and
pepper and let rest in the refrigerator for 30 minutes.
Shape into 24 small patties. Flatten patties properly.

Mix the ingredients for the dressing.

Melt the butter in a grill pan or skillet. Grill the
patties on medium heat for a few minutes until
brown on both sides.

Place the lettuce, beef patties, dressing, tomato,
onions, mustard, and ketchup onto the buns and
fasten with a toothpick.

Serve immediately.
See the photo on page 128.

IN ADVANCE The grilled patties can be stored
in the refrigerator for a day or in the freezer for
a month. Heat up in the oven at 300°F (150°C)
for about ten minutes just before serving. The
dressing may be prepared the day before and stored
in the refrigerator.

SLIDERS DELUXE WITH FOIE GRAS & TRUFFLE

MAKES approx. 24
TIME approx. 1 hour

1 batch of ground beef patties
   (*see* CLASSIC SLIDERS *to the left*)
butter for frying
1 batch CARAMELIZED RED ONION
   (*see the recipe on page 217*)

8 hamburger buns
1 head of lettuce
7 oz (200 g) foie gras, ½-inch (1 cm) thick slices
black truffle, thinly sliced

Punch out 3 mini hamburger buns from each
hamburger bun. Prepare the beef patties according
to the recipe to the left.

Melt the butter in a grill pan or skillet. Grill the
patties on medium heat for a few minutes until
brown on both sides.

Place lettuce, beef patties, foie gras, truffle, and
caramelized red onion onto the buns, and fasten with
a toothpick. Serve immediately.

See the photo on page 128.

IN ADVANCE The patties can be prepared like the
CLASSIC HAMBURGER SLIDERS (*see the recipe to
the left*).

LAMB SLIDERS WITH CHÈVRE & BEETS

MAKES approx. 24
TIME approx. 1 hour

1 ¾ lbs (800 g) ground lamb
2 eggs
1 clove garlic, pressed
½ tsp salt
½–1 tsp freshly ground black pepper
butter for frying

8 hamburger buns
⅔ lb (300 g) fresh beets
5 oz (150 g) chèvre
1 head of lettuce
fresh thyme

DRESSING
4 tbsp mayonnaise
2 tsp honey
2 tsp Dijon mustard

Punch out 3 mini hamburger buns from each hamburger bun.

Mix the ground lamb, eggs, garlic, salt, and pepper and let sit the refrigerator.

Boil the beets until tender. Peel and cut them into thin slices. Cut the chèvre into thin slices.

Mix the ingredients for the dressing. Shape the lamb mixture into patties and flatten properly. Melt the butter in a grill pan or skillet. Grill the patties on medium heat for a few minutes until brown on both sides.

Place lettuce, lamb patties, dressing, beets, chèvre, and thyme onto the buns, and fasten with a toothpick. Serve immediately.

See the photo on page 128.

IN ADVANCE For the lamb sliders, *see* CLASSIC HAMBURGER SLIDERS *on page 129.* Beets can be boiled and the dressing can be prepared the day before serving. Keep refrigerated.

TUNA SLIDERS WITH MANGO SALSA & WASABI MAYO

MAKES approx. 24
TIME approx. 1 hour

1 ½ lbs (700 g) fresh tuna
salt and pepper
oil for frying

8 hamburger buns
1 head of lettuce

MANGO SALSA
½ of a mango, diced
4 oz (100 g) watermelon, diced
1 avocado, diced
½ cucumber (approx. 4 oz [100 g]), diced
1 tomato, diced
½ of a small red onion, finely chopped
1 tsp red chili pepper, seeded and finely chopped
2 tbsp cilantro, finely chopped
3 tbsp (50 ml) freshly squeezed lime juice

WASABI MAYO
½ cup (100 ml) MAYONNAISE, **store bought**
(or *see the recipe on page 74*)
approx. 1 tsp wasabi paste

Punch out 3 mini hamburger buns from every hamburger bun.

Mix the ingredients for the mango salsa.

Mix the ingredients for the wasabi mayo.

Cut the tuna into slices, approx. 1 ½ inches × 1 ½ inches (4 cm × 4 cm). Heat the oil in a grill pan or a frying pan to medium-high heat. Quickly sear the tuna on both sides until the outside is light brown and the inside is still pink. Season with salt and pepper.

Place salad, tuna, mango salsa, and wasabi mayo into the buns, and fasten with a toothpick. Serve immediately.

See the photo on page 128.

IN ADVANCE The wasabi mayo can be stored in the refrigerator for 1 day. The mango salsa should be made the same day. Slice the tuna and sear it just before serving.

BBQ BABY BACK RIBS
WITH COLESLAW

MAKES approx. 30
TIME approx. 1 hour and 45 minutes

3 ⅓ lbs (1 ½ kg) baby back pork ribs
1 tsp of salt per 4 cups (1 liter) of water
5 black peppercorns
1 bay leaf

BBQ SAUCE
1 ⅓ cups (300 ml) ketchup
3 tbsp Dijon mustard
3 tbsp red wine vinegar
1 ½ tbsp Worcestershire sauce
3 tbsp brown sugar
½ tsp garlic salt
½ tsp freshly ground black pepper
a few drops of Tabasco
1 tsp chipotle paste (optional)
a few drops liquid smoke (optional)

COLESLAW (approx. 2 cups [500 ml])
1 ¾ cups (400 ml) shredded cabbage
½ cup (100 ml) grated carrot
3 tbsp mayonnaise
2 tbsp sour cream
1 tbsp white wine vinegar
salt and pepper

Place the ribs in a large pot of water, so that it is entirely covered. Add salt, pepper, and bay leaf. Bring to a boil, and simmer for about 1 hour or until the meat is tender. Remove the ribs from the pot and let cool.

Mix all the ingredients for the sauce, except the liquid smoke, in a saucepan. Simmer for about 20 minutes or until the sauce thickens. Stir in the liquid smoke. Let the sauce cool.

Mix together all the ingredients for the coleslaw, and season with salt and pepper.

Preheat the oven to 400°F (200°C).

Wipe the meat dry with a paper towel, and separate the ribs between the bones. Place on a baking dish and coat with barbecue sauce. Broil the ribs in the oven or on a grill for about 10 minutes. Turn halfway through baking time. Serve immediately.

See the photo on page 126.

IN ADVANCE The meat can be boiled about 2 days in advance and stored in the refrigerator. The sauce can be prepared and stored in the refrigerator for up to a week. The coleslaw tastes even better when prepared the day before serving.

BUFFALO CHICKEN WINGS
WITH BLUE CHEESE DIP

MAKES approx. 24
TIME approx. 45 minutes

24 chicken wings
4 cups (1 liter) of oil for deep frying
4 tbsp butter, melted
Tabasco or other hot sauce to taste

3–4 celery stalks

BLUE CHEESE DIP
5 oz (150 g) blue cheese
½ cup (100 ml) MAYONNAISE, store bought
(or *see the recipe on page 74*)
½ cup (100 ml) sour cream
salt and pepper

Cut the celery into sticks. Mix the ingredients for the dip. Season with salt and pepper.

Heat the oil in a heavy-bottomed saucepan to 340°F (170°C). Fry a few chicken wings at a time until golden brown—about 7 minutes. Drain on paper towels.

Mix the butter with the Tabasco and coat the chicken wings so they are covered completely. Serve immediately with dip and celery sticks.

See the photo on page 126.

IN ADVANCE The dip can be made the day before, but the chicken wings will taste best if they are fried right before serving.

FRIED CHICKEN WITH HONEY MUSTARD SAUCE

MAKES approx. 24
TIME approx. 1 hour and 15 minutes

1 lb (500 g) chicken fillets

1 ⅓ cups (300 ml) all-purpose flour
1 tsp paprika
1 tsp garlic salt
1 tsp onion powder
1 tsp cayenne pepper
1 tsp chili powder
1 tsp dried thyme
1 tsp dried oregano
2–3 tsp salt
½ tsp black pepper
½ tsp white pepper
1 ⅓ cups (300 ml) breadcrumbs

11 oz (300 g) macadamia nuts, finely chopped
2 eggs, lightly beaten
4 cups (1 liter) of oil for deep frying

HONEY MUSTARD SAUCE
1 ⅓ cups (300 ml) MAYONNAISE, store bought
   (or *see the recipe on page 74*)
1 tbsp Dijon mustard
1 tbsp honey

Cut the chicken fillets into strips. Mix the flour with the spices.

Mix the breadcrumbs and nuts.

Coat the chicken first in flour, then in the eggs, and then in the breadcrumbs. Refrigerate for about 30 minutes.

Mix the ingredients for the dipping sauce.

Heat oil in a heavy-bottomed saucepan to 320°F (160°C). Fry the chicken pieces a few at a time for about a minute and a half or until golden brown. Drain on paper towels.

Serve immediately with dipping sauce.

See the photo on page 126.

IN ADVANCE The sauce can be stored in the refrigerator for about 2 days. The chicken tastes best when freshly fried.

ZUCCHINI CORNBREAD

MAKES approx. 45
TIME approx. 1 hour

2 eggs
7 tbsp (100 g) melted butter
1 ½ cups (350 ml) buttermilk
1 ⅓ cups (300 ml) cornmeal
⅔ cup (150 ml) all-purpose flour
1 tbsp sugar
2 tsp baking powder
½ tsp baking soda
½ tsp salt
2 small zucchini (approx. ½ lb [250 g]), grated

Preheat the oven to 400°F (200°C). Grease and flour one rectangular baking pan (approx. 8 × 12 inches [20 cm × 30 cm]).

Beat the eggs in a bowl, and pour in the melted butter and buttermilk.

Mix the dry ingredients in another bowl and combine with the buttermilk mixture until smooth. Add the zucchini. Pour the batter into a pan, and bake it in the oven for about 40 minutes or until the bread is baked through and a toothpick inserted in the middle comes out clean.

See the photo on page 127.

IN ADVANCE Cornbread can be stored in the refrigerator for about 3 days or in the freezer for 3 months.

PIGS IN A BLANKET

MAKES approx. 24
TIME approx. 1 hour and 15 minutes

3 oz (85 g) puff pastry sheets
24 cocktail sausages or mini hot dogs
3 oz (75 g) Cheddar cheese, grated
1 egg, lightly beaten
sesame seeds for garnish
ketchup, mustard, and/or chili sauce
   for serving

Preheat the oven to 440°F (225°C).

Cut the puff pastry into strips of about 3 inches × 1 inch (7 cm × 2 ½ cm). Brush lightly with the egg, and place about 1 tsp of cheese and a mini hot dog on one edge. Roll up the hot dog in the puff pastry. Place the finished rolls, faced down, on a baking sheet lined with parchment paper. Brush the puff pastry with a little more egg. Sprinkle with sesame seeds, and refrigerate for about 15 minutes.

Bake for about 20 minutes. Serve immediately with ketchup, mustard, or chili sauce.

See the photo on page 126.

IN ADVANCE Unbaked pigs in a blanket can be stored in the refrigerator for 1 day, but brush and bake them right before serving.

CORN DOGS

MAKES approx. 24
TIME approx. 45 minutes

> 24 cocktail sausages or mini hot dogs
> 1 cup (250 ml) all-purpose flour
> 1 cup (250 ml) cornmeal
> 2 tbsp sugar
> 2 tsp baking powder
> ½ tsp salt
> 1 cup (250 ml) milk
> 1 egg
> 4 cups (1 liter) oil for deep frying
>
> 24 wooden skewers
> ketchup, mustard, and/or chili sauce for serving

Dry the mini sausages with paper towels, otherwise the batter will not stick. Mix all dry ingredients together. Stir in the milk and egg, and whisk until smooth.

Heat oil in a heavy-bottomed saucepan to 340°F (170°C). Dip the mini sausages in the batter and then in the hot oil a few at a time. Fry until the sausages are golden brown and crispy, turning them occasionally so that they fry evenly. Drain them on paper towels. Pierce the corn dogs on wooden skewers, and serve immediately with chili sauce, ketchup, and/or mustard.

See the photo on page 127.

IN ADVANCE Corn dogs are best when freshly fried.

CORN ON THE COB

MAKES approx. 24
TIME approx. 15 minutes

> 4 ears of fresh corn
> FLAVORED BUTTER, optional *(see the recipe on page 246)*
> salt

Boil the fresh corn in salted water for 7–10 minutes. For frozen, follow the instructions on the package.

Cut the corn into pieces, spread with herb butter, and sprinkle with salt. Serve warm.

See the photo on page 127.

IN ADVANCE Corn on the cob tastes best freshly cooked.

HUSH PUPPIES

MAKES approx. 16
TIME approx. 45 minutes

> 1 cup (250 ml) cornmeal
> 1 tsp salt
> 2 tbsp sugar
> ½ tsp baking powder
> ½ cup (100 ml) corn
> 1 shallot, finely chopped
> ½ cup (100 ml) sour cream
> 1 egg
> 4 cups (1 liter) oil for deep frying

Mix the dry ingredients. Blend the corn, onion, and sour cream in a food processor or with a hand blender. Mix everything together into a thick batter.

Heat the oil in a heavy-bottomed saucepan to approximately 340°F (170°C). Fry a few dollops of dough at a time for about 3 minutes, or until golden brown and cooked through. Drain on paper towels. Serve immediately.

See the photo page 126.

WITH BACON & SCALLION Mix 4 oz (100 g) fried, crumbled bacon, and 3 tbsp thinly sliced scallions.

IN ADVANCE Hush puppies are best when fresh.

QUESADILLAS

CHORIZO & JALAPEÑO FILLING

TUNA FILLING

CHEESE & GOLDEN SALSA

The recipes are available on pages 146–147

134

TACOS

SHRIMP & CILANTRO-LIME SAUCE

TUNA &
PINEAPPLE SALSA

FRIED COD &
COLESLAW

The recipes are available on pages 144–145

SWEET POTATO &
BEAN DIP

TORTILLA CHIPS

CHORIZO & CORN DIP

CLASSIC TACO
FILLING

CHICKEN

TORTILLAS

The recipes are available on pages 141–144 and 228 (tortilla
chips and tortillas)

CHILI CON CARNE

SOUR CREAM

PICO DE GALLO

GUACAMOLE

BLACK BEAN DIP

137

JALAPEÑO POPPERS

The recipe is available on page 146

EMPANADAS

CHICKEN & ORANGE

CHEESE, CORN & CHILI

SPICY BEEF

The recipes are available on pages 140–141

139

TEX-MEX

*An excellent way to serve Tex-Mex at a casual gathering is to fill
the table with an array of dishes, such as hearty chili, piquant
pico de gallo, and creamy guacamole—served with
homemade tortilla chips, of course.*

EMPANADAS WITH CHICKEN & ORANGE

MAKES approx. 24
TIME approx. 1 hour

EMPANADA DOUGH
2 cups (500 ml) all-purpose flour
2 tsp salt
1 tsp sugar
1 tsp active dry yeast
1 tbsp melted butter
1 egg
1 tbsp canola oil
½–⅔ cup (100–150 ml) water

FILLING
1 small onion, chopped
2 tbsp olive oil
7 oz (200 g) ground chicken
1 tsp grated fresh ginger
½ tsp ground cinnamon
1 tbsp parsley finely chopped
1 tsp coriander finely chopped
½ orange, zested
1 egg, beaten
salt and pepper

1 egg, lightly beaten

Start with the dough by mixing the flour, salt, sugar, and yeast. Add butter, eggs, and oil into the flour mixture. Heat the water to 100°F (40°C), add the flour mixture, and knead the dough smooth. Let it rise for 30–40 minutes under a kitchen towel.

Preheat the oven to 400°F (200°C).

Sauté the onion in the oil. Add the chicken, ginger, and cinnamon, and cook until the chicken is cooked through. Put it in a bowl and add parsley, coriander, and orange zest. Stir in the egg.

Season with salt and pepper and let it cool.

Remove the dough, and knead until smooth. Roll it out thin, and using a round cutter, cut out rounds about 3 inches (8 cm) in diameter. Place 1 tbsp of filling on each round. Brush the edges with water, and fold the circle in half, forming a half moon. Press and seal the edges with a fork. Place empanadas on a baking sheet covered with parchment paper. Brush with egg.

Bake for 13–15 minutes or until golden brown.
See the photo on page 139.

IN ADVANCE Ready-baked empanadas can be stored in the refrigerator for about 1 day or in the freezer for about 3 months. Heat them in the oven at 300°F (150°C) for 7–8 minutes just before serving. They taste best when fresh, but can be baked the day they are to be served.

EMPANADAS WITH CHEESE, CORN & CHILI

MAKES approx. 24
TIME approx. 1 hour

1 batch EMPANADA DOUGH (*see the recipe to the left*)

FILLING
1 small onion, chopped
1 tbsp olive oil
2 cups (500 ml) corn
1 tsp seeded, finely chopped green chili
3 tbsp heavy cream
3 tbsp grated Cheddar

2 scallions, sliced
1 tbsp chopped parsley
1 tbsp chopped cilantro
salt and pepper

Sauté the onion in oil. Add the corn and chili, and sauté for another few minutes. Stir in the cream and cheese. Stir until the cheese has melted. Add the scallions, parsley, and cilantro. Season with salt and pepper. Let cool.

See the photo page 139.

IN ADVANCE *See* EMPANADAS WITH CHICKEN & ORANGE *on the opposite page.*

EMPANADAS WITH SPICY BEEF

MAKES approx. 24
TIME approx. 1 hour

1 batch EMPANADA DOUGH (*see the recipe on the opposite page*)

FILLING
1 small onion, finely chopped
1 clove garlic, pressed
1 tbsp olive oil
⅔ lb (300 g) ground beef
1 tsp salt
½ tsp black pepper
½ tsp white pepper
½ tsp ground cardamom
½ tsp ground cinnamon
½ tsp ground nutmeg
½ tsp ground ginger
½ tsp paprika powder
a pinch of ground cloves

Sauté the onion and garlic in olive oil for a few minutes. Stir in the ground beef, and cook until it cooked through. Mix the dry spices and stir into the ground beef, and cook for a few more minutes. Let the filling cool.

See the photo on page 139.

IN ADVANCE *See* EMPANADAS WITH CHICKEN & ORANGE *on the opposite page.*

PICO DE GALLO

MAKES approx. 1 ⅓ cups (300 ml)
TIME approx. 15 minutes

3 tomatoes, seeded and diced
½ red onion, chopped
2 tbsp chopped fresh cilantro
½–1 jalapeño, seeded and finely chopped
2 tbsp freshly squeezed lime juice
salt and pepper

Stir together all ingredients. Season with salt and pepper.

Serve with tortilla chips, for example, and/or TORTILLA BREAD (*see the recipe on page 228*).

See the photo page 137.

IN ADVANCE The pico de gallo can be refrigerated for a few hours to allow the flavors to marry.

BLACK BEAN DIP

MAKES approx. 1 ⅓ cups (300 ml)
TIME approx. 5 minutes

14 oz (400 g) cooked black beans, drained
½ cup (100 ml) taco sauce
salt and pepper

Mix beans and sauce in a food processor or with a hand blender. Season with salt and pepper.

Serve with tortilla chips, for example, and/or TORTILLAS (*see the recipe on page 228*).

See the photo on page 137.

IN ADVANCE The dip can be stored in the refrigerator for about 2 days.

TORTILLA CHIPS WITH CHICKEN

MAKES approx. 24
TIME approx. 1 hour

5 oz (150 g) chicken fillets
1 lime, freshly squeezed juice
½ onion, chopped
1 clove garlic, pressed
1 tbsp olive oil
½ tsp ground cumin
1 tomato, chopped
1 tbsp chopped fresh cilantro
1 tsp freshly squeezed lemon juice
salt and pepper

approx. 24 TORTILLA CHIPS (*see the recipe on page 228*) or store bought
½ cup (100 ml) sour cream
fresh cilantro for garnish

Cut the chicken into small cubes. Mix with lime juice, and marinate for at least an hour.

Sauté the onion and garlic in oil for a few minutes. Add in the chicken and cumin, and cook until the chicken is cooked through. Add the tomato, cilantro, and lemon juice, and stir. Season with salt and pepper.

Plate the tortilla chips, and top with chicken, sour cream, and fresh cilantro.

See the photo on page 136.

IN ADVANCE The chicken topping can be stored in the refrigerator for 1 day. Heat just before serving.

CLASSIC TACO FILLING

MAKES approx. 24
TIME approx. 30 minutes

Here we've made it easy for ourselves with store bought taco seasoning mix, tortilla chips, and salsa. Of course, making your own tortilla chips tastes even better (see the recipe on page 228)—but then, of course, it takes a little longer to get the food on the table.

½ lb (250 g) ground beef
½ packet of taco seasoning mix

24 round tortilla chips
¾ cup (200 ml) corn
4 oz (100 g) Cheddar, grated
¾ cup (200 ml) sour cream
¾ cup (200 ml) taco salsa
fresh cilantro for garnish

Preheat the oven to 400°F (200°C).

Cook the ground beef as directed on the seasoning packet.

Plate the tortilla chips. Add a dollop of ground beef and some corn to each chip. Sprinkle some cheese on top. Bake in the oven for 5–10 minutes or until cheese has melted.

Top with a dollop of sour cream and salsa on each chip. Garnish with a little cilantro, and serve immediately.

See the photo on page 136.

IN ADVANCE The filling can be made a day in advance and stored in the refrigerator. Bake right before serving.

CHORIZO & CORN DIP

MAKES approx. 4 cups (1 liter)
TIME approx. 45 minutes

½ onion, chopped
1 tbsp olive oil
7 oz (200 g) chorizo, cut into small pieces
14 oz (410 g) canned black beans, drained
7 oz (190 g) canned corn, drained
¾ cup (200 ml) taco sauce
¾ cup (200 ml) finely grated Cheddar
1 onion, sliced
salt and pepper

approx. 24 TORTILLA CHIPS, (*see the recipe on page 228*) or store bought tortilla chips

Preheat the oven to 440°F (225°C).

Sauté the onion in olive oil. Add the chorizo, and cook for a couple of minutes more. Add in the beans and corn, and stir. Place mixture into a food processor, and blend for a few seconds until chopped.

Blend the mixture and taco sauce, ½ cup (100 ml) of the cheese, and scallions. Season with salt and pepper.

Pour the mixture into a greased ovenproof dish. Sprinkle over the rest of the cheese, and let it cook in the oven for about 10 minutes.

Serve the chorizo and corn dip on tortilla chips. *See the photo on page 136.*

IN ADVANCE The dip can be made completely the day before and stored in the refrigerator. Heat in the oven at 400°F (200°C) for about 5 minutes right before serving.

SWEET POTATO & BEAN DIP

MAKES approx. 2 cups (500 ml)
TIME approx. 40 minutes

14 oz (400 g) sweet potatoes, peeled
1 onion, chopped
2 cloves garlic, pressed
1 tbsp olive oil
½ green chili pepper, seeded and chopped
1 tsp ground coriander

2 tsp ground cumin
1 ¾ cups (400 ml) cooked white beans
freshly squeezed juice of 1 lime
2 tbsp chopped fresh cilantro
salt and pepper

fresh cilantro for garnish

Cut the sweet potato into pieces. Boil in salted water until soft—about 15 minutes. Drain.

Sauté the onion and garlic for a few minutes in olive oil. Add the chili, ground cilantro, and cumin. Sauté for a few more minutes. Allow to cool slightly.

Mix all ingredients, except for the cilantro, in a food processor or with a hand blender. Stir in the cilantro, and season with salt and pepper.

Serve with tortilla chips, and/or tortillas (*see the recipe on page 228*).

See the photo on page 136.

IN ADVANCE The dip can be stored in the refrigerator for about 2 days.

GUACAMOLE

MAKES approx. 2 cups (500 ml)
TIME approx. 10 minutes

6 avocados
1 clove garlic, pressed
2 tbsp freshly squeezed lime or lemon juice
approx. 1 tsp chopped red chili pepper, seeded
salt and pepper

Halve the avocados, pit, and scoop out the flesh. Mix all ingredients in a food processor or with a hand blender until smooth. Season with salt and pepper.

Serve with tortilla chips, for example, and/or tortillas (*see the recipe on page 228*).

See the photo on page 137.

IN ADVANCE As avocados discolor quickly, the guacamole should be served fresh.

All dips in this chapter can also be served as canapés on tortilla chips. Likewise, the CHORIZO & CORN DIP can be served with tortillas on the side.

CHILI CON CARNE

MAKES approx. 2 cups (500 ml)
TIME approx. 30 minutes + 1 ½ hour of cooking

⅔ lb (300 g) prime rib
1 tbsp olive oil
1 onion, finely chopped
2 cloves garlic, pressed
1 jalapeño, seeded and finely chopped
1 tsp ancho chili pepper
1 tsp chili powder
1 tsp cocoa powder
½ tsp ground cumin
½ tsp dried oregano
½ tsp ground coriander
2 tbsp brown sugar
1 tbsp water
1 cup chopped tomatoes
2 tbsp tomato paste
¾ cup (200 ml) beef broth
¾ cup (200 ml) cooked kidney beans, drained
salt and pepper

Trim the meat, and cut it into small pieces.

Heat the oil in a casserole pot, brown the meat and set aside. Reduce the heat and sauté the onion, garlic, and jalapeño until tender.

Mix all the spices with water until it reaches a pasty consistency. Stir the spice paste into the pan and simmer for a few minutes. Add the meat, crushed tomatoes, tomato paste, and broth. Bring to a boil, and simmer for 1 ½–2 hours or until most of the liquid has been absorbed. Add the kidney beans approximately 30 minutes before the stew is finished. Season with salt and pepper.

Serve immediately with, for example, TORTILLA CHIPS and TORTILLAS (see the recipes on page 228), PICO DE GALLO (see the recipe on page 141), GUACAMOLE (see the recipe on page 143), and sour cream.

See the photo on page 137.

IN ADVANCE The chili con carne can be cooked 2–3 days in advance. Cool down quickly by placing the pot in cold water. Store in the refrigerator. Heat slowly, possibly with some water if the chili is too thick.

SHRIMP TACOS WITH CILANTRO-LIME SAUCE

MAKES approx. 24
TIME approx. 30 minutes + 2 hours marinating

24 raw large shrimp, peeled

MARINADE
5 tbsp olive oil
2 cloves garlic, chopped
1 tsp ground cumin
1 tsp chili powder
1 tsp salt
a pinch cayenne pepper

CILANTRO-LIME SAUCE
⅔ cup (150 ml) sour cream
2 tbsp chopped fresh cilantro
freshly squeezed juice from ½ lime
salt and pepper

6 large soft tortillas, store bought (or *see the recipe on page 228*)
2 tomatoes, finely cubed
2 avocados, finely cubed
7 oz (200 g) iceberg lettuce, finely chopped

Mix together the marinade ingredients. Add in the shrimp, and marinate for a few hours. Stir the ingredients for the cilantro-lime sauce.

Preheat the oven to 400°F (200°C).

With a round cutter, cut out rounds of tortilla bread, about 3 ½ inches (7 cm) in diameter. Lay them on a baking sheet, and place in the oven for about a minute and a half. Remove from the oven, and drape over a thin rolling pin or similar. Let cool.

Heat a grill pan to medium-high heat. Sauté the shrimp for about 5 minutes or until they are cooked through.

Fill the tortilla with lettuce, tomato, avocado, and a shrimp. Top with a little sauce. Serve immediately.

See the photo on page 135.

TIP To save time, you can skip shaping the tortillas. Instead, add the filling directly to the cut tortilla circles.

IN ADVANCE The sauce can be made the day before and kept cold. The rest tastes best prepared the same day.

FISH TACOS WITH FRIED COD & COLESLAW

MAKES approx. 24
TIME approx. 30 minutes

7 oz (200 g) cod
¾ cup (200 ml) all-purpose flour
2 tbsp cornstarch

2 tsp salt
1 egg
¾ cup (200 ml) beer

COLESLAW
4 oz (100 g) cabbage, shredded
1 small carrot, grated
5 tbsp mayonnaise
4 tbsp sour cream
freshly squeezed juice from ½ lime
1 tsp seeded finely chopped jalapeño
½ tsp dried oregano
a pinch ground cumin
a pinch cayenne pepper
salt and pepper

4 cups (1 liter) oil for deep frying
6 large tortillas, store bought (or *see the recipe on page 228*)
some sliced jalapeño for garnish

Cut the cod into pieces and place on paper towels.

Mix the flour, cornstarch, and salt. Add the eggs and beer, and mix to a smooth batter. Mix ingredients for the coleslaw. Season with salt and pepper.

Preheat the oven to 400°F (200°C). With a round cutter, cut out rounds from the tortilla bread, about 3 ½ inches (7 cm) in diameter. Lay the rounds on a baking sheet, and place in the oven for about a minute and a half. Remove from the oven, and drape over a thin rolling pin or similar. Let cool.

Heat the oil to 340°F (170°C) in a heavy-bottomed saucepan. Coat the pieces of cod with the batter and drain excess batter. Fry the cod, a few pieces at a time, for about 1 minute or until golden brown. Drain on a paper towel.

Fill the tortillas with coleslaw and top with the cod. Garnish with jalapeño. Serve immediately.

See the photo on page 135.

IN ADVANCE The coleslaw can be made the day before and stored in the refrigerator. The rest tastes best prepared the same day.

FISH TACOS WITH TUNA & PINEAPPLE SALSA

MAKES approx. 24
TIME approx. 20 minutes + 2 hours marinating

½ lb (250 g) fresh tuna

MARINADE
½ cup (100 ml) pineapple juice
½ cup (100 ml) lime juice, freshly squeezed
½ tsp salt
1 tsp chopped fresh oregano
1 clove garlic, pressed

PINEAPPLE SALSA
⅔ cup (150 ml) chopped pineapple
3 tbsp chopped red tomato
3 tbsp chopped yellow tomato
freshly squeezed juice from ½ lime
1 small clove garlic, pressed
½–1 tsp seeded and finely chopped red chili pepper
1 tsp grated fresh ginger
1 tbsp fresh cilantro, finely chopped
1 tsp fresh mint, finely chopped
salt and pepper

6 large tortillas, store bought (or *see the recipe on page 228*)
fresh mint for garnish

Cut the tuna into smaller pieces. Whisk the ingredients for the marinade, and mix with the tuna. Refrigerate for at least 2 hours.

Preheat the oven to 400°F (200°C). Stir together the ingredients for the salsa. Season with salt and pepper.

With a round cutter, cut out rounds from the tortilla bread, about 3 ½ inches (7 cm) in diameter. Lay the rounds on a baking sheet, and place in the oven for about a minute and a half. Remove from the oven, and drape over a thin rolling pin or similar. Let cool.

Brush a grill pan with oil. Quickly sear the tuna until the outside is light brown and the inside is still pink. Fill the tortillas with a piece of tuna in each tortilla, and top with pineapple salsa. Garnish with mint. Serve immediately.

See the photo on page 135.

IN ADVANCE Salsa can be made the day before and stored in the refrigerator. The rest tastes best prepared the same day.

JALAPEÑO POPPERS

MAKES approx. 20
TIME approx. 45 minutes

20 fresh jalapeño peppers
approx. 4 oz (100 g) Cheddar, grated
a few drops of Tabasco
1 tsp salt
a pinch ground black pepper
3 eggs
approx. 1 ⅓ cups (300 ml) breadcrumbs
2 tsp dried oregano
4 cups (1 liter) of oil for deep-frying

Cut a slit lengthwise in each jalapeño without cutting through. Gently scrape out the seeds.

Carefully fill each jalapeño with cheese. Press lightly to close opening.

Beat the eggs in a bowl. Mix the breadcrumbs and oregano in a separate bowl.

Dip the jalapeño first in egg and then in breadcrumbs. Repeat for all the jalapeños.

Heat oil in a heavy-bottomed saucepan to 320°F (160°C). Fry a few jalapeños at a time in the hot oil for about a minute and twenty seconds. Drain on paper towels. Serve warm.

See the photo on page 138.

IN ADVANCE Jalapeños can be filled a few hours before they are to be breaded and fried. Serve freshly fried.

QUESADILLAS WITH CHORIZO & JALAPEÑO FILLING

MAKES approx. 24
TIME approx. 30 minutes

CHORIZO & JALAPEÑO FILLING
½ onion, chopped
1 clove garlic, pressed
1 tbsp oil
11 oz (300 g) chorizo, finely chopped
½ jalapeño, seeded and finely chopped
2 tbsp chopped cilantro
salt and pepper
4 oz (100 g) Cheddar, grated
6 small soft tortillas, store bought (or *see the recipe on page 228*)

Sauté the onion and the garlic in oil for a few minutes. Add the chorizo and jalapeño, and cook for another few minutes. Stir in the cilantro, and season with salt and pepper.

Spread the filling and cheese on half of the tortillas. Cover with the remaining tortillas. Fry both sides in a frying pan until golden brown and the cheese is melted. Place on a cutting board to cool slightly. Cut each quesadilla into 8 triangles.

See the photo on page 134.

IN ADVANCE The mixture can be made the day before and stored in the refrigerator. Put together the quesadillas and fry just before serving. The quesadillas taste best freshly made but can also be made several hours in advance.

QUESADILLAS WITH
TUNA FILLING

MAKES approx. 24
TIME approx. 30 minutes

TUNA FILLING

7 oz (185 g) canned tuna, drained
2 tbsp mayonnaise
1–2 pickled jalapeños, finely chopped
2 tbsp red onion finely chopped
2 oz (50 g) Cheddar cheese, grated
salt and pepper

6 small tortillas, store bought (or *see the recipe on page 228*)

Stir together all ingredients for the mixture. Season with salt and pepper. Spread the tuna filling on half of the tortilla breads. Cover with the remaining tortillas, and fry both sides in a frying pan until golden brown and the cheese is melted. Place on a cutting board to cool slightly. Cut each quesadilla into 8 triangles.

See the photo on page 134.

IN ADVANCE The tuna mixture can be made the day before and stored in the refrigerator. Put together the quesadillas, and fry just before serving. The quesadillas taste best freshly made, but can also be made several hours in advance.

QUESADILLA FILLINGS
Substitute the different fillings in the quesadillas with, for example, SWEET POTATO & BEAN DIP (*see the recipe on page 143*) or BLACK BEAN DIP (*see the recipe on page 141*). Feel free to add cheese for even more flavor.

QUESADILLAS WITH
CHEESE & GOLDEN SALSA

MAKES approx. 24
TIME approx. 30 minutes

GOLDEN SALSA

1 scallion, finely chopped
1 clove garlic, pressed
1 yellow tomato, seeded and finely chopped
2 tbsp finely chopped yellow bell peppers
3 tbsp corn
3 tbsp diced cantaloupe
1 tsp freshly squeezed lime juice
½ tsp seeded finely chopped red chili pepper
salt and pepper

6 small soft tortillas, store bought (or *see the recipe on page 228*)
4 oz (100 g) Cheddar, grated
cilantro for garnish

Mix all ingredients for the salsa. Season with salt and pepper.

Spread the cheese over half of the tortillas. Cover with the remaining tortillas, and fry both sides in a frying pan until golden brown and the cheese is melted. Place on a cutting board to cool slightly. Cut each quesadilla into 8 triangles.

Top with salsa and garnish with cilantro.
See the photo on page 134.

TIP Replace the golden salsa with PICO DE GALLO (*See the recipe on page 141*).

IN ADVANCE The salsa can be made the day before and stored in the refrigerator. Put together the quesadillas and fry just before serving. The quesadillas taste best freshly made, but can also be made several hours in advance.

GYOZA WITH
VEGETABLE FILLING

GYOZA WITH
PORK FILLING

CHAR SIU BAO BUNS

DUMPLINGS WITH
CRAB FILLING

DUMPLINGS WITH
SHRIMP FILLING

The recipes are available on pages 158–160

CHAR SIU BAO

SUSHI STACKS

MAKI ROLLS

INSIDE-OUT
MAKI ROLLS

The recipes are available on page 169

SESAME SOBA NOODLES

TOFU & EDAMAME WITH LEMON SESAME SAUCE

FRIED COCONUT SHRIMP

FISH CAKES

SHRIMP TOAST

FRIED SPRING ROLLS

The recipes are available on pages 162–163

will have a wonderful evening.

FORTUNE COOKIES

The recipe is available on page 161

153

CHA PLU BUNDLES

PEKING DUCK

The recipes are available on pages 166–167

FRESH SPRING ROLLS

The recipe is available on page 167

NOODLES & SEAFOOD
IN LETTUCE LEAVES

TUNA-FILLED NOODLE BASKETS

GREEN PAPAYA SALAD
IN LETTUCE LEAVES

ASIAN BEEF SALAD IN CUCUMBER CUPS

SPICY PORK FILLING
IN LETTUCE LEAVES

The recipes are available on pages 164–166

ASIA

*In this chapter, we take a journey through the exciting culinary palate
of the Far East and sample such savory dishes as Chinese
Char Siu Bao, Japanese sesame soba noodles, and
spicy Thai green papaya salad.*

GYOZA WITH PORK FILLING

MAKES approx. 24
TIME approx. 1 hour

approx. 24 gyoza wrappers
1 egg, lightly beaten
approx. 1 tbsp of canola oil

PORK FILLING
7 oz (200 g) ground pork
½ carrot, finely chopped
1 clove garlic, finely chopped
1 red chili pepper, seeded and finely chopped
2 tbsp finely chopped bamboo shoots
1 scallion, finely chopped
1 tbsp Japanese soy sauce
1 tbsp fish sauce
1 tbsp mirin
2 tsp grated fresh ginger
1 tbsp sesame seeds, toasted
1 tbsp finely chopped fresh cilantro
½ tsp sugar

SAUCE
4 tbsp Japanese soy sauce
2 tbsp rice vinegar
a few drops of sesame oil
1 tsp sesame seeds

Mix ingredients for the filling. Mix ingredients for
the sauce.

Brush a gyoza wrapper with egg. Add a dollop of
filling—approximately 1 ½ tsp—to the center of the
dough. Fold dough into a crescent shape and make
small pleats along the edge so that it closes tightly. Do
the same with the rest of the sheets and filling.

Heat the oil in a frying pan. Sauté a few
dumplings at a time—1 minute on each side until
they color. Pour a tiny bit of water in the pan so
that the bottom is just covered. Cover the pan with
a lid, and steam the dumplings for approximately
3 minutes. Check the water every so often to ensure
the right amount. Too much water will boil the
dumplings, and too little will rapidly evaporate,
frying the dumplings instead of steaming them. You
can also steam the dumplings in a bamboo steam
basket or in a steam oven (*see the text box* STEAMING
on page 161).

Serve the gyoza immediately with sauce on
the side.

See the photo on page 148.

TIP You can also simply steam the dumplings for
7–10 minutes.

IN ADVANCE The filling and the sauce can be
stored in the refrigerator for 1 day. The dumplings
should be prepared right before serving. They
can be stored uncooked in the freezer for
up to 3 months.

GYOZA WITH VEGETABLE FILLING

MAKES approx. 24
TIME approx. 1 hour

approx. 24 gyoza wrappers
1 egg
approx. 1 tbsp of canola oil

VEGETABLE FILLING

2 oz (40 g) dried shiitake mushrooms
4 oz (100 g) bamboo shoots, finely chopped
½ cup (100 ml) carrots, finely chopped
3 tbsp celery, finely chopped
2 scallions, finely chopped
2 cloves garlic, finely chopped
2 tsp canola oil
1 tsp soy sauce
½ tsp sugar
2 tbsp cornstarch
3 tbsp water
salt and pepper

Soak the mushrooms in boiling hot water for about 30 minutes or until soft. Remove the tough stems. Chop finely.

Sauté the mushrooms, vegetables, scallions, and garlic in oil for about 3 minutes or until the vegetables start to get soft. They should still have a little crunch to them. Add the soy sauce and sugar. Mix the cornstarch in the water, and pour it onto the vegetables. Sauté for about 1 minute. Let cool.

Brush a gyoza wrapper with egg. Add a dollop of filling—approximately 1 ½ tsp—into the center of the dough. Fold dough into a crescent shape and make small pleats along the edge, so that it closes tightly. Do the same with the rest of the sheets and filling.

Follow the description to fry and steam (or just steam) the gyozas in the recipe for GYOZA WITH PORK FILLING *on the opposite page.* Serve immediately with soy sauce, or see the sauce for GYOZA WITH PORK FILLING.

See the photo on page 148.

IN **ADVANCE** *See* GYOZA WITH PORK FILLING *on the opposite page.*

DUMPLINGS WITH SHRIMP FILLING

MAKES approx. 20
TIME approx. 1 hour

approx. 20 wonton wrappers

SHRIMP FILLING

½ lb (250 g) raw shrimp, peeled and finely chopped
4 oz (100 g) water chestnuts, finely chopped
2 scallions, finely chopped
1 tsp Japanese soy sauce
1 egg
½ tsp sesame oil

Mix ingredients for the filling.

Add about 1 tbsp of filling to the center of the wonton wrapper. Push the edges up and shape the dough into a small "cup" shape that is open at the top.

Brush the bottom of a bamboo basket with a little oil. Pour water into the bottom of a saucepan—keep in mind that the dumplings are to be steamed, not boiled. Put the basket in the saucepan, or use a folding metal steaming basket. Place a few dumplings at a time in the basket, and put a lid on the saucepan. Steam for 7–10 minutes. Serve immediately with soy sauce or *see the sauce for* GYOZA WITH PORK FILLING *on the opposite page.*

See the photo on page 148.

IN **ADVANCE** These dumplings should be prepared right before they are to be served because the filling contains raw shrimp. If the shrimp are fresh and have not been frozen, you can store the uncooked dumplings in the freezer for up to 3 months.

DUMPLINGS WITH CRAB FILLING

MAKES approx. 35
TIME approx. 1 ½ hours

approx. 35 wonton wrappers

CRAB FILLING

1 cooked crab
2 tsp grated fresh ginger
1 stalk lemongrass, white part only,
    finely grated
1 tsp sugar
1 clove garlic, finely chopped
1 scallion, finely chopped
2 tbsp finely chopped fresh cilantro
2 egg yolks

Remove all the crabmeat from the shell. Mix it with the remaining ingredients for the filling.

Brush the edge of a wonton wrapper with water. Add about 1 tsp crab filling in the center, and pinch the dumpling closed. Do the same with the rest of the wonton wrappers. Follow the instructions for steaming in the recipe DUMPLINGS WITH SHRIMP FILLING on page 159. Steam for 7–10 minutes. Serve immediately with soy sauce or see the sauce for GYOZA WITH PORK FILLING on page 158.

See the photo on page 148.

IN ADVANCE The filling can be stored in the refrigerator for 1 day. Prepare the dumplings right before serving. They can also be stored uncooked in the freezer for up to 3 months. Thaw in the refrigerator.

CHAR SIU BAO

MAKES approx. 30
TIME approx. 1 ½ hrs. + 1 hrs. 40 minutes for
    marinating and rising

¾ lb (350 g) pork tenderloin
approx. 3 scallions, sliced

SAUCE

1 clove garlic, pressed
2 tbsp Chinese soy sauce
3 tbsp Japanese soy sauce
2 tbsp sugar
2 tbsp sherry
2 tbsp hoisin sauce
1 tbsp honey
1 tsp sesame oil
½ tsp five spice powder
½ tbsp cornstarch, dissolved in water

DOUGH

1 cup (250 ml) water
1 tbsp active dry yeast
3 tbsp sugar
2–2 ½ cups (500–600 ml) all-purpose flour
2 tbsp canola oil
approx. 3 tbsp sesame oil

Whisk together all ingredients for the sauce except the cornstarch. Set aside ½ cup (100 ml) sauce, and let the tenderloin marinate in the rest. Refrigerate for at least 1 hour—preferably overnight.

Heat water for the dough to 100°F (40°C). Dissolve the yeast, and let it stand for 10 minutes. Mix in the sugar, flour, and canola oil. Knead into a smooth dough. Pour about 1 tsp sesame oil in a bowl. Turn the dough over in oil, so that it is completely covered. Cover with plastic wrap, and let it rise for about an hour.

Roll out the dough about ½ inch (1 cm) thick. Punch out small circles, approximately 2 ⅓ inches (6 cm) in diameter. Place rounds on a baking sheet that has been brushed with sesame oil. Brush the rounds with sesame oil. Let them rise for another 40 minutes.

Meanwhile, take out the marinated tenderloin. Fry the meat in a bit of oil until it is cooked through. Cut into smaller pieces.

Whisk cornstarch into the sauce that was set aside. Boil the sauce, and let simmer for 2 minutes. Stir in the meat. Let cool.

Brush the bottom of the steam basket with oil. Place in a few bread rounds at a time, and steam for 5–6 minutes; alternately, you can steam them on a baking sheet in a steam oven.

Arrange the meat on the bread rounds, and top with scallions.

Serve immediately.

See the photo on page 149.

CHAR SIU BAO BUNS
To make the "authentic" char siu bao, chop the meat into even smaller pieces. Put meat in the middle of each dough round, and pinch the dough into a bun before letting it rise a second time. Steam for about 10 minutes as described above.

IN ADVANCE The meat can be stored in the refrigerator for about 2 days. The rest of the dish should be prepared on the day it is to be served.

FORTUNE COOKIES

MAKES approx. 35
TIME approx. 1 ½ hours

4 egg whites
1 cup (250 ml) sugar
¾ cup (200 ml) all-purpose flour
3 tbsp cornstarch
a pinch of salt
1 tsp vanilla extract
5 tbsp butter, melted and cooled
1 lemon, zested

Preheat the oven to 400°F (200°C). Grease a baking sheet.

Write short messages on strips of paper approximately 2 inches (5 cm) long.

Beat the egg whites until stiff. Add the sugar a little at a time, and whisk into a meringue-like batter.

Combine the dry ingredients and sift it into the meringue batter. Mix well. Add the butter and lemon zest, and stir.

Dollop tablespoons of batter on a baking sheet at least 4 inches (10 cm) apart from one another. Spread the batter into thin circles with the back of a spoon—approximately 2 ¾ inches (7 cm) in diameter. Bake only a few cookies at a time because they need to be folded quickly before they set. Bake for about 8 minutes or until the edges begin to color.

While the cookies are still hot, place a message in the center of each, and fold. Bend them over the edge of a bowl. Let cool.

See the photo on page 153.

IN ADVANCE Fortune cookies can be stored in an airtight container for up to 3 weeks.

STEAMING
There are different ways to steam wonton and gyoza dumplings. The traditional way is to use bamboo baskets, which are available in different sizes. Remember that the basket will have to fit in a saucepan.

You can buy bamboo baskets in Asian grocery stores and in places that sell kitchenware. These baskets are also practical and beautiful for serving dumplings, and the basket lid will keep them warm.

You can also steam in a folding stainless steel steaming basket or in a standard convection oven with a steam function.

When using a steaming basket of either bamboo or stainless steel, you should always brush the bottom with a little oil so that the dumplings don't stick.

Don't put too much water in the saucepan, so that the dumplings are steamed, not boiled. Also, tightly secure the lid on the saucepan so that no steam escapes.

In a steam oven, place the dumplings on a baking sheet covered with parchment paper that has been brushed with a little oil. Follow the oven's instructions for how to use the steam function.

FISH CAKES

MAKES approx. 20
TIME approx. 30 minutes

If the fish is frozen and thawed, you must first drain it of all water. If the fish mixture is still too wet, add another egg.

1 red chili pepper, seeded
1 stalk lemongrass, white part only
2 cloves garlic
1 tsp grated fresh ginger
1 lb (500 g) fish fillet, cod or perch
1 tbsp fish sauce
1 egg
½ cup (100 ml) coconut milk
1 tbsp brown sugar
approx. 1 tsp salt
3 tbsp finely chopped fresh cilantro

approx. 2 tbsp canola oil for frying

SAUCE
½ red chili pepper, seeded and finely chopped
3 tbsp sugar
3 tbsp water
1 tbsp rice vinegar

Mix the chili and lemongrass in a food processor with the garlic and ginger. Add the fish, and blend to a smooth mixture. Add the fish sauce, eggs, coconut milk, brown sugar, and salt. Mix for a few more seconds. Add the cilantro.

Mix sauce ingredients.

Shape the fish mixture into small patties. Cook the patties in the oil for about a minute on each side until they are nicely browned and cooked through. Serve immediately.

See the photo on page 152.

IN ADVANCE The fish mixture and the sauce can be stored in the refrigerator for 1 day, but do not add the cilantro until the patties are cooked. Fried patties can be stored in the refrigerator for about 2 days or in the freezer for 3 months. Heat in the oven at 300°F (150°C) for 5–6 minutes.

SHRIMP TOAST

MAKES approx. $^{32}/_{64}$
TIME approx. 30 minutes

SHRIMP MIXTURE
1 lb (450 g) raw shrimp, peeled
1 scallion, finely chopped
1 tbsp grated fresh ginger
1 clove garlic, pressed
1 tsp sugar
1 egg
½ tsp salt
a few drops of Tabasco

8 slices white sandwich bread
3 tbsp canola oil

3 tbsp sesame seeds, black and white

In a food processor, blend all the ingredients for the shrimp mixture—except the sesame seeds—to a smooth mixture.

Trim the crusts from the bread. Spread a thin layer of the shrimp mixture on each bread slice. Sprinkle with sesame seeds, and cut each slice into either 4 or 8 triangles.

Heat the oil in a frying pan. Fry a few triangles at a time on both sides until golden brown. Serve immediately.

See the photo on page 152.

IN ADVANCE The shrimp mixture should be prepared the same day and stored in the refrigerator until it is ready to be used.

FRIED SPRING ROLLS

MAKES approx. $^{12}/_{24}$
TIME approx. 1 hour

1 oz (20 g) dried shiitake mushrooms
1 clove garlic, finely chopped
1 red chili pepper, seeded and finely chopped
2 tsp canola oil
5 oz (150 g) ground pork or beef
3 oz (75 g) cabbage, shredded finely
2 medium carrots, shredded
3 tbsp fish sauce
salt and pepper

24 spring roll papers (spring roll pastry)
1 egg yolk, lightly beaten

4 cups (1 liter) oil for deep frying

Soak the mushrooms in boiling water for about 30 minutes or until soft. Remove the tough stems and cut the mushrooms into strips.

Fry the garlic and chili in oil for a minute. Add the ground meat and cook until it has browned. Add the cabbage, carrots, and mushrooms, and cook until the vegetables begin to soften, but are still a bit crunchy. Add the fish sauce, and season with salt and pepper. Let cool.

Place some filling in the middle of the spring roll paper. Fold in the left and right edges, and then roll up from the bottom into a cylindrical shape. Brush the edge with egg yolk so that it secures tightly.

Heat oil to 340–355°F (170–180°C). Fry a few spring rolls at a time until golden brown.

Serve with NUOC CHAM SAUCE (*see the recipe on page 167*) or with sweet chili sauce.

See the photo on page 152.

FRIED VEGETARIAN SPRING ROLLS
Follow the recipe for spring rolls, but replace ground meat with 2 oz (50 g) cooked thin rice noodles. You can also omit the fish sauce.

IN ADVANCE The filling can be stored in the refrigerator for 1 day. Spring rolls taste best when they are filled and fried just before serving. You can deep-fry them a few hours in advance and reheat them in the oven at 300°F (150°C) for 5-6 minutes, but they lose will their crispiness.

FRIED COCONUT SHRIMP

MAKES approx. 24
TIME approx. 40 minutes

¾ cup (200 ml) all-purpose flour
½ tsp salt
24 raw shrimp, peeled
3 eggs, lightly beaten
1 ⅓ cups (300 ml) coconut flakes

4 cups (1 liter) oil for deep frying
sweet chili sauce for serving

Mix the flour and salt in a bowl. Roll the shrimp first in flour, then in egg and, lastly, in coconut flakes.

Heat oil in a heavy saucepan to 355°F (180°C). Add the shrimp, a few at a time, in the hot oil, and fry for 1–2 minutes or until golden brown and crispy. Drain on paper towels.

Serve immediately with sweet chili sauce.
See the photo page 152.

TIP Replace coconut flakes with sesame seeds.

IN ADVANCE The shrimp tastes best freshly fried.

NOODLES & SEAFOOD IN LETTUCE LEAVES

MAKES approx. 24
TIME 40 minutes + 30 minutes in the refrigerator

approx. 3 oz (75 g) glass noodles
1 tbsp canola oil
4 oz (100 g) calamari, chopped
4 oz (100 g) cooked shrimp, peeled and
    chopped
½ cup (100 ml) finely chopped cucumber
2 tbsp red onion finely chopped
2 tbsp chopped fresh mint
2 tbsp chopped fresh cilantro

gem salad or other small lettuce leaves

SAUCE

1 stalk lemongrass, white part only
½ red chili pepper, seeded and sliced
1 clove garlic, finely chopped
2 tbsp freshly squeezed lime juice
    (approx. 1 lime)
2 tbsp fish sauce
1 tbsp sugar

Cook the noodles according to the instructions on the packet. Rinse them in cold water.

Heat oil in a pan, and cook the calamari for a few minutes. Allow it to cool.

Crush the lemongrass and cut into thin slices. Mix with the rest of the ingredients for the sauce.

Mix the sauce with the noodles, calamari, shrimp, cucumber, red onion, and herbs. Refrigerate for about 30 minutes for the flavors to mix.

Pick the leaves from the lettuce head, and distribute the noodles and seafood salad on them.

See the photo on page 157.

IN ADVANCE The noodle and seafood salad without the mint and coriander can be stored in the refrigerator for 1 day. Do not add the herbs until the filling is to be spooned into salad leaves.

GREEN PAPAYA SALAD IN LETTUCE LEAVES

MAKES approx. 24
TIME approx. 45 minutes

1 green papaya
3–4 red chili peppers, seeded
3 cloves garlic
2 tbsp freshly squeezed lime juice
    (approx. 1 lime)
2 tbsp fish sauce
1 tbsp brown sugar
½ tsp salt
2 tomatoes or 10 cherry tomatoes
4 oz (100 g) fresh green beans
½ cup (100 ml) salted peanuts, finely chopped

gem salad or other small lettuce leaves

Peel the papaya, halve it lengthwise, and remove the seeds. Grate the flesh, and put it in cold water for about 30 minutes. Strain and squeeze out as much water as possible.

Mash the chili with the garlic in a mortar or in a food processor. Add the lime juice, fish sauce, brown sugar, and salt. Mix with the papaya.

Halve the tomatoes, remove the seeds, and cut into thin wedges. Cut the green beans into thin strips. Stir together the tomatoes and the green beans with the papaya salad.

Pick the leaves from the lettuce head. Fill the leaves with the papaya salad, and sprinkle with peanuts.

See the photo on page 157.

IN ADVANCE The papaya salad can be stored in the refrigerator for 1 day without the peanuts. Add them when the lettuce leaves are filled with the papaya salad.

SPICY PORK FILLING IN LETTUCE LEAVES

MAKES approx. 24
TIME approx. about 45 minutes

PORK FILLING

1 oz (20 g) dried shiitake mushrooms
1 shallot, finely chopped
2 cloves garlic, finely chopped
1 red chili pepper, seeded and finely chopped
1 tbsp grated fresh ginger
1 tbsp canola oil
7 oz (200 g) ground pork
2 ⅔ oz (75 g) bamboo shoots, finely chopped
2 tbsp light soy sauce
½ tsp sesame oil
2 tbsp cilantro, finely chopped
½ cup (100 ml) roasted cashews, finely chopped

little gem salad or small lettuce
24 mandarin or clementine wedges (2–3 fruits)
1 scallion, thinly sliced

Soak the mushrooms in boiling water for about 30 minutes or until soft. Remove the tough stems and finely chop the mushrooms.

Sauté the shallot, garlic, chili, and ginger in oil for a few minutes. Add the ground pork, and cook until the meat is done. Add the bamboo shoots, mushrooms, soy sauce, and sesame oil, and cook for another minute. Stir in the cilantro and cashews. Allow to cool slightly.

Pick the leaves from the lettuce head, and top with the filling. Add a mandarin or clementine wedge, and sprinkle with scallions.

See the photo on page 157.

IN ADVANCE The filling can be stored in the refrigerator for 1 day without the cilantro and cashews. Add them when the lettuce leaves are filled with pork filling.

ASIAN BEEF SALAD IN CUCUMBER CUPS

MAKES approx. 20
TIME approx. 40 minutes

½ lb beef fillet or entrecôte
1 tbsp canola oil
6 cherry tomatoes, cut into wedges
2–3 cucumbers
1 red chili pepper, seeded and sliced

SAUCE

1 tbsp light soy sauce
1 tbsp freshly squeezed lime juice
1 tbsp fish sauce
½ tsp sugar
2 tbsp chopped fresh cilantro
2 tbsp chopped fresh mint
¼ of a red chili pepper, seeded and finely chopped
2 tsp sesame seeds, toasted
1 tsp lime zest

Cook the meat to medium rare in oil in a skillet on high heat. Allow it to cool. Cut it into strips.

Stir together all the ingredients for the sauce, and mix with the meat and tomatoes.

Cut the cucumbers into about 1-inch (2 ½ cm) thick slices. Scoop out the insides with a small melon baller so that they form cups.

Fill the cucumber cups with the steak salad and garnish with chili.

See the photo on page 157.

IN ADVANCE The meat can be stored in the refrigerator for 1 day. Add the mint and cilantro when the cucumber cups are filled with the meat salad.

TUNA-FILLED NOODLE BASKETS

MAKES approx. 24
TIME approx. 45 minutes

5 oz (150 g) egg noodles
1 tsp canola oil
4 oz (100 g) fresh tuna
½ mango, diced
1 avocado, diced
½ of a red chili pepper, seeded and
    finely chopped
1 tbsp finely chopped mint

3 tbsp mayonnaise
½–1 tsp wasabi paste

1 lime
watercress for garnish

Preheat the oven to 400°F (200°C).

Cook the noodles according to the instructions on the packet. Drain and mix them with the oil. Place the noodles in the bottom of a mini muffin pans or form small baskets on a baking sheet. Bake for 15–20 minutes or until golden brown. Allow them to cool.

Cut the tuna into small cubes. Mix the tuna with the mango, avocado, chili and mint.

Stir together the mayonnaise and wasabi paste.

Fill the noodle baskets with the tuna mixture. Drizzle over the lime juice, and top with a dollop of wasabi mayonnaise. Garnish with watercress.

See the photo on page 157.

TIP Replace the tuna with salmon.

IN ADVANCE The noodle baskets can be prepared and stored in a tightly sealed jar for 1 day. The rest should be made right before serving.

PEKING DUCK

MAKES approx. 24
TIME approx. 2 hours + marinating overnight

2 duck breasts with skin
2 tbsp canola oil
5 scallions
1 cucumber
24 pancakes for Peking duck or rice paper

MARINADE
4 tsp honey
1 tsp dark soy sauce
2 tsp five spice powder
2 tsp brown sugar

SAUCE
2 tbsp sesame oil
6 tbsp hoisin sauce
6 tbsp sugar
6 tbsp water
1 tbsp dark soy sauce
1 tbsp cornstarch
1 tbsp water

Score the duck skin in a crisscross pattern. Mix the marinade. Let the duck marinate overnight in the refrigerator.

Mix all the ingredients for the sauce—except cornstarch and water—in a saucepan. Bring to a boil. Whisk the cornstarch and water, and add to the sauce. Simmer until sauce thickens. Allow it to cool.

Cut the scallions into long thin strips. Seed the cucumber, and cut it into long thin strips.

Preheat the oven to 260°F (125°C). Brush an oven rack with oil. Place the rack in the oven over a baking sheet covered with foil to catch the drippings. Heat the oil in a frying pan and brown the duck breasts on both sides, starting with the skin-side down, for about 3 minutes per side. Place the duck breasts on a oven rack in the oven, skin-side up, and cook for about 45 minutes.

Prepare pancakes or rice paper according to the instructions on the package. To eat, cut the duck into slices.

Plate everything individually. Fill a pancake or rice paper with a piece of duck, cucumber, and scallions. Drizzle with sauce and roll up.

See the photos on pages 154–155.

IN ADVANCE The sauce can be stored in the refrigerator for about 3 days. The rest should be prepared right before serving.

CHA PLU BUNDLES

MAKES approx. 24
TIME approx. 30 minutes

These small dumplings offer a real firework of flavor!

2 limes
2 oz (50 g) fresh ginger
4 red chilies peppers, seeded
½ cup (100 ml) coconut flakes
½ cup (100 ml) crispy fried onions
3 tbsp small dried shrimp
24 cha plu leaves or small lettuce leaves
SAUCE
¼ tsp shrimp paste (gkapi)
¾ cup (200 ml) palm or brown sugar
½ tsp finely grated galangal
½ cup (100 ml) tamarind paste

Mix the sauce ingredients in a heavy-bottomed saucepan. Bring to a boil, and simmer to a thick syrup. Pour it into a small serving bowl and let cool.

Cut thick slices of lime peel with a knife, and then cut into small cubes. Peel the ginger and cut it evenly into small cubes. Slice the chili.

Roast the coconut flakes in a dry pan until they are golden brown.

Put all the ingredients in separate bowls. To eat, fill a cha plu leaf with a dollop of sauce, shrimp, chili, lime, and ginger. Sprinkle with fried onions and coconut flakes, and fold together into a bundle.

See the photo on page 154.

IN ADVANCE The sauce and coconut flakes can be prepared about 3 days in advance. Store the sauce in the refrigerator. The rest of the dish can be made right before serving.

FRESH SPRING ROLLS

MAKES approx. ¹²⁄₂₄
TIME approx. 1 hour

4 oz (100 g) thin rice noodles
½ cucumber
1 carrot, cut into thin strips
¾ cup (200 ml) shredded iceberg lettuce
¾ cup (200 ml) fresh bean sprouts
12 cooked shrimp, split lengthwise
12 sheets of rice paper
12 sprigs of fresh mint
12 sprigs fresh cilantro

NUOC CHAM SAUCE
1 red chili pepper, seeded and finely chopped
1 clove garlic, finely chopped
5 tbsp sugar
3 tbsp boiling water
3 tbsp fish sauce
½ cup freshly squeezed lime juice
  (approx. 3 limes)

Cook the noodles according to the package instructions. Rinse them in cold water, and cut them into 2-inch (5 cm) pieces. Mix the sauce ingredients and refrigerate for about 30 minutes.

Halve the cucumber lengthwise, and discard the seeds. Cut the cucumber into 2-inch (5 cm) sticks. Mix the cucumbers, carrot, lettuce, and bean sprouts.

Dip a rice paper in warm water. In the center of the paper, place some mint and coriander followed by vegetables and noodles, and finally 2 shrimp halves. Fold the edges both from the left and the right, and then roll into a tight cylindrical shape.

Rolls can be served either whole or divided diagonally. Serve with nuoc cham sauce or sweet-chili sauce.

See the photo on page 156.

FRESH VEGETARIAN SPRING ROLLS Replace the shrimp with fresh shredded mango.

IN ADVANCE The sauce, noodles, and vegetables can be stored in the refrigerator for 1 day. Roll the spring rolls a few hours before serving, and store them cold.

SESAME SOBA NOODLES

MAKES approx. 24
TIME approx. about 1 hour

7 oz (200 g) soba noodles or egg noodles
1 cucumber

1 red chili pepper, seeded and finely chopped
1 bunch cilantro, finely chopped
1 bunch mint, finely chopped
3 tbsp soy sauce
4 tbsp mirin
1 tbsp sesame oil

toasted sesame seeds for garnish

Cook the noodles according to the package instructions. Rinse in cold water.

Halve the cucumber lengthwise. Discard the seeds, and cut it into small cubes. Mix with the chili, herbs, soy sauce, mirin, and sesame oil in a bowl. Add the noodles, and refrigerate the mixture for at least 30 minutes.

Twirl some noodles around 2 chopsticks into a small bundle. Then carefully remove the bundle from the sticks, and place in an Asian spoon or a small bowl. Do the same with the rest of noodles. Top the bundles with the remaining soy mixture and cucumbers. Sprinkle with toasted sesame seeds.

See the photo on page 151.

IN ADVANCE The noodle mixture can be stored in the refrigerator for up to a day. Add the mint and cilantro right before serving.

TOFU & EDAMAME WITH LEMON SESAME SAUCE

MAKES approx. 24
TIME approx. about 45 minutes

4 oz (120 g) edamame beans, in their pods
4 oz (120 g) broccoli, cut into small florets
5 oz (125 g) fried tofu, diced
1 tbsp oil

LEMON SESAME SAUCE
2 tbsp freshly squeezed lemon juice
2 tbsp sweet chili sauce
2 tbsp rice vinegar
2 tbsp tahini
2 tsp sugar
1 ½ tsp soy sauce
1 ½ tsp sesame oil
½ tsp dried chili flakes

Start by making the sauce; cook all ingredients, and let simmer for a few minutes. Remove from the heat and mix with a hand blender to make a smooth sauce. Keep warm.

Place the edamame in a saucepan, and cover with water. Bring to a boil, remove from the heat, and strain. Let cool slightly, and remove the beans from their pods.

Blanche the broccoli in salted water for a few minutes. Fry the tofu in the oil until crispy. Stir in the broccoli, beans, and sauce, and stir until warm.

Arrange in small Asian spoons or bowls, and serve immediately.

See the photo on page 151.

IN ADVANCE The sauce as well as the pre-cooked beans and broccoli can be stored in the refrigerator for 1–2 days. The entire dish should be prepared right before serving.

MAKI ROLLS

MAKES approx. 36
TIME approx. 1 ½ hours

½ lb (250 g) fresh tuna, salmon, or crab sticks
2 oz (60 g) cucumber, seeded
1 avocado
3 nori sheets
2 tsp wasabi paste

SUSHI RICE

1 ⅓ cup (300 ml) sushi rice
1 ⅓ cup (300 ml) cold water
3 tbsp rice vinegar

1 tbsp sugar
½ tsp mirin
¼ tsp salt

Wash the rice thoroughly under cold running water. Place in a pot with ⅓ cup (300 ml) of water. Let soak for 30 minutes. Bring the water to a boil, reduce the heat, and let the rice simmer, covered, for about 20 minutes. Remove from the heat, and let stand covered for about 15 minutes.

Heat up the rice vinegar, sugar, mirin, and salt at low temperature, and stir until the sugar is dissolved. Let cool.

Place the rice in a large plastic bowl. Pour the rice vinegar mixture over the rice and mix gently without mashing the rice. Let cool.

Cut the fish, cucumber, and avocado into thin sticks. Place one nori sheet with the glossy side down and with the long side facing you on a rice rolling mat. Spread a third of the rice over the entire sheet. Add a string of wasabi paste along the side facing you. Add the fish or crab sticks, cucumber, and avocado on the wasabi. Take the edge of the rolling mat, and roll the sushi to a compact roll. Cut the roll into 12 pieces with a sharp knife. Repeat with the other 2 nori sheets.

See the photo on page 150.

INSIDE-OUT MAKI ROLLS

Spread the rice on a nori sheet as above. Place plastic wrap on the rice, and turn gently so that the nori sheet is on top. Then, follow the rest of the description in the recipe above to create the maki roll. Finish by rolling in toasted sesame seeds and shiso leaves.

IN ADVANCE Maki rolls should be made on the day they will be eaten. Store in the refrigerator until ready to be served.

SUSHI STACKS

MAKES approx. 16
TIME approx. 1 ½ hours

1 batch of SUSHI RICE (*see* MAKI ROLLS *to the left*)
3 nori sheets
approx. 1 tbsp sesame seeds, black and/or white
6 oz (170 g) fresh salmon, thinly sliced (*see* RAW FISH *text box on page* 75)
approx. ½ tbsp wasabi paste

gari (pickled ginger)
cilantro or chervil for garnish

CREAMY SWEET CHILI SAUCE

¾ cup (200 ml) MAYONNAISE, store bought (or *see the recipe on page* 74)
½ cup (100 ml) sweet chili sauce

Place a nori sheet on a cutting board. Spread one third of the rice over the sheet, and cover with a thin layer of wasabi paste on top. Lay out the salmon in a thin layer. Repeat again, and finish with a nori sheet and a layer of rice.

Cover with plastic wrap, and place a cutting board on top. Set some weights on the cutting board, and let stand in the refrigerator for about 1 hour. Remove the plastic wrap and sprinkle with sesame seeds. Cut into squares with a sharp knife.

Mix the mayonnaise and sweet chili sauce.

Cut the ginger into thin slices. Roll into roses, and put one on top of each cube. Garnish with cilantro or chervil. Serve with the sauce.

See the photo on page 150.

IN ADVANCE Maki rolls and sushi cubes should be made the same day they will be eaten and kept cold until served.

See text box RAW FISH *on page* 75.

GRISSINI WITH ARUGULA &
BRESAOLA

PANZANELLA

The recipes are available on the page 180

CROSTINI

GARLIC

BRUSCHETTA

PESTO & MOZZARELLA

RED PESTO & SALAMI

PEAR & GORGONZOLA

SHRIMP, ARUGULA & TOMATO

FIGS & PECORINO

ROASTED VEGETABLES & MORTADELLA

SAUTÉED CHICKEN LIVER

RICOTTA & BAKED TOMATO

SPINACH, PINE NUTS & GOLDEN RAISINS

CANNELLINI BEAN DIP

The recipes are available on the pages 176–180

POLENTA WITH SUN-DRIED
TOMATOES & OLIVES

MELON & PROSCIUTTO

SALTIMBOCCA
ALLA ROMANA

FIGS WITH GORGONZOLA &
BRESAOLA

CRISPY FRIED RISOTTO BALLS

The recipes are available on the pages 180–182

GRILLED MUSHROOMS WITH MOZZARELLA

The recipe is available on page 182

PICKLED VEGETABLES

MARINATED OLIVES,
FENNEL & ORANGE

GRILLED MARINATED
VEGETABLES

MARINATED OLIVES,
CORIANDER & CHILI

MARINATED ARTICHOKE
HEARTS

CARAMELIZED
GARLIC

MARINATED CHERRY TOMATOES

MARINATED CAPERS

PUFF PASTRY-BAKED OLIVES

MARINATED OLIVES,
LEMON & HERB

ITALY

Over the years, we have eaten our way across much of Italy, and these trips have inspired many of the recipes that we share with you here. "Antipasti" means "before the meal" and may consist of crostini, cured meats like prosciutto and salami, cheeses, marinated vegetables, and olives. Traditionally, antipasti is served as an appetizer, but it is also excellent to eat standing with a glass of red wine or prosecco.

CROSTINI WITH GARLIC

MAKES approx. 24
TIME approx. 15 minutes

1 baguette
4 tbsp olive oil
2 cloves garlic
course-ground sea salt

Preheat the oven to 440° F (225°C).
    Cut the baguette into slices. Brush with oil, and bake in the oven for a few minutes until golden brown. Halve the garlic cloves, and rub the cut surfaces on the bread slices. Sprinkle with sea salt.
    See the photo on page 171.

IN ADVANCE Crostini taste best served right away.

CROSTINI WITH FIGS & PECORINO

MAKES approx. 24
TIME approx. 15 minutes

4 fresh figs, sliced
approx. 4 oz (100 g) pecorino, sliced
balsamic syrup

1 baguette
4 tbsp olive oil

Preheat the oven to 440°F (225°C).
    Cut the baguette into slices. Brush with oil, and bake in the oven for a few minutes until golden brown. Put a slice of pecorino and a slice of fig on each piece of bread. Drizzle with balsamic syrup.
    See the photo on page 171.

IN ADVANCE The breads can be roasted the day before and kept at room temperature.

CROSTINI WITH CANNELLINI BEAN DIP

MAKES approx. 24
TIME approx. 25 minutes

BEAN DIP
2 shallots, finely chopped
2 cloves garlic, pressed
2 tbsp butter
1 tsp sugar
2 tsp rosemary
15 oz (410 g) cooked white beans, drained
zest of ½ of lemon
2 tbsp lemon juice, freshly squeezed
2 tbsp olive oil
rosemary for garnish

1 baguette
4 tbsp olive oil

Preheat the oven to 440° F (225°C).
    Sauté the shallots and the garlic in butter over low heat. Raise the heat, add sugar and rosemary. Cook for another minute. Allow to cool.

Mix the shallots with beans, lemon zest, lemon juice, and olive oil in a food processor to a creamy consistency. Season with salt and pepper.

Cut the baguette into slices. Brush with oil, and bake in the oven for a few minutes until golden brown. Spread the bean dip on the bread, and garnish with rosemary.

See the photo on page 171.

IN ADVANCE Both the bread and the bean dip can be made the day before. Keep the bread at room temperature and refrigerate the bean dip.

CROSTINI WITH RICOTTA & BAKED TOMATO

MAKES approx. 24
TIME approx. 3 hours and 15 minutes

50 cherry tomatoes
1 tbsp olive oil

5 oz (150 g) ricotta
2 oz (50 g) pecorino or Parmesan, grated
salt and black pepper

fresh basil for garnish

1 baguette
4 tbsp olive oil

Preheat the oven to 210°F (100°C).

Put the cherry tomatoes in an ovenproof dish. Drizzle with olive oil and salt. Bake in the oven for 3 hours. Remove the tomatoes, and raise the heat to 440° F (225°C).

Stir together ricotta and pecorino or Parmesan. Season with salt and pepper. Cut the baguette into slices. Brush with oil, and bake in the oven for a few minutes until golden brown. Spread the ricotta dip on the bread, and top with cherry tomatoes. Garnish with basil.

See the photo on page 171.

IN ADVANCE Bread can be roasted the day before and kept at room temperature. The cherry tomatoes can be baked 1–2 days in advance and stored in the refrigerator.

CROSTINI WITH ROASTED VEGETABLES & MORTADELLA

MAKES approx. 24
TIME approx. 45 minutes

½ fennel bulb
1 red bell pepper, seeded
1 yellow bell pepper, seeded
4 oz (100 g) zucchini
½ red onion
1 tsp dried oregano
1 tsp dried basil
salt and pepper
2 tbsp olive oil
5 oz (125 g) mortadella, cut in strips

1 baguette
4 tbsp olive oil

Preheat the oven to 440°F (225°C).

Slice the fennel. Cut the bell peppers, zucchini, and red onion into pieces. Place the vegetables in a roasting pan, and sprinkle with oregano and basil. Drizzle with olive oil. Roast the vegetables in the oven for about 20 minutes or until browned. Allow to cool slightly. Season with salt and pepper.

Cut the baguette into slices. Brush with oil, and bake in the oven for a few minutes until golden brown. Top the bread with the vegetables and mortadella.

See the photo on page 171.

IN ADVANCE The bread can be roasted the day before and kept at room temperature. The vegetables may be roasted the day before serving and stored in the refrigerator.

CROSTINI WITH RED PESTO & SALAMI

MAKES approx. 24
TIME approx. 20 minutes

RED PESTO
12 sun-dried tomatoes in oil
1 clove garlic
¾ cup (200 ml) fresh basil
3 tbsp olive oil
2 oz (50 g) Parmesan
salt and pepper

1 baguette
4 tbsp olive oil
5 oz (125 g) salami, sliced

Preheat the oven to 440°F (225°C).

Mix sun-dried tomatoes, garlic, and basil in a food processor or with a hand blender. Pour the oil in a thin stream while the machine is running. Add the Parmesan, and blend until smooth. Season with salt and pepper.

Cut the baguette into slices. Brush with oil, and bake in the oven for a few minutes until golden brown. Spread with pesto and top with salami.

See the photo on page 171.

IN ADVANCE The bread can be roasted the day before and stored at room temperature. The pesto can be stored for about 3 days in the refrigerator.

CROSTINI WITH PESTO & MOZZARELLA

MAKES approx. 24
TIME approx. 20 minutes

PESTO
¾ cup fresh basil
1 clove garlic, pressed
1 tbsp pine nuts
3 tbsp olive oil
2 tbsp grated Parmesan
salt and pepper

1 baguette
4 tbsp olive oil
11 oz (300 g) buffalo mozzarella

Preheat the oven to 440°F (225°C).

Blend the basil, garlic, and pine nuts in a food processor or with a hand blender. Pour the oil in a thin stream while the machine is running. Add the Parmesan cheese, and pulse for a few more seconds. Season with salt and pepper. Tear the mozzarella into pieces.

Cut the baguette into slices. Brush with oil, and bake in the oven for a few minutes until golden brown. Place the mozzarella on the bread and top with pesto.

See the photo on page 171.

IN ADVANCE The bread can be roasted the day before and stored at room temperature. The pesto can store for about 3 days in the refrigerator.

CROSTINI WITH SPINACH, PINE NUTS & GOLDEN RAISINS

MAKES approx. 24
TIME approx. 20 minutes

3 tbsp golden raisins
1 clove garlic, finely chopped
2 tbsp olive oil
5 oz (150 g) fresh spinach
3 tbsp toasted pine nuts
a pinch of ground nutmeg
salt and pepper

1 baguette
4 tbsp olive oil

Preheat the oven to 440°F (225°C).

Soak the raisins in a bit of cold water.

Sauté the garlic in olive oil for a few minutes. Add the spinach, and continue sautéing for another minute.

Strain the water from the raisins and add them to the pan.

Cook for another minute. Stir in the pine nuts, and season with nutmeg, salt and pepper.

Cut the baguette into slices. Brush with oil, and bake in the oven for a few minutes until golden brown. Spread the spinach mixture on the bread.

See the photo on page 171.

IN ADVANCE The bread can be roasted the day before and stored at room temperature, and the spinach mixture can be done the day before and reheated before serving. Store in the refrigerator.

CROSTINI WITH SAUTÉED CHICKEN LIVER

MAKES approx. 24
TIME approx. 40 minutes

1 ⅓ cups (300 ml) golden raisins
½ cup (100 ml) Marsala wine
1 onion, finely chopped
1 tbsp butter
3 tbsp olive oil
1 lb (450 g) chicken livers
7 anchovies in oil, finely chopped
4 tbsp capers, chopped

1 baguette
4 tbsp olive oil

Preheat the oven to 440°F (225°C). Soak the raisins in the wine.

Sauté the onion in butter and olive oil for a few minutes. Add the chicken livers, and cook for another 10 minutes or until the livers are cooked through. Allow to cool slightly.

Chop the livers, and mix with the anchovies and capers.

Cut the baguette into slices. Brush with oil and bake in the oven for a few minutes until golden brown. Place the chicken liver on the bread and top with the marinated raisins.

See the photo on page 171.

IN ADVANCE The bread can be roasted the day before and kept at room temperature. The liver mixture can also be made the day before. Keep in the refrigerator.

CROSTINI WITH PEAR & GORGONZOLA

MAKES approx. 24
TIME approx. 20 minutes

1 small pear, peeled and cored
1 tbsp butter
1 tbsp sugar
½ lb (250 g) gorgonzola, crumbled
1 oz (25 g) walnuts, roughly chopped

1 baguette
3 tbsp olive oil

Preheat the oven to 440°F (225°C).

Cut the pear into small pieces. Fry in butter and sugar on low heat for a few minutes.

Cut the baguette into slices. Brush with oil, and bake in the oven for a few minutes until golden brown. Arrange the gorgonzola, pears, and walnuts on the bread slices.

See the photo on page 171.

IN ADVANCE The bread can be roasted the day before and kept at room temperature.

CROSTINI WITH SHRIMP, ARUGULA & TOMATO

MAKES approx. 24
TIME approx. 30 minutes

1 ⅓ lbs (600 g) cooked shrimp, peeled
1 shallot, finely chopped
1 clove garlic, pressed
⅓ cup (75 ml) olive oil
24 cherry tomatoes, cut into wedges
2 oz (40 g) arugula
salt and black pepper

1 baguette
4 tbsp olive oil

Preheat the oven to 440°F (225°C).

Sauté the shallots and garlic in 1 tbsp of olive oil for a few minutes. Add the cherry tomatoes, and cook for a few more minutes. Allow to cool.

Combine the shrimp with the tomato mix, arugula, and 2 tbsp of olive oil. Season with salt and pepper.

Cut the baguette into slices. Brush with oil and bake in the oven for a few minutes until golden brown. Arrange the mixture on the bread.

See the photo on page 171.

IN ADVANCE The bread can be roasted the day before and stored at room temperature. The shrimp and the cherry tomatoes can be mixed a couple of hours before serving.

BRUSCHETTA

MAKES approx. 24
TIME approx. 20 minutes

14 oz (400 g) tomatoes, finely chopped
4 tbsp chopped basil
1 clove garlic, pressed
2 tbsp olive oil
salt and black pepper

1 baguette
4 tbsp olive oil

Preheat the oven to 440°F (225°C).
 Mix the tomatoes, basil, garlic, and olive oil. Season with salt and pepper.
 Cut the baguette into slices. Brush with oil and bake in the oven for a few minutes until golden brown. Spread the tomato mixture on the bread.
 See the photo on page 171.

IN ADVANCE The bread can be roasted the day before and stored at room temperature. The tomato mixture can be made a couple of hours before serving.

GRISSINI WITH ARUGULA & BRESAOLA

MAKES approx. 24
TIME approx. 15 minutes

24 grissini breadsticks, store bought (*or see the recipe on page 229*)
1 oz (25 g) arugula
5 oz (125) bresaola and/or prosciutto

Cut the prosciutto and/or bresaola into strips lengthwise. Wrap the arugula and grissini in the prosciutto or bresaola.
 See the photo on page 170.

TIP Serve as is or with a dip (*see* DIPS & SPREADS *in the index*).

IN ADVANCE The grissini taste best if served right away.

PANZANELLA

MAKES approx. 20
TIME approx. 30 minutes

TOMATO SALAD
8 oz (225 g) tomatoes, seeded and diced
2 oz (50 g) cucumber, diced
½ red bell pepper, seeded and diced
½ yellow bell pepper, seeded and diced
2 tbsp red onion, finely chopped
2 oz (60 g) day-old bread, diced

DRESSING
2 tsp red wine vinegar
1 small clove garlic, pressed
3 tbsp finely chopped basil
2 tbsp olive oil

Stir together the ingredients for the dressing. Mix all ingredients for the tomato salad. Blend the dressing with the tomato salad, and arrange the panzanella in small glasses.
 See the photo on page 170.

IN ADVANCE The panzanella tastes best if prepared and refrigerated a couple of hours before serving.

MELON & PROSCIUTTO

MAKES approx. 24
TIME approx. 20 minutes

5 oz (125 g) prosciutto
9 oz (240 g) melon, cut into cubes

Cut the prosciutto into strips lengthwise. Wrap the melon cubes in the prosciutto. Secure with a toothpick or serve with toothpicks on the side.
 See the photo on page 172.

IN ADVANCE Can be prepared a few hours in advance and stored in the refrigerator.

SALTIMBOCCA ALLA ROMANA

MAKES approx. 20
TIME approx. 45 minutes

    14 oz (400 g) veal cutlet, thinly sliced
    2 oz (50 g) prosciutto
    20 sage leaves
    2 tbsp butter
    2 tbsp olive oil
    1 tsp all-purpose flour
    ½ cup (100 ml) white wine
    ½ cup (100 ml) veal broth
    salt and pepper

Lay out the slices of veal, slightly overlapping each other, on a cutting board covered with plastic. Cover the slices with plastic and gently pound with a meat mallet until thin. Cut the veal and the prosciutto into 2-inch (5 cm) wide strips. Place a slice of prosciutto and a sage leaf on each piece of veal, roll them up, and secure with a toothpick.

Cook the rolls in butter and olive oil. When they are almost cooked through (make sure the rolls don't loosen during this step), gently pull out the toothpicks, and continue cooking until browned. Place on a plate, and cover to keep warm.

Whisk the flour into the leftover fat in the pan. Whisk in the wine and broth and let the mixture simmer on low heat while stirring until the sauce is reduced by half. Season with salt and pepper. Gently put the rolls back into the pan, spooning the sauce over them, and raise the heat slightly.

Stick a new toothpick in each roll and put them on a plate, or serve with toothpicks on the side. Pour the rest of the sauce over the rolls. Serve immediately.

See the photo on page 172.

IN ADVANCE The rolls and the sauce can be made the day before and stored separately in the refrigerator. Heat up the rolls and the sauce together just before serving.

CRISPY FRIED RISOTTO BALLS

MAKES approx. 15
TIME approx. 1 hour and 30 minutes

    approx. 2 cups (500 ml) chicken broth
    1 shallot, finely chopped
    1 tbsp olive oil
    ½ cup (100 ml) Arborio rice
    3 tbsp white wine
    1 oz (30 g) Parmesan, grated
    3 tbsp chopped fresh basil
    salt

    2 oz (50 g) mozzarella

    ½ cup (100 ml) all-purpose flour
    ¼ tsp salt
    2 eggs, lightly beaten
    ⅔ cup (150 ml) breadcrumbs
    4 cups (1 liter) oil for deep frying

Boil the broth and keep it warm over low heat.

Heat the olive oil in a saucepan. Fry the shallot for a few minutes on low heat. Add the rice and sauté until it becomes transparent. Add the wine and stir until absorbed. Pour in some broth. Let simmer while stirring. Continue by adding broth a little at a time until the rice is soft and creamy, but still chewy. Add the Parmesan and basil, and stir until the cheese has melted. Season with salt. Let the risotto cool to room temperature before refrigerating.

Cut the mozzarella into small cubes. With wet hands, roll a piece of mozzarella in about 1 tbsp of risotto, so that the cheese is completely covered.

Mix flour and salt. Put the flour, eggs, and breadcrumbs into 3 separate bowls. Dip the risotto balls first in the flour, then in eggs, and lastly in the breadcrumbs.

Heat the oil to 320°F (160°C) in a heavy-bottomed saucepan. Add a few risotto balls at a time into the hot oil, and fry until golden brown. Drain on paper towels. Serve immediately.

See the photo on page 172.

IN ADVANCE The risotto balls can be made the day before and stored in the refrigerator. Bread and fry right before serving.

POLENTA WITH SUN-DRIED TOMATOES & OLIVES

MAKES approx. 24
TIME approx. 45 minutes

2 ½ cups (600 ml) water
¾ cup (200 ml) polenta
salt
2 tbsp butter

PARMESAN CREAM
3 oz (70 g) Parmesan, finely grated
4 oz (100 g) cream cheese
1 tbsp chopped basil

2 oz (50 g) black olives, sliced
2 oz (50 g) sun-dried tomatoes in oil, sliced

Boil the water. Stir in the polenta and simmer for approximately 10 minutes while stirring, or until the polenta is soft. Season with salt.

Spread it into about a ½-inch (1 cm) thick layer in a water rinsed pan and let cool. Refrigerate until firm.

Mix the ingredients for the Parmesan cream.

Cut the polenta into small squares. Melt the butter in a frying pan, and fry the polenta on both sides until lightly browned. Allow to cool.

Add a dollop of Parmesan cream onto each piece of polenta. Garnish with olives and sun-dried tomatoes.

See the photo on page 172.

TIP Top the polenta with other spreads, such as BACON & CHEDDAR SPREAD or SPINACH & FETA SPREADS WITH SUN-DRIED TOMATOES (*see the recipes on page 236*).

IN ADVANCE Before being fried, the polenta can be stored in the refrigerator for one day. Fry and garnish right before serving.

FIGS WITH GORGONZOLA & BRESAOLA

MAKES approx. 24
TIME approx. 15 minutes

4 fresh figs
2 oz (50 g) bresaola
2 oz (50 g) gorgonzola cheese

Slice each fig into 6 wedges. Cut the bresaola into slices lengthwise. Put a piece of gorgonzola on each fig, and wrap in a slice of bresaola. Fasten with toothpicks or serve with toothpicks on the side.

See the photo on page 172.

IN ADVANCE Can be made a few hours in advance and stored in the refrigerator.

GRILLED MUSHROOMS WITH MOZZARELLA

MAKES approx. 20
TIME approx. 20 minutes

14 oz (400 g) button mushrooms, sliced
11 oz (300 g) mozzarella
1 tbsp fresh thyme
course-ground sea salt and black pepper
olive oil

Preheat the oven to 440°F (225°C).

Spread out the mushrooms on a baking sheet or in an ovenproof dish. Break the mozzarella into pieces, and arrange them over the mushrooms. Sprinkle the thyme leaves over the mushrooms. Season with salt and pepper, and drizzle with olive oil.

Broil in the upper part of the oven for about 12 minutes or until the cheese has melted and is golden brown. Serve the mushrooms warm with toothpicks.

See the photo on page 173.

IN ADVANCE The mushrooms taste best served freshly made.

MARINATED CHERRY TOMATOES

MAKES approx. 1 lb (500 g)
TIME approx. 10 minutes + 2 hours marinating

1 lb (500 g) cherry tomatoes, cut in half

MARINADE
approx. ½ cup (100 ml) extra virgin olive oil
2 tbsp red wine vinegar
2 tbsp chopped basil
1 tbsp dried marjoram
1 tsp salt
½ tsp black pepper

Mix the marinade ingredients. Stir in the tomatoes, and let sit at room temperature for about 2 hours before serving.
See the photo on page 175.

IN ADVANCE Can be stored in the refrigerator for 2 days.

MARINATED ARTICHOKE HEARTS

MAKES approx. 1 lb (425 g)
TIME approx. 10 minutes + 1 hour marinating

1 lb (425 g) canned artichoke hearts

MARINADE
½ cup (100 ml) extra virgin olive oil
2 cloves garlic, sliced
1 tbsp chopped fresh thyme
1 tbsp chopped fresh rosemary
1 tbsp chopped fresh basil
zest of ½ lemon
course-ground sea salt

Drain the artichoke hearts and halve them.
Mix the olive oil, garlic, spices, and lemon zest. Gently blend the marinade with the artichoke hearts. Sprinkle with some sea salt and refrigerate for at least 1 hour.
See the photo on page 175.

IN ADVANCE Can be stored in the refrigerator for 2 days.

GRILLED MARINATED VEGETABLES

MAKES approx. 6–8 ½ cups (1 ½–2 liters)
TIME approx. 30 minutes + 1 hour marinating

⅔ lb (300 g) eggplant, sliced
½ lb (250 g) zucchini, sliced
½ lb (250 g) red bell pepper, cut in pieces
½ lb (250 g) green bell pepper, cut in pieces
2 red onions, cut into wedges

chopped basil for garnish

MARINADE
3 tbsp olive oil
1 tbsp balsamic vinegar
1 tbsp freshly squeezed lemon juice
2 cloves garlic, pressed
1 tsp dried parsley
1 tsp dried oregano
1 tsp dried thyme
½ tsp salt
½ tsp chili flakes

Mix all the ingredients for the marinade, and blend with the vegetables. Let sit for about 1 hour.
Preheat the oven to 440°F (225°C).
Remove the vegetables from the marinade, and spread them in a roasting pan. Roast in the oven for 10–15 minutes. Garnish with basil right before serving. The vegetables can be served cold or hot.
See the photo on page 174.

TIP Sprinkle with Parmesan or pecorino after grilling!

IN ADVANCE The roasted vegetables can be stored for 1 day in the refrigerator. If serving warm, heat in the oven at 300°F (150°C) for 10 minutes.

CARAMELIZED GARLIC

MAKES approx. 1 garlic bulb
TIME approx. 45 minutes

  1 garlic bulb
  2 tbsp butter
  ¾ cup (200 ml) veal broth
  2 tbsp sugar
  ¼ tsp salt
  1 tsp red wine vinegar
  1 tsp sherry

Separate the cloves from the bulb and peel them.
Mix them with the other ingredients in a
heavy-bottomed saucepan. Bring to a boil,
and let simmer with the lid on for about
30 minutes or until the garlic has softened a bit.
Remove the lid, raise the heat, and cook until the
liquid is reduced to a glaze. Serve warm.

See the photo on page 175.

IN ADVANCE Once the garlic has cooled, it can
be stored in the refrigerator for up to 3 days. Heat
gently until the butter melts.

PICKLED VEGETABLES

MAKES approx. 4 cups (1 liter)
TIME approx. 20 minutes + 1 day of pickling

  approx. 5 oz (150 g) cauliflower florets
  1 carrot, peeled and cut into half moons
  10 radishes, cut into wedges
  4 scallions, sliced
  ½ red onion, sliced

  PICKLING LIQUID
  ¾ cup (200 ml) white vinegar
  ¾ cup (200 ml) water
  ½ cup (100 ml) sugar
  1 tsp whole cloves
  6 all spice berries
  2 bay leaves

Put the cauliflower and carrots in a bowl or a jar.
Boil the vinegar, water, sugar, and spices. Pour the
hot pickling liquid over the cauliflower and carrots.
Allow to cool. Add the radishes, scallions, and red
onion. Cover and let stand in the refrigerator for at
least 1 day.

See the photo on page 174.

IN ADVANCE Can be stored in the refrigerator for
2 months.

PUFF PASTRY–BAKED OLIVES

MAKES approx. 24
TIME approx. 45 minutes

  24 filled olives of choice
  1 puff pastry sheet (3 oz [85 g])
  1 egg, lightly beaten

Preheat the oven to 440°F (225°C).
Roll the pastry out slightly. Cut it into small
squares large enough wrap around an olive.
Wrap each olive in a piece of pastry, so that
it is covered completely.
Put the puff pastry–covered olives on a greased
or parchment paper–covered baking sheet, and
brush them with the egg. Bake in the oven for about
10 minutes or until the pastry is golden brown.

See the photo on page 175.

IN ADVANCE The olives can be wrapped 1 hour
before they are brushed with the egg and baked.

MARINATED OLIVES

MAKES 11 oz (300 g)
TIME approx. 10 minutes + 2 hours marinating

11 oz (300 g) olives
marinade of your choice 9 (*see the recipe below*)

LEMON & HERB

2 cloves garlic, sliced
2 tbsp dried oregano
1 tbsp dried rosemary
1 tbsp dried thyme
1 tbsp dried marjoram
1 lemon, zested
approx. ½ cup (100 ml) extra virgin olive oil

Put the olives, herbs, and lemon zest in a bowl or
a jar, and cover with olive oil. Marinate for at least
2 hours.

*See the photos of the different olive varieties on pages
174 and 175.*

CORIANDER & CHILI

4 cloves garlic, pressed
2 tbsp coriander seeds, coarsely ground
1 tbsp whole black pepper
1 tsp chili flakes
approx. ½ cup (100 ml) extra virgin olive oil

Put the olives and spices in a bowl or a jar, and cover
with olive oil. Marinate for at least 2 hours.

FENNEL & ORANGE

3 tbsp freshly squeezed orange juice
1 tbsp orange zest
½ cup (100 ml) thinly sliced fennel bulb
1 tsp fennel seeds
approx. ½ cup (100 ml) extra virgin olive oil

Simmer the juice, orange zest, and fennel slices in a
pan for a few minutes. Allow it to cool slightly. Pour
the olives and fennel seeds into a bowl or jar, and
add the mixture from the pan. Cover in olive oil and
marinate for at least 2 hours.

MARINATED CAPERS

MAKES approx. 5 oz (150 g)
TIME approx. 10 minutes + 2 hours marinating

approx. 5 oz (150 g) capers
2–3 cloves garlic
1 lemon, zested
approx. ½ cup (100 ml) extra virgin olive oil

Put the capers, garlic, and lemon zest in a bowl
or a jar, and cover with olive oil. Marinate for
at least 2 hours.

See the photo on page 175.

IN ADVANCE The marinated olives and capers
can be stored in the refrigerator for 3 days. Let sit at
room temperature 1 hour before serving.

CHARCUTERIE PLATTER

Serving a spread of charcuterie, vegetables,
and homemade marinated olives requires
surprisingly little effort. Some of our favorite
meats include sausages and cured hams such
as the Spanish *pata negra bellota* and Italian
prosciutto di parma. Why not add some spicy
chorizo and a fragrant truffle salami? And
there's always room to add a selection of
cheeses (*see page 206*).

Don't forget the freshly baked bread and a
good red wine!

OTHER GOODIES FOR A MEAT PLATTER

→ FIG TAPENADE (*see the recipe on page 199*)
→ GREEN TAPENADE (*see the recipe on page 200*)
→ BAKED GARLIC (*see the recipe on page 202*)
→ ROASTED BONE MARROW (*see the recipe
  on page 202*)
→ PORK RILLETTE (*see the recipe on page 204*)
→ DUCK RILLETTE (*see the recipe on page 205*)
→ FOCACCIA (*see the recipe on page 232*)

**PROSCIUTTO, FIGS,
CHÈVRE & RED ONION**

**ZUCCHINI, MUSHROOMS &
TOMATO**

**SALAMI, OLIVES &
ARUGULA**

BRESAOLA & ARTICHOKE HEARTS

QUATTRO FORMAGGI

**POTATOES, BACON, ROSEMARY &
PARMESAN**

The recipes are available on pages 188–190
(pizzas in the photo are not baked)

SALSICCIA, TOMATO & PINE NUTS

PISSALADIÈRE

SHRIMP, SPINACH, PARMESAN & LEMON

The recipes are available on page 191

PIZZA

A steaming slice of pizza, piping hot and slathered in melted cheese, is a guilty pleasure few of us can resist. Here we reinvent this classic street food as dainty mini pizzas. Not as greasy—but still finger-licking good!

PIZZA DOUGH

MAKES approx. 30
TIME approx. 1 hour

- 1 cup (250 ml) warm water, 110°F (40°C)
- 2 tsp active dry yeast
- ½ tsp salt
- ½ tsp sugar
- 2 tbsp olive oil
- 2 ½–3 cups (600–700 ml) all-purpose flour

Pour the warm water into a bowl. Sprinkle in the yeast and stir until dissolved. Add the salt and sugar. Mix in almost all the flour and work the dough, adding more flour if needed, until the dough is smooth. Cover with a kitchen towel, and let rise for 40 minutes. Follow any of the pizza recipes below.

IN ADVANCE Pizza dough can be rolled out and prepared 1 hour before baking. Baked pizza can be stored in the refrigerator for 1 day or in the freezer for about 3 months. Heat at 400°F (200°C) for 7–8 minutes before serving.

TOMATO SAUCE

MAKES approx. 30
TIME approx. 30 minutes

- 1 small onion, chopped
- 1 clove garlic, finely chopped
- 1 tbsp olive oil
- 14 oz (400 g) chopped tomatoes
- 2 tbsp tomato paste
- 1 tsp dried basil
- ½ tsp dried oregano
- 1 bay leaf
- 1 tsp sugar
- salt and pepper

Sauté the onion and garlic in olive oil for a few minutes in a saucepan. Add the tomatoes, tomato paste, herbs, and sugar. Let simmer for about 20 minutes. Season with salt and pepper.

IN ADVANCE The tomato sauce can be stored in the refrigerator for about 3 days or in the freezer for about 3 months.

PIZZA WITH BRESAOLA & ARTICHOKE HEARTS

MAKES approx. 30
TIME approx. 30 minutes

- 1 batch PIZZA DOUGH (*see the recipe on the opposite page*)
- 1 batch TOMATO SAUCE (*see the recipe on the opposite page*)
- 9 oz (250 g) mozzarella, cut into small pieces
- 5 oz (125 g) bresaola, cut into strips
- 6 oz (175 g) artichoke hearts, cut into wedges
- 2 ⅔ oz (75 g) ROASTED BELL PEPPERS (*see the recipe on page 118*), thinly sliced

Make the pizza dough and the tomato sauce. Preheat the oven to 440°F (225°C).

Roll out the dough into large oblong pizzas or into small rounds. Place on baking sheets lined with parchment paper. Spread the tomato sauce and add mozzarella, bresaola, artichoke hearts, and bell peppers on top.

Bake the small pizzas for about 12 minutes and the large pizzas for about 20 minutes.

See the photo on page 186.

IN ADVANCE *See* PIZZA DOUGH *and* TOMATO SAUCE *on the opposite page.*

PIZZA WITH PROSCIUTTO, FIGS, CHÈVRE & RED ONION

MAKES approx. 30
TIME approx. 30 minutes

- 1 batch PIZZA DOUGH (*see the recipe on the opposite page*)
- 1 lb (500 g) red onion, thinly sliced
- 2 tbsp olive oil
- 1 tbsp butter
- 1 tbsp balsamic vinegar
- 1 tbsp brown sugar
- 5 oz (125 g) prosciutto, cut into strips
- 5 oz (125 g) chèvre, crumbled
- 5 fresh figs, cut into wedges

Make the pizza dough. Heat the oven to 440°F (225°C).

Heat the oil and the butter in a frying pan. Sauté the onion on low heat for about 15 minutes. Stir occasionally. Add the balsamic vinegar and brown sugar, and raise the heat. Cook for another few minutes.

Roll out the dough into large oblong pizzas or into small rounds. Place on baking sheets covered with parchment paper.

Spread the onion, prosciutto, chèvre, and figs on the pizza dough.

Bake the small pizzas for about 12 minutes and the large pizzas for about 20 minutes.

See the photo on page 186.

PIZZA WITH SALAMI, OLIVES & ARUGULA

MAKES approx. 30
TIME approx. 30 minutes

- 1 batch PIZZA DOUGH (*see the recipe on the opposite page*)
- 1 batch TOMATO SAUCE (*see the recipe on the opposite page*)
- 9 oz (250 g) mozzarella, cut into small pieces
- 5 oz (125 g) sliced salami, cut into strips
- 5 oz (125 g) olives
- 2 oz (50 g) arugula

Make the pizza dough and the tomato sauce. Preheat the oven to 440°F (225°C). Roll out the dough into large oblong pizzas or into small rounds. Place on baking sheets lined with parchment paper. Spread the tomato sauce, mozzarella, salami, and olives on the pizza dough.

Bake the small pizzas for about 12 minutes and the large pizzas for about 20 minutes. Garnish with arugula salad.

See the photo on page 186.

IN ADVANCE *See* PIZZA DOUGH *and* TOMATO SAUCE *on the opposite page.*

PIZZA WITH ZUCCHINI, MUSHROOMS & TOMATO

MAKES approx. 30
TIME approx. 30 minutes

1 batch PIZZA DOUGH (*see the recipe on page 188*)
1 batch TOMATO SAUCE (*see the recipe on page 188*)

9 oz (250 g) mozzarella, cut into small pieces
4 oz (120 g) zucchini, cut into half moons
2 oz (50 g) sun-dried tomatoes in oil, sliced
3 oz (75 g) fresh mushrooms, sliced
1 bunch basil, chopped

Make the pizza dough and tomato sauce. Preheat the oven to 440°F (225°C).

Roll out the dough into large oblong pizzas or into small rounds. Place on baking sheets lined with parchment paper.

Spread the tomato sauce and add mozzarella, zucchini, sun-dried tomatoes, and mushrooms on the pizza dough.

Bake the small pizzas for about 12 minutes and the large pizzas for 20 minutes. Garnish with basil.

See the photo on page 186.

IN ADVANCE *See* PIZZA DOUGH *and* TOMATO SAUCE *on page 188.*

PIZZA QUATTRO FORMAGGI

MAKES approx. 30
TIME approx. 30 minutes

1 batch PIZZA DOUGH (*see the recipe on page 188*)
1 batch TOMATO SAUCE (*see the recipe on page 188*)

3 oz (75 g) gorgonzola, crumbled
3 oz (75 g) chèvre, crumbled
3 oz (75 g) mozzarella, cut into small pieces
3 oz (75 g) Parmesan, grated
15 cherry tomatoes, cut into wedges
2 oz (50 g) arugula

Make the pizza dough and tomato sauce. Preheat the oven to 440°F (225°C).

Roll out the dough into large oblong pizzas or into small rounds. Place on baking sheets covered with parchment paper. Spread the tomato sauce and add the different cheeses on the pizza dough.

Bake the small pizzas for about 12 minutes and the large pizzas for about 20 minutes.

Garnish with cherry tomatoes and arugula.

See the photo on page 186.

IN ADVANCE *See* PIZZA DOUGH *and* TOMATO SAUCE *on page 188.*

PIZZA WITH POTATOES, BACON & PARMESAN

MAKES approx. 30
TIME approx. 30 minutes

1 batch PIZZA DOUGH (*see the recipe on page 188*)

½ lb (250 g) potatoes, thinly sliced
3 oz (75 g) Parmesan, grated
5 oz (140 g) bacon, chopped
2 tbsp chopped fresh rosemary

Make the pizza dough. Preheat the oven to 440°F (225°C).

Roll out the dough into large oblong pizzas or into small rounds. Place on baking sheets lined with parchment paper.

Arrange the potatoes, Parmesan, bacon, and rosemary on the pizza dough.

Bake the small pizzas for about 12 minutes and the large pizzas for about 20 minutes.

See the photo on page 186.

IN ADVANCE *See* PIZZA DOUGH *on page 188.*

PIZZA WITH SALSICCIA, TOMATO & PINE NUTS

MAKES approx. 30
TIME approx. 30 minutes

1 batch PIZZA DOUGH (*see the recipe on page 188*)
1 batch TOMATO SAUCE (*see the recipe on page 188*)

9 oz (250 g) mozzarella, cut into small pieces
5 oz (125 g) fresh salsiccia
15 cherry tomatoes, halved
3 tbsp pine nuts

Make the pizza dough and tomato sauce. Preheat the oven to 440°F (225°C).

Roll out the dough into large oblong pizzas or into small rounds. Place on baking sheets covered with parchment paper.

Cut the sausages open and remove the meat. Using wet hands, roll it into small balls.

Arrange the tomato sauce, mozzarella, salsiccia balls, cherry tomatoes, and pine nuts on the pizza dough.

Bake the small pizzas for about 12 minutes and the large pizzas for about 20 minutes.

See the photo on page 187.

IN ADVANCE *See* PIZZA DOUGH and TOMATO SAUCE on *page 188.*

PIZZA WITH SHRIMP, SPINACH, PARMESAN & LEMON

MAKES approx. 30
TIME approx. 30 minutes

1 batch PIZZA DOUGH (*see the recipe on page 188*)
1 batch TOMATO SAUCE (*see the recipe on page 188*)

1 clove garlic, finely chopped
1 tbsp olive oil
3 oz (80 g) fresh spinach
2 ⅔ lb (300 g) raw shrimp, peeled
approx. 4 oz (100 g) Parmesan, grated
½ lemon

Make the pizza dough and tomato sauce. Preheat the oven to 440°F (225°C). Roll out the dough into large oblong pizzas or into small rounds. Place on baking sheets lined with parchment paper.

Sauté the garlic in oil for a minute. Add the spinach and cook for about 30 seconds; remove it and put aside. Add the shrimp to the pan and sauté for about 30 seconds.

Spread the tomato sauce and add the Parmesan, spinach, and shrimp on the pizza dough.

Bake the small pizzas for about 12 minutes and the large pizzas for about 20 minutes.

Squeeze lemon juice over the baked pizzas.
See the photo on page 187.

IN ADVANCE *See* PIZZA DOUGH and TOMATO SAUCE on *page 188.*

PISSALADIÈRE

MAKES approx. 30
TIME approx. 30 minutes

1 batch PIZZA DOUGH (*see the recipe on page 188*)

1 lb (500 g) onions, thinly sliced
2 tbsp olive oil
1 tbsp butter
1 clove garlic, finely chopped
1 tsp French herbs (herbes de Provence)
1 tbsp sugar
1 oz (35 g) anchovies, split lengthwise
5 oz (150 g) black olives

Make the pizza dough. Preheat the oven to 440°F (225°C).

Heat the oil and butter in a frying pan. Sauté the onions, garlic, and herbs on low heat for about 15 minutes. Stir occasionally. Sprinkle with sugar and raise the heat. Sauté for another few minutes.

Roll out the dough into large oblong pizzas or into small rounds. Place on baking sheets covered with parchment paper.

Arrange the onions, anchovies, and olives on the pizza dough.

Bake the small pizzas for about 12 minutes and the large pizzas for about 20 minutes.

See the photo on page 187.

IN ADVANCE See PIZZA DOUGH on *page 188.*

FOIE GRAS & RASPBERRY ONION CHUTNEY

CHÈVRE & WALNUTS

CHÈVRE CREAM & GOLDEN RAISINS

TRUCHA

GREEN TAPENADE WITH ARMAGNAC

FIG TAPENADE

BRANDADE

ROQUEFORT & POMEGRANATE

FENNEL & ALMOND ANCHOÏADE

The recipes are available on pages 199–202

DUCK RILLETTE

PORK RILLETTE

SALMON RILLETTE

The recipes are available on pages 204–205

ROASTED CHESTNUTS

SNAILS WITH GARLIC & PARSLEY

BAKED GARLIC

FRENCH ONION SOUP

ROASTED BONE
MARROW

The recipes are available on pages 202–203

195

STEAK TARTARE

The recipe is available on page 205

CREAMY PESTO DIP

CHIVE DIP

LEMON BUTTER

BROWNED BUTTER

HOLLANDAISE SAUCE

COOKED ARTICHOKES

The recipes are available on page 198

FRANCE

We began this book by renting a house in the south of France for two months. Our goal was to have a place where we could work in peace, but not many recipes were actually written—we were simply too busy eating! For our meals, we used fresh produce from the local village market and wine from a neighboring vineyard. Here we offer the inspiration and flavors from our wonderful experience in Provence.

ARTICHOKE WITH DIPPING SAUCE

MAKES 1
TIME approx. 30–50 minutes

> 1 artichoke
> dipping sauce of your choice *(see the recipes below)*

Put the artichoke in a large pot and cover with water. Lightly season with salt. Cook for 30–50 minutes. The cooking time depends on the size of the artichoke. It's ready when the leaves can be plucked off easily. Serve hot or cold.
  See the photo on page 197.

IN ADVANCE The artichoke can be cooked the day before and served cold.

LEMON BUTTER
> 4 oz (100 g) melted butter
> ½ of a lemon, zest
> approx. 2 tsp course-ground sea salt

Mix the butter with lemon zest and salt.

BROWNED BUTTER
> 4 oz (100 g) butter

Melt the butter over medium heat while stirring until it becomes a light brown color with a nutty aroma. Be careful that it does not burn.

CREAMY PESTO DIP
> ¾ cup (200 g) sour cream or crème fraîche
> approx. 3 tbsp PESTO *(see the recipe on page 178)*

Mix sour cream and pesto.

HOLLANDAISE SAUCE
> ½ lb (250 g) butter
> 3 egg yolks
> 2 tbsp water
> 2 tsp freshly squeezed lemon juice
> ¼ tsp cayenne pepper
> salt

Melt the butter over low heat. Remove the pan from the heat and set it aside.
  Beat the egg yolks and water in a small stainless steel bowl. Place over a pan of hot water, and whisk until the egg mixture thickens. Lift the bowl from the pan of hot water, and whisk in the butter a little at a time. Add the lemon juice and cayenne pepper. Season with salt.

CHIVE DIP
> ¾ cup (200 g) sour cream
> 3 tbsp mayonnaise
> 2–3 tbsp chives, finely chopped
> herbal salt

Mix the ingredients. Season with herbal salt.

IN ADVANCE The pesto dip and the chive dip can be refrigerated for 3 days. Other sauces should be made right before serving.

CROUTON WITH TRUCHA

MAKES approx. 16
TIME approx. 40 minutes

The trucha can be served in 2 ways: in 16 triangle pieces, or as in the picture, in thin slices on a baguette.

- 2 tbsp pastis
- 2 tbsp water
- 2 tbsp golden raisins
- 14 oz (400 g) chard
- 7 eggs
- 2 oz (50 g) Parmesan, grated
- 3 tbsp pine nuts, toasted
- 2 cloves garlic, finely chopped
- 2 tbsp olive oil

Boil the pastis, water, and raisins, and simmer for 2 minutes. Strain and save raisins. Rinse the chard. Remove the stems and the coarse stem in the middle of each leaf. Coarsely chop the leaves.

Beat the eggs, and add the Parmesan and pine nuts.

Sauté the garlic in olive oil in a skillet for a few minutes. Add the chard and sauté until the leaves wilt. Pour in the egg mixture and sprinkle with raisins. Cook without stirring, until the batter begins to set. Loosen around the edge using a soft spatula, and wiggle the pan so that the egg mixture flows down the edges.

Once the top of the trucha has set, place a plate over the skillet. Flip the skillet and plate so that the trucha lands on the plate. Slide the trucha back into the skillet. Cook for a few minutes more until completely set. Plate it, and let cool slightly. Cut into triangles or thin slices.

See the photo on page 192.

IN ADVANCE The trucha can be stored in the refrigerator for about 3 days and in the freezer for 3 months. Heat it up in the oven at 300°F (150°C) for 5–10 minutes before serving.

CROUTON WITH FIG TAPENADE

MAKES approx. 30
TIME approx. 20 minutes

FIG TAPENADE
- 3 dried figs
- 1 clove garlic, pressed
- 1 cup (250 ml) pitted black olives
- 2 tbsp capers
- 1 tbsp chopped fresh basil
- approx. 3 tbsp olive oil
- salt and black pepper

- 1 baguette
- approx. 3 tbsp olive oil

- 4 fresh figs, cut into thin wedges
- fresh basil for garnish

Preheat the oven to 400°F (200°C).

Mix the figs with garlic, olives, capers, and basil in a food processor or with a hand blender. Pour the oil in a thin stream while blending. Season with salt and pepper.

Cut the baguette into slices. Brush with oil, and bake in the oven for a few minutes until golden brown.

Spread the tapenade on the bread and garnish with figs and basil leaves, or serve as a dip with slices of baguette on the side.

See the photo on page 192.

IN ADVANCE The tapenade may be stored in the refrigerator for about 3 days. Bread can be roasted the day before and kept at room temperature.

CROUTON WITH GREEN TAPENADE WITH ARMAGNAC

MAKES approx. 30
TIME approx. 20 minutes

GREEN TAPENADE

½ cup (100 ml) almonds, blanched and peeled
1 clove garlic
1 tbsp capers
1 cup (250 ml) pitted green olives
2 tbsp chopped fresh basil
2 tbsp Armagnac, brandy, or eau de vie
approx. 3 tbsp olive oil
salt and pepper

1 baguette
approx. 3 tbsp olive oil

Brown the almonds in a dry frying pan.

Add all ingredients except oil to a food processor. Pour the oil in a thin stream while blending it coarsely. Season with salt and pepper.

Cut the baguette into slices. Brush with oil, and bake in the oven for a few minutes until golden brown.

Spread the tapenade on the bread and garnish with figs and basil leaves, or serve as a dip with slices of baguette on the side.

See the photo on page 192.

IN ADVANCE The mixture can be stored in the refrigerator for about 3 days. The bread can be toasted the day before and stored at room temperature.

CROUTON WITH ROQUEFORT & POMEGRANATE

MAKES approx. 24
TIME approx. 15 minutes

7 oz (200 g) Roquefort
2 oz (50 g) pecans, chopped
seeds from ½ pomegranate

1 baguette
approx. 3 tbsp olive oil

Preheat the oven to 400°F (200°C).

Cut the baguette into slices. Brush with oil, and bake in the oven for a few minutes until golden brown. Spread the cheese on the bread. Sprinkle with pecans and pomegranate seeds.

See the photo on page 192.

IN ADVANCE The bread can be toasted the day before and kept at room temperature. Deseed the pomegranate the day before, and store the seeds in the refrigerator.

CROUTON WITH FENNEL & ALMOND ANCHOÏADE

MAKES approx. 24
TIME approx. 15 minutes

FENNEL & ALMOND ANCHOÏADE

½ fennel bulb
3 anchovies
1 clove garlic
1 tbsp pastis
2 tsp chopped fresh mint
2 tsp chopped fresh basil
2–4 tbsp olive oil
3 tbsp chopped toasted slivered almonds

1 baguette
approx. 3 tbsp olive oil
toasted slivered almonds for garnish

Preheat the oven to 400°F (200°C).

Trim the fennel bulb, cut into smaller pieces, and blend with the anchovies, garlic, pastis, mint, and basil. Pour the olive oil in a thin stream while blending. Stir in the almonds. Season with salt and pepper.

Cut the baguette into slices. Brush with oil, and bake in the oven for a few minutes until golden brown. Spread the anchoïade on the bread, or serve it as a dip with baguette on the side.

See the photo on page 192.

IN ADVANCE The anchoïade can be stored in the refrigerator for about 3 days. Stir in the almonds just before serving. The bread can be toasted the day before and kept at room temperature.

CROUTON WITH CHÈVRE & WALNUTS

MAKES approx. 24
TIME approx. 25 minutes

2 oz (50 g) walnuts, coarsely chopped
11 oz (300 g) chèvre (a small roll), sliced
1 oz (30 g) frissé lettuce, coarsely chopped
honey

1 baguette
4 tbsp olive oil

Preheat the oven to 400°F (200°C).

Toast the walnuts on a baking sheet in the oven for about 10 minutes or until golden brown.

Cut the baguette into slices. Brush with oil, and lay out on a baking sheet. Place a slice of chèvre on each baguette slice. Grill in upper part of oven for a few minutes until cheese is golden brown.

Arrange a bit of salad on each piece of toast. Sprinkle with walnuts, and drizzle with a little honey.

See the photo on page 192.

IN ADVANCE These taste best when freshly made.

CROUTON WITH FOIE GRAS & RASPBERRY ONION CHUTNEY

MAKES approx. 24
TIME approx. 15 minutes

½ lb (250 g) foie gras
RASPBERRY ONION CHUTNEY (*see the recipe on page 217*)

1 baguette
4 tbsp olive oil

Preheat the oven to 400°F (200°C).

Cut the baguette into slices. Brush with oil, and bake in the oven for a few minutes until golden brown.

Spread a little foie gras on each piece of bread, and top with a dollop of raspberry onion chutney.

See the photo on page 192.

IN ADVANCE These taste best when freshly made.

CROUTON WITH BRANDADE

MAKES approx. 30
TIME approx. 1 hour + 1 day of soaking

BRANDADE
4 oz (100 g) dried salt cod
1 baked potato
½ cup (100 ml) heavy cream
3 cloves garlic, sliced
1 bay leaf
¼ tsp dried thyme
a pinch of ground cloves
approx. 1 tbsp olive oil
salt and pepper

1 baguette
4 tbsp olive oil

Soak the fish in cold water for about 24 hours. Change the water several times.

Preheat the oven to 400°F (200°C).

Pierce the potato with a fork, and bake it in the oven for about 45 minutes or until soft. Let cool and then scoop it out the inside.

Mix the cream, garlic, bay leaf, thyme, and cloves, and let simmer for about 5 minutes. Remove the bay leaf.

Remove the fish from the water and place it in a saucepan. Cover it with fresh water, bring to a boil, and simmer for about 10 minutes. Strain the water and squeeze out all the liquid. Let it cool. Mix the fish with the potato and the cream mixture in a food processor. Run it on low speed for about 2 minutes. Add the olive oil in a thin stream, and continue mixing for about 30 seconds. Season with salt and pepper.

Cut the baguette into slices. Brush with oil, and bake in the oven for a few minutes until golden brown.

Spread the brandade on the bread, or serve it as a dip with baguette on the side.

See the photo on page 192.

IN ADVANCE The mixture can be stored in the refrigerator for 3 days. The bread can be roasted the day before and kept at room temperature.

CROUTON WITH CHÈVRE CREAM & GOLDEN RAISINS

MAKES approx. 24
TIME approx. 40 minutes

4 oz (100 g) golden raisins
½ cup (100 ml) Sautérnes
5 oz (150 g) chèvre
4 oz (100 g) cream cheese

1 baguette
4 tbsp olive oil

Marinate the raisins in the wine for at least 30 minutes.

Preheat the oven to 400°F (200°C).

Stir together the chèvre and the cream cheese.

Cut the baguette into slices. Brush with oil, and bake in the oven for a few minutes until golden brown. Spread the chèvre cream mixture on the bread, and top with raisins.

See the photo on page 192.

IN ADVANCE The raisins marinate for about 2 days. The bread can be grilled the day before and kept at room temperature.

BAKED GARLIC

MAKES 1 garlic head
TIME approx. 35 minutes

1 head of garlic
approx. 2 tbsp olive oil

sea salt and fresh thyme leaves for garnish

Preheat the oven to 400°F (200°C).

Halve the head of garlic. Place the halves on a baking sheet with the cut side up. Drizzle with olive oil. Bake in the oven for about 30 minutes until the garlic is completely soft. Garnish with sea salt and thyme leaves.

Serve immediately with a knife to scoop out the garlic and spread it on slices of toasted baguette.

See the photo on page 194.

IN ADVANCE The garlic tastes best freshly baked.

ROASTED BONE MARROW

MAKES approx. 8 marrow bones / 32 small portions of marrow
TIME approx. 25 minutes

8 veal or ox marrow bones approx. 2-inch (5 cm) long

baguette or rustic style bread
½ cup (100 ml) finely chopped parsley
2 lemons, zested
approx. 1 tsp course-ground sea salt

Preheat the oven to 400°F (200°C).

Cut the baguette into slices. Brush with oil, and bake in the oven for a few minutes until golden brown.

Put the marrow bones in a baking pan, and roast them in the oven for about 20 minutes or until the marrow is soft and creamy—however, it should not be runny.

Meanwhile, mix the parsley, lemon zest, and salt.

Serve the marrow with the parsley mixture and slices of baguette on the side, or spread the bone marrow on the baguette slices and sprinkle with the parsley mixture. Serve immediately.

See the photo on page 195.

IN ADVANCE Everything should be prepared right before serving.

ROASTED CHESTNUTS

MAKES approx. 24
TIME approx. 25 minutes

24 chestnuts
butter and course-ground sea salt for serving

Preheat the oven to 400°F (200°C).

Carve a cross into the top of each chestnut. Place the chestnuts on a baking sheet and toast them in the oven for about 20 minutes. The chestnuts are ready when the interior is soft.

Serve immediately with butter and sea salt.

See the photo on page 194.

IN ADVANCE Chestnuts taste best freshly roasted.

SNAILS WITH GARLIC & PARSLEY

MAKES approx. 24
TIME approx. 30 minutes

24 canned snails + 24 snail shells
1 shallot, finely chopped
1 tbsp butter
½ cup (100 ml) dry white wine
8 cloves garlic
½ cup (100 ml) parsley
½ cup (125 g) butter, cold
salt and pepper

Preheat the oven to 480°F (250°C).

Sauté the shallots with 1 tsp butter in a skillet over medium heat. Add the snails and the wine, and let simmer for about 5 minutes. Strain the wine.

Mix the garlic and parsley in a food processor to a finely chopped mixture. Add the butter and mix it into a paste. Season with salt and pepper.

Place a snail in each shell, and fill with the butter mixture. Place the shells in an ovenproof dish or on a snail plate. Grill in the upper part of the oven for 5–6 minutes or until the butter begins to bubble.

Serve immediately, preferably with bread to soak up the butter.

See the photo on page 194.

IN ADVANCE The snails stuffed with garlic butter can be stored uncooked in the refrigerator for 1 day or in the freezer for about 1 month. They do not need be thawed before grilling but expect the grilling to take a few minutes longer.

FRENCH ONION SOUP

MAKES approx. 24
TIME approx. 1 hour

1 ⅔ lbs (750 g) onions, sliced
3 tbsp butter
2 tsp sugar
¾ cup (200 ml) dry white wine
4 cups (1 liter) chicken or vegetable broth
1 tsp chopped fresh thyme
salt and pepper

¾ cup (200 ml) diced day-old bread
1 tbsp olive oil
approx. 1 oz (30 g) Gruyère, grated

Sauté the onions in butter in a saucepan over low heat under a lid for about 20 minutes. Stir occasionally. Add the sugar and sauté for another 10 minutes without a lid. Pour in the wine, broth, and thyme. Bring to a boil and let simmer for another 20 minutes. Season with salt and pepper.

Preheat the oven to 400°F (200°C).

Mix the bread and oil in a roasting pan. Roast for about 5 minutes until the bread is golden brown.

Pour the soup into small bowls, and serve immediately with croutons and cheese.

See the photo on page 195.

ROSÉ ONION SOUP
Replace the onion with red onion and the white wine with rosé.

IN ADVANCE The soup can be stored in the refrigerator for about 2 days.

PORK RILLETTE

MAKES approx. 4 cups (1 liter)
TIME approx. 3 hours and 45 minutes

2 lbs (1 kg) boneless pork shoulder
3 cloves
1 onion, halved
1 carrot, sliced
1 stalk celery, sliced
6 cloves garlic, lightly pressed
5 black peppercorns
a handful of fresh thyme
3 bay leaves
2 cups (500 ml) white wine
water
salt and pepper

approx. 3 oz (100 g) lard
thyme sprigs for garnish

Cut the pork into cubes of approximately 2 inches (5 cm). Push the cloves into one of the onion halves. Add all ingredients except lard into a large saucepan, and fill it with water until the meat is covered. Simmer on low heat with the lid on for about 3 hours. Stir occasionally.

Remove the meat and shred it using 2 forks. Mix the meat with a bit of the resulting broth, and stir until creamy. Season with salt and pepper. Pour the mixture into well-cleaned glass jars. Smooth the surface and make sure the edges are clean.

Melt the lard over low heat until you get about ½ cup (100 ml) of melted fat. Allow it to cool slightly, and pour it into the jars so it covers the meat. Stir a few sprigs of thyme into the lard. Seal the jars and store them in the refrigerator.

Serve the rillette at room temperature.
See the photo on page 193.

IN ADVANCE The rillette tastes best if refrigerated for a few days. Unopened and refrigerated, it can last for a month, but as soon as you break the lid of fat it should be eaten in about 2 days.

SALMON RILLETTE

MAKES approx. 2 cups (500 ml)
TIME approx. 40 minutes

1 lb (500 g) fresh salmon
¾ cup (200 g) butter, unsalted
2 shallots, finely chopped
1 tbsp crème fraîche or sour cream
7 oz (200 g) smoked salmon, finely chopped
1 lemon, zested
2 tbsp freshly squeezed lemon juice
1 tbsp olive oil
2 egg yolks, lightly beaten
3 tbsp finely chopped chives
salt and pepper

Steam the salmon for 5-8 minutes. It should not be fully cooked.

Sauté the shallots in 1 tbsp of butter over low heat until it is soft, but not browned. Set aside.

Beat together half of the butter and the crème fraîche.

Break the salmon into large pieces. Stir in the shallots, smoked salmon, lemon zest, lemon juice, olive oil, yolks, and chives. Stir together. Lastly, mix in the crème fraîche and the butter mixture. Season with salt and pepper.

Distribute the salmon mixture among well-cleaned glass jars. Smooth the surface and make sure the edges are clean.

Melt the remaining butter over low heat. Carefully pour the butter over the salmon rillette so that it is completely covered. Seal the jars and store them in the refrigerator.

Serve the rillette at room temperature.
See the photo on page 193.

IN ADVANCE The rillette tastes best if refrigerated for a few days. Unopened and refrigerated, it can last for a week, but as soon as you break the lid of butter it should be eaten in about 2 days.

DUCK RILLETTE

MAKES approx. 4 cups (1 liter)
TIME approx. 4 hours + 1 night in the fridge

4 duck legs
1 ¾ lbs (800 g) duck or goose fat
2 tbsp coarse salt
2 cloves garlic, pressed
2 bay leaves
1 bunch thyme
approx. 2 tbsp cognac
1 orange, zested
salt and pepper

Sprinkle 1 tbsp coarse salt in the bottom of a pan. Add the garlic, bay leaves, and half of the thyme sprigs. Spread out the duck legs in the pan, and then sprinkle with the rest of the salt and thyme sprigs. Cover with plastic wrap and let stand in the refrigerator overnight.

Preheat the oven to 300°F (150°C).

Scrape away the salt from the duck legs. Place them into a casserole with the garlic, thyme sprigs, and bay leaves. Melt the fat, and pour it over the duck legs so they are covered. Cover with a lid, and allow the casserole to stand in the oven for about 3 hours.

Let the duck legs cool in the fat, then take them out and remove the meat from the bones. Shred the meat using 2 forks. Mix in some of the fat so that the rillette becomes creamy. Add the cognac and orange zest, and season with salt and pepper.

Distribute the mixture among well-cleaned glass jars. Smooth the surface and make sure the edges are clean.

Strain a little of the melted fat into the glass jars so that it covers the meat. Lay a few thyme leaves gently in the fat. Seal the jars and store them in the refrigerator.

Serve the rillette at room temperature. *See the photo on page 193.*

IN ADVANCE *See* PORK RILLETTE *on the opposite page.*

STEAK TARTARE

MAKES approx. 24
TIME approx. 30 minutes

approx. 1 ⅓ lbs (600 g) beef tenderloin, chilled
2 egg yolks
2 tbsp Dijon mustard
1 tsp Worcestershire sauce
approx. 3 tbsp canola oil
approx. 1 tsp cognac
a few drops of Tabasco
salt and pepper
2 tbsp finely chopped gherkins
2 tbsp capers, finely chopped
2 tbsp parsley, finely chopped
3 tbsp red onion, finely chopped

6 slices of whole wheat or white sandwich bread
parsley, finely chopped red onion, and large capers for garnish

Chop the meat as finely as possible.

Mix the egg yolks, Dijon mustard, and Worcestershire sauce. Pour the oil in a thin stream while whisking. Stir in the cognac and season with Tabasco, salt, and pepper. Stir in the gherkins, capers, parsley, and red onion. Add the meat and mix well.

Press a round cutter into the bread. Without removing the cutter, fill it with the meat mixture. Press the mixture and gently lift the cutter. Garnish with parsley, red onion, and capers.

See the photo on page 196.

IN ADVANCE Can be stored in the refrigerator for about 2 hours.

PECAN CARAMELIZED BRIE

BRIE EN CROUTE WITH
WALNUTS & FRUIT

CHEESE WHEEL

FRIED CAMEMBERT
WITH CLOUDBERRIES

FIG & ALMOND
COVERED BRIE

The recipes are available on pages 213–215

BAKED RICOTTA WITH
CAPERS & SAGE

BLUE CHEESE & WALNUT
COVERED GRAPES

CHÈVRE BALLS

The recipes are available on pages 212–213

RASPBERRY & ONION CHUTNEY

RHUBARB & GINGER CHUTNEY

WALNUTS IN BALSAMIC VINEGAR

BALSAMIC POACHED APRICOTS

CANDIED GINGER

The recipes are available on pages 215–217 and 231 crackers

FIGS POACHED
IN PORT

ROASTED PINE
NUTS IN HONEY

PEAR & PECAN
COMPOTE

209

MARINATED MOZZARELLA

MARINATED FETA

MARINATED HALLOUMI

The recipes are available on page 211

CHEESE PLATTERS

It's time to breathe new life into the cheese platter! Why limit yourself to Cheddar and Brie when there is a cornucopia of delicious cheeses from around the world? On our platter, we often serve a creamy well-aged chèvre from France with a Spanish Manchego, and a pungent Stilton from England. We also like to pair cheeses with condiments that offer a novel contrast in flavors.

MARINATED MOZZARELLA

MAKES approx. 11 oz (300 g)
TIME approx. 15 minutes + 1 day in the refrigerator

11 oz (300 g) bocconcini (small mozzarella balls)

approx. 1 ⅓ cups (300 ml) olive oil
1 tsp chopped red chili pepper, seeded
3 tbsp finely chopped fresh basil
1 tsp lemon zest
salt and pepper

Drain the mozzarella, and mix it with the rest of the ingredients. Season with salt and pepper. Marinate for at least 1 day in the refrigerator.

See the photo on page 210.

IN ADVANCE The marinated cheese can be stored for about 3 days in the refrigerator. If the olive oil has solidified, place the container at room temperature 1 hour before serving.

MARINATED FETA

MAKES approx. 11 oz (300 g)
TIME approx. 15 minutes + 1 day in the refrigerator

11 oz (300 g) feta, diced

approx. 1 ⅓ cups (300 ml) olive oil
1 lemon, zested + 1 tbsp freshly squeezed juice
2 tbsp toasted sesame seeds

1 tbsp fennel seeds
1 tsp coarsely ground black pepper

Mix all ingredients except the feta. Gently fold the feta into the oil so that it does not break. Marinate for at least 1 day in the refrigerator.

See the photo on page 210.

IN ADVANCE *See* MARINATED MOZZARELLA.

MARINATED HALLOUMI

MAKES approx. 7 oz (200 g)
TIME approx. 20 minutes + 1 day in the refrigerator

7 oz (200 g) halloumi, sliced

approx. 1 ⅓ cups (300 ml) olive oil
1 tbsp chopped fresh thyme
1 tbsp chopped fresh rosemary
2 cloves garlic, thinly sliced
1 lemon, zested
1 tsp whole black peppercorns
1 tsp whole pink peppercorns

Mix all the ingredients except the halloumi.
    Grill the cheese on both sides in a hot grill pan until it gets grill marks. Let cool, and then place it in the marinade. Marinate for at least 1 day in the refrigerator.

See the photo on page 210.

IN ADVANCE *See* MARINATED MOZZARELLA.

BAKED RICOTTA WITH CAPERS & SAGE

MAKES approx. 9 oz (250 g)
TIME approx. 1 hour

9 oz (250 g) ricotta cheese
approx. 1 tbsp olive oil
1 egg
salt and pepper

3 tbsp olive oil
½ cup (100 ml) fresh sage
2 tbsp capers
1 lemon, zested
freshly squeezed juice from ½ lemon
salt and pepper

Preheat the oven to 400°F (200°C).

Brush a small but deep ovenproof form that holds approximately 1 ¾ cups (400 ml), with oil. Alternately, use a baking tray for large muffins.

Mix the ricotta and the eggs. Season with salt and pepper. Fill the dish with the cheese mixture, and press it properly. Bake it in the oven for about 40 minutes. Let cool slightly before plating.

Heat the oil in a frying pan or small skillet. Fry the sage and capers until the sage is crispy. Remove the pan from the heat, and stir in the lemon zest and juice. Season with salt and pepper, and pour the mixture over the ricotta. Serve immediately with a rustic style bread.

See the photo on page 207.

RICOTTA WITH RED CHILI PEPPER
Use seeded and finely chopped red chili pepper instead of capers.

RICOTTA WITH PARSLEY
Use parsley instead of sage.

RICOTTA WITH OLIVES
Add 3 tbsp finely chopped olives to the caper mixture.

IN ADVANCE The cheese can be prepared a few hours in advance and reheated at 260°F (125°C) for 10 minutes before serving. Fry capers and sage at the last minute.

BLUE CHEESE & WALNUT COVERED GRAPES

MAKES approx. 48
TIME approx. 30 minutes + 1 hour in the refrigerator

¾ cup (200 ml) finely chopped walnuts
5 oz (150 g) blue cheese
4 oz (100 g) cream cheese
24 seedless grapes

Preheat the oven to 350°F (175°C).

Roast the walnuts in the oven for about 8 minutes or until they become golden brown. Stir after 4 minutes.

Blend the blue cheese and cream cheese into a smooth cream. Refrigerate for about 30 minutes.

Cover each grape with about 1 tbsp of the cheese by rolling it in your hands.

Place the cheese covered grapes on a tray, and refrigerate for about 30 minutes. Then, roll the grapes in the walnuts. Refrigerate for another 30 minutes or until firm. Cut the grapes into halves with a sharp knife. Serve immediately.

See the photo on page 207.

IN ADVANCE Grapes covered with cheese can be prepared several hours in advance if refrigerated. Roll in the walnuts about 30 minutes before serving. The walnuts can be roasted the day before.

CHÈVRE BALLS

MAKES approx. 20
TIME approx. 1 hour

> 7 oz (200 g) chèvre
> 4 oz (100 g) cream cheese
>
> ½ cup (100 ml) golden raisins, dried
> cranberries, fresh herbs, pecans *and/or*
> walnuts, finely chopped

Mix the chèvre and cream cheese. Refrigerate the mixture for about 30 minutes or until firm. Roll into small balls.

Pour one or a few of the chopped ingredients on separate plates, and roll each ball so that they are covered. Keep cold until ready to be served.
See the photo on page 207.

IN ADVANCE The cheese mixture can be mixed and stored in the refrigerator for 1 day. Shape into balls, and roll them in the chopped ingredients a few hours before serving.

WINE & CHEESE

Part of the joy of planning a cheese plate is in choosing the right wines to complement it. Finding a balance between the saltiness, fat content and maturity of the cheese and the freshness, astringency and sweetness of the wine is key to achieving a perfect pairing. The general rule of thumb is to match lighter wines with lighter cheeses, and more full-bodied wines with heavier cheeses. Mature cheeses tend to be better served with well-ages wines. Despite convention, white wine often is easier to pair with a wider variety of cheeses, as it lacks the tannins in red wines which can overwhelm the palate.

For goat cheese, white wine is the traditional partner. However, a light red wine is a fine complement to an aged goat cheese. Full-bodied red wines stand up well to the saltiness of sheep milk's cheese. Blue cheeses are often paired with aged, sweet reds such as port wines though sweet white wines are also a delicious alternative. Brie and camembert, often served with red wine, can also be paired with medium-bodied white wines.

BRIE EN CROUTE WITH WALNUTS & FRUIT

MAKES approx. 8 pieces
TIME approx. 1 hour

> ½ cup (100 ml) chopped apricots,
> fresh or dried
> 3 tbsp peeled and chopped apple
> 3 tbsp chopped walnuts
> 1 tbsp raspberry jam
> 1 whole brie cheese (9 oz [250 g])
> approx. 6 oz (170 g) puff pastry sheets
> 1 egg yolk, beaten

Preheat the oven to 400°F (200°F).

Place the apricots, apple, and walnuts on a baking sheet. Roast in the oven for about 15 minutes or until the fruit begins to color. Allow to cool, and mix with the raspberry jam.

Cut the brie horizontally to make a top and bottom. Spread the fruit and the nut mixture on the bottom piece, and place the upper piece of brie on top.

Roll out a puff pastry sheet into a circle of about ¾ inch (2 cm) larger than the brie. Brush the pastry with egg yolk, and place the cheese in the middle.

Roll out the other pastry sheet about 2 inches (5 cm) larger than the brie and place it on top. Smooth down the pastry over the edges and press gently on the bottom pastry to seal. Cut away excess dough so that there is a ¾-inch (2 cm) border around the cheese. Brush with the rest of the egg yolk.

Bake it in the center of the oven for 10 minutes. Reduce the heat to 350°F (175°C) and bake for an additional 15–20 minutes or until the pastry is golden brown. Let it rest for about 10 minutes before serving.
See the photo on page 206.

TIP For a more aesthetic touch, trim the edge in a decorative way and cut decorative shapes with the left over puff pastry and lay on top.

IN ADVANCE The fruit and nut mixture can be prepared days before serving. The cheese can be filled, wrapped and refrigerated about 3 hours before baking. Brush with the egg yolk, and bake right before serving.

FRIED CAMEMBERT WITH CLOUDBERRIES

MAKES approx. 8
TIME approx. 5 minutes

1 whole camembert (approx. 9 oz [250 g])
½ cup (100 ml) water
½ cup (100 ml) all-purpose flour
½ cup (100 ml) breadcrumbs
1 egg, beaten
4 cups (1 liter) oil for deep frying
approx. ½ cup (100 ml) cloudberries or cloudberry jam

Pour the water, flour, breadcrumbs, and egg into separate bowls. Dip the cheese in water. Then dip it in the flour, then in the egg, and lastly in the breadcrumbs.

Heat the oil in a saucepan to 350°F (180°C). Fry the cheese for about 3 minutes or until it is golden brown. Drain on paper towels. Serve with cloudberries.

See the photo on page 206.

IN ADVANCE Prepare right before serving.

CHEESE WHEEL

MAKES approx. 16
TIME approx. 20 minutes

1 whole brie or camembert (1 lb [500 g])
4 oz (100 g) cream cheese
2 tbsp finely chopped chives
2 tbsp finely chopped walnuts
2 tbsp finely chopped golden raisins
2 tbsp finely chopped dried cranberries

Spread a thin layer of cream cheese on the brie or camembert. Mark 8 wedges on the cheese with a knife. Carefully sprinkle on the toppings, filling each marked wedge.

See the photo on page 206.

IN ADVANCE The cheese wheel can be stored in the refrigerator for a couple of hours before serving.

FIG & ALMOND COVERED BRIE

MAKES approx. 16
TIME approx. 30 minutes

½ cup (100 ml) brown sugar
2 tbsp water
2 fresh figs, cut into wedges
½ cup (100 ml) roasted almond flakes
½ tsp vanilla extract
1 whole brie (1 lb [500 g])

Preheat the oven to 350°F (175°C).

Heat the sugar and water in a saucepan until the sugar melts. Add the figs, stir, and simmer for a couple of minutes. Mix the vanilla extract and the almonds into the syrup.

Place the brie on a baking sheet lined with parchment paper. Pour the syrup with the figs and almonds over it. Bake in the oven for about 10 minutes or until the brie has softened—however not completely melted. Serve immediately.

See the photo on page 206.

IN ADVANCE Prepare right before serving.

PECAN CARAMELIZED BRIE

MAKES approx. 8
TIME approx. 30 minutes

1 whole brie (approx. 9 oz [250 g])
¾ cup (200 ml) sugar
3 tbsp water
approx. 10 pecans

Place the brie on a baking rack. Set the rack on a baking sheet covered with parchment paper.

Mix the sugar and water in a heavy-bottomed saucepan. Let the sugar melt over medium heat without stirring. Remove any sugar on the sides of the pan with a wet brush. Boil the syrup until a golden caramel color.

Pour the hot caramel over the brie, covering it completely. Press the pecans into the caramel, and be careful not to burn your fingers. Let the caramel harden and then serve the brie immediately.

See the photo on page 206.

IN ADVANCE   The brie tastes best if served immediately.

WALNUTS IN BALSAMIC VINEGAR

MAKES   approx. 1 ⅓ cups (300 ml)
TIME   approx. 15 minutes

½ cup (100 ml) brown sugar
¾ cup (200 ml) balsamic vinegar
2 tbsp honey
¾ cup (200 ml) walnuts

Bring the brown sugar and balsamic vinegar to a boil, and simmer for about 5 minutes. Stir in the honey and let it cool. Mix the syrup with the walnuts.

See the photo on page 208.

IN ADVANCE   The walnuts may be stored in a jar with a lid for a few weeks.

ROASTED PINE NUTS IN HONEY

MAKES   approx. ½ cup (100 ml)
TIME   approx. 10 minutes

½ cup (100 ml) pine nuts
2 tbsp honey, preferably flavored

Roast the pine nuts in a dry pan. Be careful not to burn them. When they have browned slightly, drizzle with the honey. Stir and remove the pan from the heat.

See the photo on page 209.

IN ADVANCE   Can be stored in an air-tight jar for 1 week.

COMPOSING A CHEESE PLATTER

To create a great cheese plate, you should seek out cheeses that complement each other in terms of taste, smell, shape, and texture. Select a combination of mild, aged, and stronger cheeses, and ensure that both hard and soft cheeses are represented. And be sure to include a pungent blue cheese to round off the plate.

If only wine and cheese are being served, plan on a total of 9 oz (250 g) of cheese per person. If you plan to have other food, count 5 oz (150 g) of cheese per person.

A wooden cutting board makes a lovely option to display the cheese. Always plate the cheeses in order of strength, starting with the milder cheeses and ending with the one with the punchiest flavor. Each cheese should have its own knife and a label, noting its name and the type of milk from which it is made.

Crispy crudites like celery, bell peppers, cucumber and radishes work well on a cheese plate as their crunchiness provides a counterpoint to the texture of the cheeses. Pears, peaches, and figs all pair well with cheese. Dried fruits like apricots also work well on a cheese plate but avoid tropical fruits and the cliché of grapes.

For the best taste and texture, cheeses should not be served straight from the refrigerator, but rather at room temperature. Cheese will keep just fine outside the refrigerator, and taste better if left covered at room temperature for three to fours hours before serving.

RHUBARB & GINGER CHUTNEY

MAKES approx. 1 cup (250 ml)
TIME approx. 30 minutes

> 1 lb (500 g) rhubarb
> 3 tbsp water
> 2 red onions, sliced
> 2 cloves garlic, pressed
> ¾ cup (200 ml) sugar
> 2 tbsp red wine vinegar
> 1 tsp salt
> 1 tbsp grated fresh ginger

Rinse and cut the rhubarb into approximately ¾-inch (2 cm) pieces (only peel it if the skin is thick).

Mix the rhubarb with the other ingredients in a heavy saucepan. Bring to a boil and let simmer for about 20 minutes. Stir occasionally. Pour the chutney into a well-cleaned and hot glass jar. Seal it immediately and store it in a cool place.

See the photo on page 208.

IN ADVANCE The chutney can be stored in the refrigerator for about 3 months.

FIGS POACHED IN PORT

MAKES approx. ¾ cup (200 ml)
TIME approx. 25 minutes

> 8 fresh figs, cut into wedges
> 3 tbsp water
> 3 tbsp port wine
> ½ cup (100 ml) brown sugar

Mix all the ingredients in a saucepan, and bring to a boil. Let it simmer for about 20 minutes or until all liquid has been absorbed. Pour into a clean warm jar, and seal it.

See the photo on page 209.

IN ADVANCE *See* RHUBARB & GINGER CHUTNEY *above.*

PEAR & PECAN COMPOTE

MAKES approx. 1 ⅓ cups (300 ml)
TIME approx. 20 minutes

> 14 oz (400 g) pears, peeled and pitted
> 1 cinnamon stick
> ½ tsp ground cardamom
> 1–2 tbsp water
> ½ cup (100 ml) coarsely chopped pecans

Cut the pear into small pieces. Boil with the cinnamon stick, cardamom, and water. Simmer until the fruit is soft. Stir occasionally.

Remove the pan from the heat and discard the cinnamon stick. Mix with a hand blender or in a food processor to a desired consistency. Allow to cool. Stir in the pecans.

See the photo on page 209.

IN ADVANCE The compote can be stored in the refrigerator for about 2 days. Add the pecans just before serving.

CANDIED GINGER

MAKES approx. 1 lb (500 g)
TIME approx. 2 hours

> 1 lb (500 g) fresh ginger, peeled
> water
>
> SYRUP
> 1 ¾ cups (400 ml) water
> 2 ⅓ cups (550 ml) sugar
> 2 tbsp corn syrup
> 1 cinnamon stick
> 2 cloves

Thinly slice the ginger and place it in a saucepan. Cover with water. Bring to a boil, and simmer for about 2 hours or until the ginger is soft. Strain out the water.

Prepare the syrup while the ginger is simmering. Bring the water and sugar to a boil, and add the corn syrup, cinnamon, and cloves. Simmer uncovered, on low heat, and without stirring for about 40 minutes.

Put the ginger in a clean jar, pour over the syrup and let it cool before screwing the lid on.

See the photo on page 208.

IN ADVANCE Candied ginger can be stored in an air tight jar in the refrigerator for 2 months.

BALSAMIC POACHED APRICOTS

MAKES approx. ¾ cup (200 ml)
TIME approx. 15 minutes

20 dried apricots, sliced
¾ cup (200 ml) water
3 tbsp raw sugar
2 tsp balsamic vinegar

Simmer all ingredients over low heat for about 10 minutes. Allow it to cool.

See the photo on page 208.

IN ADVANCE The apricots can be stored in the refrigerator for 1 week.

RASPBERRY ONION CHUTNEY

MAKES approx. 1 ¾ cups (400 ml)
TIME approx. 1 hour

2 tbsp butter
4 red onions, thinly sliced
9 oz (250 g) raspberries
½ cup (100 ml) sugar
1 ½ tbsp raspberry balsamic vinegar or
   regular balsamic vinegar
salt

Melt the butter in a pan. Add the onion, and cook on low heat for about 30 minutes or until soft.

Add the raspberries, sugar, and balsamic vinegar, and let simmer for another 20 minutes. Season with salt.

Pour it into a well-cleaned and warm glass jar. Serve at room temperature.

See the photo on page 208.

IN ADVANCE The compote can be stored in the refrigerator for about 3 weeks.

CARAMELIZED RED ONION

MAKES approx. 2 cups (500 ml)
TIME approx. 1 ½ hours

8 red onions, thinly sliced
3 ½ tbsp butter
5 tbsp brown sugar
3 tbsp balsamic vinegar
salt

Melt the butter in a pan. Add the onion, and cook on low heat for about 30 minutes or until soft. Add the brown sugar and balsamic vinegar, and let simmer on low heat for an additional 40 minutes. Season with salt and let cool.

Is not pictured.

IN ADVANCE Can be stored in the refrigerator for about 3 weeks.

LEMON & DILL GRISSINI

SUN-DRIED TOMATOES GRISSINI

PARMESAN GRISSINI

PARSLEY & BASIL GRISSINI

GRISSINI

CARROT BREADSTICKS

TOMATO BREADSTICKS

PARSLEY BREADSTICKS

GRUYÈRE BREADSTICKS

BEET BREADSTICKS

BREADSTICKS

218

The recipes are available on page 229

PARMESAN
& ROSEMARY

WHOLE-WHEAT CRACKERS
WITH FENNEL SEEDS

BLUE CHEESE &
PECANS

CHEDDAR & CARAWAY

PECORINO & OLIVES

CHEDDAR & THYME

GRUYÈRE, DIJON MUSTARD & BACON

The recipes are available on page 231

MUFFINS

FETA & SPINACH

PARMESAN, HAM & DIJON

BRIE, HONEY & PECANS

BISCOTTI

CHÈVRE, DRIED FIGS & WALNUTS

PARMESAN, ROSEMARY & PINE NUTS

OLIVES & SUNDRIED TOMATOES

The recipes are available on page 230

OLIVES

COURSE-GROUND SEA SALT & ROSEMARY

FETA & SALAMI

PITA BREAD

FLATBREAD STRIPS WITH
CHEDDAR & CARAWAY

MINI-BAGELS

ROASTED PITA
BREAD WITH
CUMIN &
SESAME

GARLIC BREAD
WITH PARSLEY

FLATBREAD STRIPS
WITH MIXED SEEDS

TORTILLA CHIPS

FLATBREAD STRIPS WITH
FLEUR DE SEL & HERBS

TORTILLA BREAD

The recipes are available on pages 226–229

The recipe is available on page 232

LARGE WONTON CUPS

TOASTED
BREAD CUPS

PITA BREAD

SMALL
WONTON CUPS

CROSTINI

TARTLET SHELLS

TOAST POINTS

TORTILLA CUPS

PHYLLO CUPS

VOL-AU-VENTS

PIZZA ROUNDS

PÂTE À CHOUX PUFFS

The recipes are available on pages 233 and 27 (pâte-à choux puffs), 28 (vol-au-vents), and 227 (pita bread)

BREAD

Bread plays a prominent role in hors d'oeuvres—both as a vehicle for scooping up delectable dips and a base for tasty toppings and spreads. Here we also give tips on how to make bread cups and bowls made from tortilla, phyllo, and wonton. Of course we haven't forgotten classics such as grissinis and savory biscottis and muffins—delicious just as they are.

FLATBREAD STRIPS

MAKES approx. 20
TIME approx. 10 minutes

5 oz (140 g) soft flatbreads
1 egg white, beaten
seasoning of your choice (*see the recipe below*)

Preheat the oven to 400°F (200°C).

Brush the flatbreads with the egg white. Sprinkle with the seasoning of your choice. Cut the bread into approximately ½-inch (1 ½ cm) wide strips, and place them on a baking sheet. Bake in the oven for 2–3 minutes or until golden brown. Let cool.

See the photo on page 222.

MIXED SEEDS

approx. 4 oz (100 g) mixed poppy seeds,
sunflower seeds, flaxseeds, and sesame seeds
course-ground sea salt

FLEUR DE SEL & HERBS

3 tbsp French herbs (herbes de Provence)
fleur de sel or course-ground sea salt

CHEDDAR & CARAWAY

approx. 3 oz (75 g) Cheddar, grated
⅔ cup (150 ml) caraway seeds

IN ADVANCE All the flatbread strips can be prepared the day before serving. Keep at room temperature.

GARLIC BREAD WITH PARSLEY

MAKES approx. 30
TIME approx. 30 minutes + 40 minutes to rise

1 batch PIZZA DOUGH (*see the recipe on page 188*)
3 cloves garlic, pressed
approx. ½ cup extra virgin olive oil
3 tbsp finely chopped parsley
**course-ground sea salt and freshly ground
black pepper**

Preheat the oven to 440°F (225°C).

Make the pizza dough. When the dough has risen, roll it out thinly and place it on a baking sheet, greased or lined with parchment paper.

Mix the garlic with 4–5 tbsp olive oil into a paste. Spread the garlic paste over the dough and sprinkle with parsley, sea salt, and black pepper. Cut small slits in the dough and stretch it out with your hands to create holes in it.

Bake for about 15 minutes or until golden brown. Drizzle with extra olive oil and cut into pieces.

See the photo on page 222.

IN ADVANCE Freshly baked garlic bread tastes best, but it is possible to make the bread a few hours in advance.

MINI-BAGELS

MAKES approx. 20
TIME approx. 1 hour and 45 minutes

½ cup (125 ml) milk
2 tsp active dry yeast
1 ½ tbsp sunflower oil
1 tbsp honey
1 tsp salt
1 cup (250 ml) rye flour, sifted
approx. ½ cup (100 ml) bread flour

8 ½ cups (2 liters) water
1 ½ tbsp salt

1 egg, beaten
sesame or poppy seeds

Warm the milk to 110°F (40°C) and pour into a bowl. Sprinkle in the yeast and stir until dissolved. Add the oil, honey, and salt. Mix in almost all the flour and work the dough by hand or using a machine, until the dough is smooth. Add more flour if needed. By hand, the dough must be worked for at least 10 minutes.

Put the dough on a floured work surface and divide it into 20 pieces. Roll 4-inch (10 cm) long lengths to form rings. Pinch the ends together tightly, and place them on a baking sheet lined with parchment paper. Cover with a kitchen towel and let it rise for about 40 minutes.

Preheat the oven to 400°F (200°C).

Boil the water and salt in a saucepan. Add a few bagels at a time, and boil for 1-2 minutes. Remove them with a slotted spoon, drain, and place on a plate.

Brush the bagels with the beaten egg. Sprinkle with sesame or poppy seeds. Bake for about 15 minutes or until golden brown. Cool on a rack.

See the photo on page 222.

IN ADVANCE Bagels can be stored airtight for 1 day or in the freezer for 3 months.

PITA BREAD

MAKES approx. 8 large/24 small
TIME approx. 45 minutes + 1 hour to rise

2 cups (500 ml) water
2 tsp active dry yeast
1 ½ tbsp salt
1 tbsp honey
2 tbsp olive oil
5–5 ½ cups flour

Warm the water to 110°F (40°C) and pour into a bowl. Sprinkle in the yeast and stir until dissolved. Add the remaining water, salt, honey, and olive oil. Mix in almost all the flour and work the dough by hand or machine, until the dough is smooth. Add more flour if needed. Cover with a kitchen towel and let rise for approximately 1 hour.

Preheat the oven to 480°F (250°C).

Place the dough on a floured work surface and divide it into 8 pieces. Roll the pieces into balls, shaped into rounds about 4 inches (10 cm) in diameter, and place them on a baking sheet lined with parchment paper. Bake for about 8 minutes. Let cool on a rack, covered by a kitchen towel.

See the photo on page 222.

IN ADVANCE Pita bread can be stored airtight for 1 day or in the freezer for 3 months. Heat at 300°F (150°C) for 5–10 minutes.

PRESERVING BREAD

To keep bread fresh it's important to store it properly. Place breads with soft crust in a plastic bag; and breads with a hard crust in a paper bag. To preserve that fresh-baked flavor, freeze the bread in a freezer bag as soon as it has cooled. Bread with a hard crust should be frozen in a paper bag, and then sealed in a plastic freezer bag. This way, the bread preserves its hard crust, even when frozen.

Dough can also be frozen. Simply take out as many unbaked buns or loafs as you need, thaw, and bake as instructed.

ROASTED PITA WITH CUMIN & SESAME

MAKES approx. 40
TIME approx. 30 minutes

> 1 batch baked PITA BREAD (*see the recipe on page 227*)
> 2 cloves garlic, pressed
> approx. ½ cup (100 ml) olive oil
> 2 tsp ground cumin
> 2 tbsp sesame seeds
> course-ground sea salt and black pepper

Preheat the oven to 400°F (200°C).

Cut the pita bread into triangles, and place them on a baking sheet lined with parchment paper.

Mix the garlic and olive oil, and brush the garlic paste on the bread. Mix the cumin and sesame seeds, and sprinkle the bread with the mixture. Top with sea salt and black pepper. Bake for about 15 minutes or until golden brown.

See the photo on page 222.

IN ADVANCE The bread can be toasted several hours ahead of time.

TORTILLA BREAD

MAKES approx. 12
TIME approx. 45 minutes

> 2–2 ½ cups (500–600 ml) all-purpose flour
> 1 ½ tsp salt
> 1 ½ tsp baking powder
> 3 ½ tbsp butter, at room temperature
> ¾ cup (200 ml) water

Mix 2 cups flour, salt, and baking powder in a bowl or food processor, and add the butter a little at a time. Add the water and work it into a slightly loose and smooth dough. Add a little more flour, if necessary. Cover and let rest for 20 minutes.

Put the dough on a floured work surface and divide it into 12 pieces. Form into balls and then roll out thin circles of approximately 6 inches (15 cm) in diameter.

Bake the tortillas in a dry skillet over medium heat. Flip over when beginning to brown on the bottom, and bake for another minute. Wrap the tortillas in a kitchen towel to keep them soft.

See the photo on page 222.

IN ADVANCE Tortillas tastes best freshly made.

TORTILLA CHIPS

MAKES approx. 40
TIME approx. 45 minutes

> 1 ¾ cups (400 ml) cornmeal
> approx. 2 ½ cups (600 ml) all-purpose flour
> 2 tsp salt
> 1 ½ cups (250 ml) water
> ⅔ cup (150 ml) beer
> 4 cups (1 liter) oil for deep frying

Preheat the oven to 480°F (250°C).

Mix all the ingredients and work them into a smooth dough, using a machine or by hand. Cut the dough into 6 pieces. Roll out each piece as thinly as possible on a floured work surface.

Carefully place the rolled-out dough on a greased or parchment paper–covered baking sheet. Bake for approximately 3 minutes.

Cut the tortilla into triangles or punch out circles with a round cutter while still soft.

Heat the oil in a heavy-bottomed saucepan to 320–340°F (160–170°C). Fry until the chips are crispy and the edges turn golden brown. (They should not become too dark!) Lift up the chips with a slotted spoon, and let drain on paper towels. Season with salt.

See the photo on page 222.

IN ADVANCE The chips can be prepared a few hours in advance.

GRISSINI

MAKES approx. 30
TIME approx. 1 hour + 1 hour to rise

¾ cup (200 ml) water
2 tsp active dry yeast
1 tsp salt
1 tbsp canola oil
1 tsp sugar
1 egg, beaten
2–2 ½ cups (500–600 ml) all-purpose flour

1 egg, lightly beaten
course-ground sea salt and/or poppy seeds
   and dried herbs

Heat the water to 110°F (40°C) and pour into a bowl. Sprinkle in the yeast and stir until dissolved. Stir in the salt, oil, sugar, and egg. Mix in almost all the flour and work the dough by hand or machine, until the dough is smooth. Add more flour if needed. Cover with a kitchen towel, and let rise for 30 minutes.

Put the dough on a floured work surface and divide it into 30 pieces. Using your hand, gently roll each piece back and forth into a long stick. Place the sticks on a greased or parchment paper–covered baking sheet, and let rise for about 20 minutes without covering.

Preheat the oven to 400°F (200°C). Brush gently with the egg. Sprinkle with salt and poppy seeds and dried herbs. Bake for about 15 minutes. Let cool on a rack.

See the photo on page 218.

WITH PARMESAN Add ½ cup (100 ml) grated Parmesan before the flour is added.

WITH LEMON & DILL Add 1 tbsp lemon zest and 1 tbsp chopped dill before the flour is added.

WITH SUN-DRIED TOMATOES Add 6 chopped sun-dried tomatoes in oil before the flour is added.

WITH PARSLEY & BASIL Add 1 tbsp chopped parsley and 1 tbsp chopped basil before the flour is added.

IN ADVANCE Grissini can be stored at room temperature for up to 1 month. Grissini with cheese stores for only 1 week.

BREADSTICKS

MAKES approx. 30
TIME approx. 45 minutes

2 cups (500 ml) all-purpose flour
½ tsp salt
1 ½ tsp baking powder
3 ½ tbsp butter, cold
½–⅔ cup (100–150 ml) ice water
2 tbsp olive oil
course-ground sea salt

Preheat the oven to 350°F (175°C).

Mix the flour, salt, and baking powder in a food processor. Add the butter a little at a time, and mix it for a few seconds. Add the ice water slowly while the machine is running until it becomes a smooth dough.

Put the dough on a floured work surface and divide it into 30 pieces. Using your hand, gently roll each piece back and forth into a medium thick log. Place the logs on a greased or parchment paper–covered baking sheet. Brush with olive oil and sprinkle with sea salt.

Bake for about 15 minutes. Let cool on a rack. *See the photo on page 218.*

WITH GRUYÈRE CHEESE Add ½ cup (100 ml) grated Gruyère to the dry ingredients.

WITH BEET Boil 1 peeled beet in water. Allow the water to cool, and then mix 2 tbsp of the beet water with about ½ cup (100 ml) of the ice water. Add to the dough.

WITH CARROT Add approx. ½ cup (100 ml) cold carrot juice instead of the ice water to the dough.

WITH TOMATO Add 2 tbsp of tomato paste mixed with approximately ½ cup (100 ml) of the ice water to the dough.

WITH PARSLEY Mix ½ cup (100 ml) finely chopped parsley and 2–3 tbsp water to form a paste. Mix with about ½ cup (100 ml) of the ice water and add it to the dough.

IN ADVANCE *See* GRISSINI *to the left.*

BISCOTTI WITH OLIVES & SUN-DRIED TOMATOES

MAKES approx. 20
TIME approx. 1 hour and 15 minutes

1 ⅓ cups (300 ml) all-purpose flour
1 tsp baking powder
½ tsp salt
⅓ cup butter
1 tbsp olive oil
1 egg
3 tbsp milk
2 oz (40 g) black olives, coarsely chopped
4 sun-dried tomatoes in oil, roughly chopped
2 tbsp chopped basil

1 egg + 1 tsp water, lightly beaten, for brushing

Preheat the oven to 350°F (175°C).

Mix the flour, baking powder, and salt in a food processor. Add the butter, a little at a time and mix until combined. Whisk together 1 tbsp olive oil, egg, and milk, and pour into the food processor. Run it for a few more seconds. Add more flour if needed. Mix the olives, tomatoes, and basil into the dough.

Form the dough into approximately two 1-inch (2 ½ cm) wide logs, and place them on a baking sheet lined with parchment paper. Brush with the egg, and bake for about 30 minutes.

Let the logs cool slightly and slice diagonally, about 1 inch wide. Reduce the heat to 260°F (125°C). Bake for an additional 20 minutes. Let them cool on a rack.

See the photo on page 220.

WITH PARMESAN, ROSEMARY & PINE NUTS
Follow the recipe above, but use 2 oz (50 g) grated Parmesan, 1 tbsp rosemary, and 3 tbsp (25 g) toasted pine nuts instead of the olives, tomatoes, and basil.

WITH CHÈVRE, DRIED FIGS & WALNUTS
Follow the recipe above, but use 3 oz (75 g) crumbled chèvre, 1 oz (25 g) chopped dried figs, and 1 oz (25 g) chopped walnuts instead of the olives, tomatoes, and basil.

IN ADVANCE The biscotti can be stored in an airtight container for a few weeks or in the freezer for 3 months.

MUFFINS WITH FETA & SPINACH

MAKES approx. 20
TIME approx. 30 minutes

1 ½ cups (350 ml) all-purpose flour
1 tsp baking powder
1 tsp baking soda
½ tsp salt
1 egg
½ cup (100 ml) milk
3 ½ tbsp butter, melted
2 oz (50 g) feta, crumbled
approx. 1 oz (20 g) fresh spinach, finely chopped
1 tbsp chopped fresh basil

Preheat the oven to 400°F (200°C). Grease and flour a mini muffin tray.

Mix all the dry ingredients. Stir in the egg, milk, and melted butter until it becomes a smooth batter. Add the feta, spinach, and basil. Pour the batter into the muffin tray. Bake for 13–14 minutes or until a toothpick comes out clean.

See the photo on page 220.

WITH BRIE, HONEY & PECANS Follow the recipe above, but use ½ cup (100 ml) of all-purpose flour with graham flour, and use 2 oz (50 g) brie, about 2 oz (50 g) pecans, and 1 tbsp of honey instead of the feta, spinach, and basil.

WITH PARMESAN, HAM & DIJON Follow the recipe above, but use 2 oz (50 g) grated Parmesan, 3 oz (75 g) chopped smoked ham, 2 tsp Dijon mustard, and 1 tsp rosemary instead of the feta, spinach, and basil.

TIP Serve as is or with a good dip (*see* DIPS *in the index*).

IN ADVANCE Muffins taste best freshly baked, but can be stored airtight for approximately 2 days or in the freezer for about 3 months. They can be heated in the oven at 300°F (150°C) for approximately 5 minutes.

WHOLE-WHEAT CRACKERS WITH FENNEL SEEDS

MAKES approx. 30
TIME approx. 1 hour

approx. 1 ⅓ cups (300 ml) all-purpose flour
½ cup (100 ml) whole-wheat flour
1 tsp baking powder
½–1 tsp salt
1 tsp fennel seeds
1 tsp sesame seeds
7 tbsp butter, melted
3 tbsp milk

Mix most of the flour with the other dry ingredients, in a food processor or mixing bowl. Mix the butter with the milk, and pour it over the dry ingredients. Work it quickly into a dough. Add more flour if necessary. Let it rest in the refrigerator for 30 minutes.

Preheat the oven to 400°F (200°C).

Divide the dough into 4 pieces and roll into thin rectangular shapes on a floured surface. To form a pattern in the dough, use a textured rolling pin or pierce with a fork. Cut into small squares. Gently lift them with a spatula and place on a baking sheet, greased or lined with parchment paper.

Bake for 10 minutes or until golden brown. Let cool on a rack.

See the photo on page 219.

IN ADVANCE The dough can be stored in the refrigerator for about 1 week or in the freezer for 3 months. Ready-baked crackers can be stored dry and kept at room temperature for up to 1 month.

CRACKERS WITH PARMESAN & ROSEMARY

MAKES approx. 20
TIME approx. 45 minutes + about 1 hour in the fridge

¾ cup (200 ml) all-purpose flour
1 tsp salt
3 tbsp butter, cold
1 cup (250 ml) Parmesan, grated
2 tsp fresh rosemary, finely chopped
⅓ cup (75 ml) sour cream
1 egg, beaten
small sprigs of fresh rosemary (optional)

Mix the flour, salt, and butter in a food processor for a few seconds. Add the Parmesan and the rosemary, and blend for a few more seconds. Add the sour cream, 1 tbsp at a time, to form a smooth dough. Put the dough on a floured work surface, and form a log of about 1 inch (2 ½ cm) thick. Roll it in plastic wrap, and refrigerate for at least 1 hour.

Preheat the oven to 350°F (175°C). Cut the roll into slices and place on a baking sheet, greased or lined with parchment paper. Dip the rosemary in the egg white and press it gently onto the crackers. Bake for about 20 minutes or until golden brown. Let cool on a rack.

See the photo on page 219.

WITH CHEDDAR & CARAWAY Use caraway seeds and Cheddar instead of the rosemary and Parmesan.

WITH PECORINO & OLIVES Use pecorino and 4 tbsp of finely chopped black olives instead of the Parmesan and the rosemary.

WITH BLUE CHEESE & PECANS Use 3 oz (75 g) blue cheese instead of the Parmesan, and add ½ cup (100 ml) chopped pecans. Omit the rosemary.

WITH CHEDDAR & THYME Use grated Cheddar and thyme instead of the Parmesan and rosemary.

WITH GRUYÈRE, DIJON MUSTARD & BACON Use Gruyère instead of Parmesan, and 1 tbsp Dijon mustard and four slices of crispy, crumbled bacon instead of the rosemary.

IN ADVANCE *See* WHOLE-WHEAT CRACKERS WITH FENNEL SEEDS. Crackers with cheese may be stored in an airtight container for 1 week.

FOCACCIA

MAKES 1 focaccia
TIME approx. 1 hour + 1 hour and 10 minutes to rise

1 ⅓ cups (300 ml) water
2 tsp active dry yeast
3 tbsp olive oil
2 tsp salt
3–4 cups (700–900 ml) all-purpose flour

olive oil
course-ground sea salt
1–2 tbsp chopped fresh rosemary

Warm the water to 110°F (40°C) and pour into the bowl. Sprinkle in the yeast and stir until dissolved. Stir in the oil and salt. Mix in almost all the flour and work the dough by hand or machine, until the dough is smooth. Add more flour if needed. Cover and let rise for about 30 minutes.

Put the dough on a floured work surface and roll it out into a rectangle, about 1 inch (2 ½ cm) thick. Place the dough on a baking sheet, greased or lined with parchment paper. Cover the dough with lightly oiled plastic wrap, and let rise for 40 minutes.

Preheat the oven to 440°F (225°C).

Remove the plastic and, with your fingers, make indentations evenly in the dough. Brush the bread gently with the olive oil. Sprinkle with salt and rosemary. Bake for 15–20 minutes or until golden brown. Let it cool on a rack.

See the photo on page 221.

WITH OLIVES Press ½–¾ cup (100–200 ml) black olives into the holes.

WITH FETA & SALAMI Press 4 oz (100 g) diced feta and 4 oz (100 g) sliced salami into the holes.

TIP Serve focaccia warm as is, or together with, for example, FIG TAPENADE (*see the recipe on page 199*), GREEN TAPENADE (*see the recipe on page 200*), or SUN–DRIED TOMATO FLAVORED CREAM CHEESE (*see the recipe on page 246*).

IN ADVANCE The focaccia tastes best if eaten on the same day.

PRETZEL BITES

MAKES approx. 50
TIME approx. 1 hour + 1 hour to rise

⅔ cup (150 ml) water
2 tsp active dry yeast
1 small egg
1 tbsp oil
½ tsp salt
1 tsp sugar
1 ⅓–1 ¾ cups (300–400 ml) all-purpose flour
½ cup (100 ml) water
2 tbsp baking soda
1 egg, beaten
1 tbsp water

FLAVORS
⇢ French herbs (herbes de Provence)
⇢ caraway and fennel seeds, lightly crushed
⇢ sesame seeds
⇢ poppy seeds
⇢ coarse salt

Warm the water to 110°F (40°C) and pour into a bowl. Sprinkle in the yeast and stir until dissolved. Add the egg, oil, salt, and sugar. Mix in almost all the flour and work the dough by hand or machine, until the dough is smooth. Add more flour if needed. Cover with a kitchen towel, and let rise for 1 hour.

Put the dough on a floured work surface and divide it into 4 pieces. Roll each piece into a roll, about ½ inch (1 cm) thick. Cut into small pieces. Place on a baking sheet lined with parchment paper.

Preheat the oven to 440°F (225°C).

Boil water in a large saucepan and dissolve the baking soda. Carefully place a few pieces of dough in the boiling water for only a few seconds. Drain them, and place back on parchment paper.

Mix the beaten egg and water. Brush the bread pieces with the egg wash, and sprinkle with a seasoning of your choice, seeds, or salt. Bake in the oven for about 12 minutes. Let cool.

See the photo on page 223.

IN ADVANCE The pretzel pieces are soft when freshly baked and crunchy after a few days. Keep at room temperature.

232 · BREAD ·

BREAD CUPS, TARTLET SHELLS & TOASTED BREADS

MAKES approx. 24
TIME *see individual recipes*

CROSTINI (about 15 minutes)
  1 baguette
  approx. 4 tbsp olive oil

Preheat the oven to 400°F (200°C). Cut the baguette into slices and brush with oil. Roast in the oven for about 10 minutes or until golden brown. For grill marks, grill the bread in a grill pan.
  See the photo on page 224.

TOAST POINTS (about 15 minutes)
  6 slices white sandwich bread
  approx. 4 tbsp melted butter or olive oil

Preheat the oven to 400°F (200°C). Cut the bread into triangles and brush them with butter or oil. Roast in the oven for about 10 minutes or until golden brown.
  See the photo on page 225.

TOASTED BREAD CUPS (about 20 minutes)
  6 slices white sandwich bread
  approx. 4 tbsp melted butter or olive oil

Preheat the oven to 400°F (200°C). Roll out the bread slices until they are somewhat thinner. Brush with oil or butter. With a round cutter, punch out circles or squares. Gently press these down into a baking tray for mini muffins. Bake for about 10 minutes.
  See the photo on page 224.

TARTLET SHELLS (about 40 minutes)
  1 batch of BISCUIT DOUGH (*see the recipe on page 231*)

Preheat the oven to 400°F (200°C). Press the dough into a baking tray for mini muffins or mini pie forms. Bake for approximately 10 minutes.
  See the photo on page 224.

WONTON CUPS (about 15 minutes)
  24 wonton dough sheets
  approx. 4 tbsp oil

Preheat the oven to 400°F (200°C). Brush both sides of the dough sheets with oil, and press them down into a baking tray for mini muffins. Alternately, flip the baking tray over and place the dough over the molds. This way, the "cups" become bigger. Bake for about 5–10 minutes until golden brown.
  See the photo on page 224.

PHYLLO CUPS (about 15 minutes)
  1–2 sheets phyllo dough
  approx. 4 tbsp oil

Preheat the oven to 400°F (200°C). Brush both sides of the dough sheets with oil, and press them down into a baking tray for mini muffins. Alternately, flip the baking tray over and place the dough over the molds. This way, the "cups" become bigger. Bake for about 5–10 minutes until golden brown. With double sheets of dough, the cups become a bit sturdier.
  See the photo on page 225.

TORTILLA CUPS (about 20 minutes)
  6 tortillas, wheat or corn
  approx. 4 tbsp olive oil

Preheat the oven to 400°F (200°C). Punch out circles with a round cutter or cut out small squares. Brush both sides with oil, and press down into a mini muffin baking tray. Bake them for about 10 minutes or until golden brown.
  See the photo on page 225.

PIZZA ROUNDS
Shape the pizza dough into 30 to 40 mini rounds, and bake them for 10–15 minutes.
  See the photo on page 225.

CRISPY CHEESE CUPS
Follow the recipe for PARMESAN & PINE NUT CRISPS (*see page 286*). Before the crisps harden, press them into a muffin baking tray.
  Is not pictured.

IN ADVANCE Everything can be prepared a day in advance and stored in an airtight container at room temperature.

MORE RELATED RECIPES
PÂTE À CHOUX PUFFS (*see the recipe on page 27*)
VOL-AU-VENTS (*see the recipe on page 28*)

ROASTED CORN DIP

SPINACH & FETA SPREAD WITH SUN-DRIED TOMATOES

CREAMY SALMON & CAVIAR DIP

BACON & CHEDDAR SPREAD

GREEN PEA & CASHEW SPREAD

CHÈVRE SPREAD WITH FIGS & PECANS

POTATO & ALMOND DIP

TURKEY & PEAR DIP WITH WALNUTS

SWEET POTATO DIP WITH GINGER & CHILI

234

The recipes are available on pages 235–237

SPREADS & DIPS

Simple and quick to prepare, spreads and dips are always appreciated—no matter what the occasion. Great for dunking bread and vegetables spreads can also be slathered on a cracker or slice of toasted baguette. Dips are so prominent in this book that they show up in several chapters; however, here we have collected some of our favorites.

POTATO & ALMOND DIP

MAKES approx. 2 cups (500 ml)
TIME approx. 45 minutes

11 oz (300 g) mealy potatoes, peeled
½ cup (100 ml) almond flakes
½ cup (100 ml) fresh breadcrumbs
3 cloves garlic
3 tbsp water
3 tsp freshly squeezed lemon juice
1 tsp lemon zest
approx. ⅔ cup (150 ml) olive oil
salt and pepper

Boil the potatoes until soft. Let cool.

Preheat the oven to 350°F (175°C). Toast the almonds and the breadcrumbs separately on a baking sheet in the oven for about 10 minutes or until golden brown.

Mix the garlic, almonds, and breadcrumbs in a food processor or with a hand blender. Add the water, lemon juice, and lemon zest, and blend it to a purée.

Mash the potatoes with a fork. Add the almond purée. Blend while slowly pouring in the olive oil. Season with salt and pepper.

See the photo on page 234.

IN ADVANCE The dip can be stored in the refrigerator for about 2 days.

SWEET POTATO DIP WITH GINGER & CHILI

MAKES approx. 2 cups (500 ml)
TIME approx. 45 minutes

approx. 1 ¾ lbs (800 g) sweet potatoes
3 tbsp olive oil
½ of a red chili pepper, seeded and finely chopped
1 clove garlic
1 tsp grated fresh ginger
freshly squeezed juice from 1 lime
salt and pepper

Preheat the oven to 400°F (200°C).

Peel the sweet potatoes and cut them into pieces. Place the potatoes in an ovenproof dish and mix them with olive oil. Bake in the oven for 20–30 minutes. Stir occasionally. Remove and let cool.

Mix the sweet potatoes with chili, garlic, ginger, and lime juice to make a smooth purée. Season with salt and pepper.

See the photo on page 234.

IN ADVANCE The dip can be stored in the refrigerator for about 2 days.

BACON & CHEDDAR SPREAD

MAKES approx. 2 cups (500 ml)
TIME approx. 20 minutes

　　4 slices bacon
　　7 oz (200 g) cream cheese
　　1 cup (250 ml) grated Cheddar
　　1 tbsp Dijon mustard
　　1 tbsp crispy fried onions
　　salt and pepper

Cook the bacon until crispy. Drain on paper towels and let cool. Crumble the bacon.

　　Stir together the cream cheese, Cheddar, mustard, fried onions, and bacon. Season with salt and pepper.

　　See the photo on page 234.

IN ADVANCE The spread can be stored, without the bacon and onion, in the refrigerator for about 2 days. Add the bacon and onions right before serving.

ROASTED CORN DIP

MAKES approx. 2 cups (500 ml)
TIME approx. 20 minutes

　　9 oz (250 g) canned corn, drained
　　2 tbsp canola oil
　　1 tsp sambal oelek
　　1 tsp lemon zest
　　salt

Roast the corn kernels in a pan with some of the oil until golden brown. Mix the corn with the other ingredients and the rest of the oil in a food processor or with a hand blender. Season with salt.

　　See the photo on page 234.

IN ADVANCE The dip can be stored in the refrigerator for about 2 days.

CREAMY SALMON & CAVIAR DIP

MAKES approx. 2 cups (500 ml)
TIME approx. 30 minutes

　　2 hard-boiled eggs, finely chopped
　　5 oz (150 g) boiled potatoes, finely chopped
　　4 oz (100 g) smoked salmon, finely chopped
　　1 tbsp caviar or fish roe
　　2 tbsp finely chopped dill
　　3 tbsp mayonnaise
　　3 tbsp sour cream
　　1 tsp lemon zest
　　salt and pepper

Stir the ingredients together. Season with salt and pepper.

　　See the photo on page 234.

IN ADVANCE The dip can be stored in the refrigerator for about 1 day.

SPINACH & FETA SPREAD WITH SUN-DRIED TOMATOES

MAKES approx. 2 cups (500 ml)
TIME approx. 15 minutes

　　7 oz (200 g) cream cheese
　　½ cup (100 ml) sour cream
　　2 oz (50 g) fresh spinach, chopped
　　2 tbsp chopped basil
　　5 oz (150 g) feta, crumbled
　　6 sun-dried tomatoes in oil, chopped
　　3 tbsp roasted sunflower seeds
　　salt and pepper

Stir together all ingredients. Season with salt and pepper.

　　See the photo on page 234.

IN ADVANCE The spread can be stored in the refrigerator for about 2 days.

CHÈVRE SPREAD WITH FIGS & PECANS

MAKES approx. 2 cups (500 ml)
TIME approx. 15 minutes

7 oz (200 g) chèvre, crumbled
½ cup (100 ml) sour cream
7 oz (200 g) cream cheese
3–4 fresh figs, coarsely chopped
½ cup (100 ml) coarsely chopped pecans

Preheat the oven to 400°F (200°C). Roast the nuts for 5–10 minutes. Let cool.

Stir together all ingredients.

See the photo on page 234.

IN ADVANCE The dip without the nuts can be stored in refrigerator for about 1 day. Stir in the nuts right before serving.

GREEN PEA & CASHEW SPREAD

MAKES approx. 2 cups (500 ml)
TIME approx. 20 minutes

1 ¾ cups (400 ml) green peas, frozen
3 tbsp sour cream
½ cup (100 ml) finely chopped roasted cashews
2 oz (50 g) Parmesan, grated
salt and pepper

Cook the peas as instructed on the package. Rinse them in cold water.

Mix the peas and sour cream to a creamy consistency. Stir in the cashew nuts and the Parmesan. Season with salt and pepper.

See the photo on page 234.

IN ADVANCE The dip can be stored in the refrigerator for about 2 days.

TURKEY & PEAR DIP WITH WALNUTS

MAKES approx. 2 cups (500 ml)
TIME approx. 20 minutes

1 pear, cored and finely chopped
7 oz (200 g) smoked turkey, finely chopped
3 tbsp mayonnaise
2 oz (50 g) cream cheese
1 clove garlic, pressed
1 tbsp Dijon mustard
1 tbsp honey
1 tbsp finely chopped fresh oregano
⅔ cup (150 ml) chopped walnuts
salt and pepper

Stir the ingredients together.

See the photo on page 234.

IN ADVANCE The dip without the nuts can be stored in the refrigerator for about 1 day. Stir in nuts right before serving.

MORE DIPS & SPREADS

→ BRIE & CRAB *(see page 28)*
→ CREAMY "SKAGEN" SHRIMP *(see page 80)*
→ EGG & ANCHOVY SALAD *(see page 90)*
→ CHANTERELLE PESTO *(see page 95)*
→ HUMMUS *(see page 118)*
→ BEETROOT HUMMUS *(see page 118)*
→ BABA GHANOUSH *(see page 119)*
→ TARAMASALATA *(see page 119)*
→ BEAN DIP WITH SAFFRON & AJVAR RELISH *(see page 119)*
→ PICO DE GALLO *(see page 141)*
→ GUACAMOLE *(see page 143)*
→ RED PESTO *(see page 178)*
→ FIG TAPENADE *(see page 200)*
→ FENNEL & ALMOND ANCHOÏADE *(see page 200)*
→ ROASTED BELL PEPPER & WALNUT DIP *(see page 118)*
→ TUNA & MANGO CHUTNEY *(see page 247)*

For more, *see* DIPS & SPREADS *in the index.*

STRIPED TEA SANDWICHES

CANAPÉS

CANAPÉS

The recipes are available on
pages 244–245

TEA
SANDWICHES

TUNA & MANGO
CHUTNEY

CURRY CHICKEN & APPLE

EGG SALAD

CUCUMBER, RADISH
& WATERCRESS

CHÈVRE, RAISINS & PECANS

HAM, CHEESE
& MUSTARD

The recipes are available on pages 247–248

239

FLAVORED CREAM CHEESE

GARLIC & HERB

CARROT, GINGER & LIME

WASABI

DIJON MUSTARD & HONEY

SUN-DRIED TOMATO & BASIL

SALMON, LEMON & DILL

BLUE CHEESE & BACON

OLIVES

BEETROOT & HORSERADISH

SWEET CHILI & SESAME SEEDS

240

The recipes are available on page 246

FLAVORED BUTTER

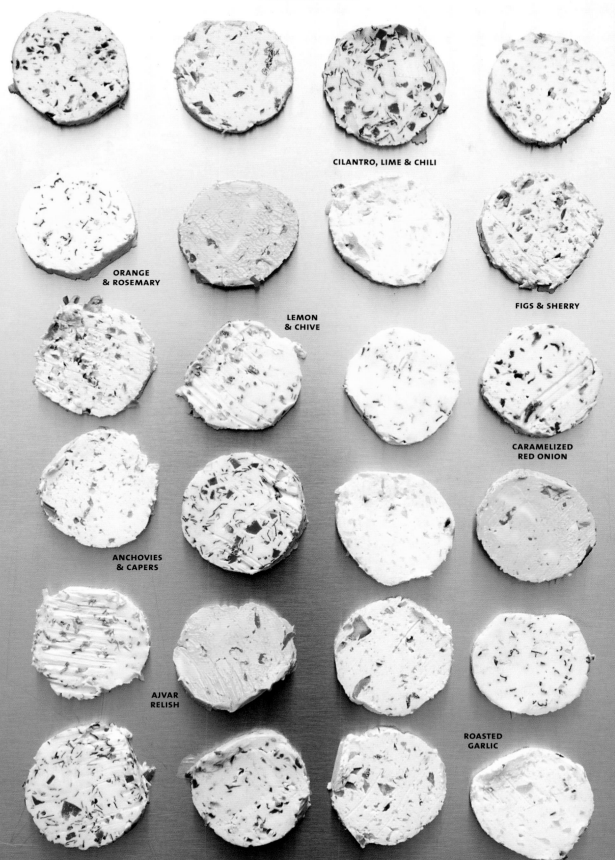

CILANTRO, LIME & CHILI

ORANGE & ROSEMARY

FIGS & SHERRY

LEMON & CHIVE

CARAMELIZED RED ONION

ANCHOVIES & CAPERS

AJVAR RELISH

ROASTED GARLIC

The recipes are available on page 246

RUSSIAN CAKES

MADELEINE CAKES

The recipes are available on page 249

LEMON CURD

CLOTTED CREAM

SCONES

243

The recipes are available on pages 248–249

AFTERNOON TEA

*Who says it has to be afternoon and who says you have to drink tea in order to
appreciate the dainty sandwiches, scones, and small pastries of this classic
British custom? Put away the porcelain cups and opt for a
chilled glass of rosé or champagne. Perfect for any festive occasion.*

CANAPÉS

MAKES approx. 24
TIME approx. 25 minutes

*Canapés can be endlessly varied. The base is bread, topped
with a thin layer of flavored butter or cream cheese. Serve as
is, or add a topping of choice.*

6 slices of white sandwich bread
toppings of your choice *(see the recipes below)*

Punch out circles with a round cutter, or cut off
the edges and cut the bread into squares. Spread on
FLAVORED CREAM CHEESE or FLAVORED BUTTER
(see the recipe on page 246) and add toppings and
garnish of your choice.
      See the photo on page 238.

OLIVES
    approx. 4 oz (100 g) OLIVE CREAM CHEESE
    (see the recipe on page 247)
    approx. 1 oz (25 g) green olives, sliced

SALMON, LEMON & CHIVE
    approx. 2 oz (50 g) LEMON & CHIVE BUTTER
    (see the recipe on page 246)
    approx. 4 oz (100 g) smoked salmon
    fresh herbs for garnish

GARLIC & HERB
    approx. 4 oz (100 g) GARLIC & HERBS CREAM
        CHEESE *(see the recipe on page 246)*
    chives for garnish

CAVIAR
    approx. 4 oz (100 g) cream cheese
    approx. 2 oz (50 g) caviar or fish roe
    chives for garnish

ROASTED BELL PEPPERS & CHIVES
    approx. 4 oz (100 g) cream cheese
    approx. 2 oz (50 g) ROASTED BELL PEPPERS
        (see the recipe on page 118)
    finely chopped chives

CUCUMBER & WATERCRESS
    approx. 4 oz (100 g) cream cheese
    24 thin cucumber slices
    watercress for garnish

FIGS, SHERRY & RADISHES
    approx. 4 oz (100 g) FIG & SHERRY CREAM
        CHEESE *(see the recipe on page 246)*
    approx. 6 radishes, sliced

CARAMELIZED RED ONION
    approx. 2 oz (50 g) CARAMELIZED RED ONION
        BUTTER *(see the recipe on page 246)*
    fresh herbs for garnish

IN ADVANCE Canapés can be made a few hours
before they are to be served.

STRIPED TEA SANDWICHES

Feel free to combine your favorite fillings. Use different kinds of sandwich bread such as white, rye, and whole wheat.

MAKES approx. 48
TIME approx. 30 minutes + 8 hours in the refrigerator

12 slices of sandwich bread of your choice

FOR EACH LAYER
approx. 7 oz (200 g) FLAVORED BUTTER **and/or**
approx. 7 oz (200 g) natural or FLAVORED CREAM CHEESE (*see the recipes on page 246*)
and/or approx. 4 oz (100 g) hard cheese of your choice
and/or approx. 4 oz (100 g) cold-cuts, such as turkey, ham, roast beef, mortadella, pastrami, prosciutto, bresaola, or smoked salmon

Lay 3 slices of bread side by side. Spread or lay out choice of the filling, overlapping on the slices of bread. Repeat 2 more layers of bread and filling. If one or more of your fillings consist of hard cheese or cold-cuts, it is important to spread the bread with plenty of butter or cream cheese in order for the sandwich to stick together.

Dampen a clean kitchen towel and wring it out thoroughly. Wrap the bread in the towel, ensuring that the layers stay intact. Place it on a cutting board and place another cutting board on top. Put a weight on the top cutting board. Let it sit in the refrigerator overnight.

Trim the edges neatly, and cut into slices. The slices can also be cut into smaller squares.

See the photo on page 238.

SUGGESTIONS ON FLAVOR COMBINATIONS
→ prosciutto • SUN-DRIED TOMATO & BASIL CREAM CHEESE • ROASTED GARLIC BUTTER (*see the recipe on page 246*)

→ SALMON • LEMON & CHIVE BUTTER • SALMON, LEMON & DILL CREAM CHEESE (*see the recipe on page 246*)

→ **CREAM CHEESE** • BEET & HORSERADISH CREAM CHEESE • AJVAR RELISH BUTTER (*see the recipe on page 246*)

→ roast beef • SWEET CHILI & SESAME SEEDS CREAM CHEESE • WASABI CREAM CHEESE (*see the recipe on page 246*)

→ bresaola • GARLIC & HERB CREAM CHEESE • OLIVE CREAM CHEESE (*see the recipe on page 246*)

The following are not pictured.
→ smoked turkey • ORANGE & ROSEMARY BUTTER (*see the recipe on page 246*) • cream cheese

→ smoked salmon • ANCHOVIES & CAPERS BUTTER • GARLIC & HERB CREAM CHEESE (*see the recipe on page 246*)

→ smoked ham • CARAMELIZED RED ONION BUTTER • DIJON MUSTARD & HONEY CREAM CHEESE (*see the recipe on page 246*)

→ smoked turkey • ROASTED GARLIC BUTTER • BLUE CHEESE & BACON CREAM CHEESE (*see the recipe on page 246*)

→ Cheddar • ANCHOVIES & CAPERS BUTTER (*see the recipe on page 246*) • cream cheese

→ smoked salmon • CILANTRO, LIME & CHILI BUTTER • CARROT, GINGER & LIME CREAM CHEESE (*see the recipe on page 246*)

→ smoked salmon • ROASTED GARLIC BUTTER (*see the recipe on page 246*) • Jarlsberg

→ mortadella • SUN-DRIED TOMATO & BASIL CREAM CHEESE • ANCHOVIES & CAPERS BUTTER (*see the recipe on page 246*)

IN ADVANCE Sandwiches must be placed in the refrigerator under a heavy weight for at least 8 hours to hold them together. They should not be made more than a day in advance. Slice right before serving.

FLAVORED BUTTER

MAKES approx. 4 oz (100 g)
TIME approx. 5–10 minutes

> 4 oz (100 g) butter, at room temperature
> flavor of your choice (*see the recipes below*)

Mix the butter with flavors of your choice
from below.
> *See the photo on page 241.*

ANCHOVIES & CAPERS
> 1 oz (35 g) anchovies, chopped
> 2 oz (50 g) capers, chopped

ORANGE & ROSEMARY
> zest of 1 orange
> 2 tbsp fresh rosemary, finely chopped

FIGS & SHERRY
> 2 fresh figs, finely chopped
> 1 tbsp sherry

AJVAR RELISH
> 2 tbsp ajvar relish
> a few drops of Tabasco (optional)

LEMON & CHIVE
> 1 tbsp freshly squeezed lemon juice
> zest of 2 lemons
> 3 tbsp finely chopped chives

ROASTED GARLIC
> 2 ROASTED GARLICS (*see the recipe on page 202*)

CILANTRO, LIME & CHILI
> 3 tbsp cilantro, finely chopped
> ½ red chili pepper, seeded and finely chopped
> zest and freshly squeezed juice from 1 lime

CARAMELIZED RED ONION
> ½ cup (100 ml) CARAMELIZED RED ONION
> (*see the recipe on page 217*)

IN ADVANCE Flavored butter lasts for about 1 week
in the refrigerator and 3 months in the freezer.

FLAVORED CREAM CHEESE

MAKES approx. 4 oz (100 g)
TIME approx. 5–10 minutes

> 7 oz (200 g) cream cheese
> flavor of your choice (*see the recipe below*)

Mix the cream cheese with any flavor from below.
> *See the photo on page 240.*

CARROT, GINGER & LIME
> 3 oz (75 g) grated carrot
> 1 tbsp fresh grated ginger
> zest from 1 orange
> salt and pepper

BEET & HORSERADISH
> 1 tbsp beet purée (½ boiled beet)
> 1 tbsp grated horseradish
> salt and pepper

GARLIC & HERB
> 1 clove garlic, pressed
> ½ cup (100 ml) chopped fresh herbs
> salt and pepper

SUN-DRIED TOMATO & BASIL
> 4 oz (100 g) sun-dried tomatoes in oil,
>   chopped
> 2 tbsp chopped basil
> salt and pepper

BLUE CHEESE & BACON
> 3 oz (75 g) blue cheese, crumbled
> 4 oz (100 g) fried bacon, crumbled
> salt and pepper

DIJON MUSTARD & HONEY
> 1 tbsp Dijon mustard
> 3 tbsp honey
> salt and pepper

SWEET CHILI & SESAME SEEDS
> ⅓ cup (75 ml) sweet chili sauce
> 1 tbsp toasted black or white sesame seeds
> salt and pepper

OLIVES

4 oz (100 g) black and/or green olives,
    finely chopped
salt and pepper

WASABI

1–2 tsp wasabi paste
salt and pepper

SALMON, LEMON & DILL

4 oz (100 g) smoked salmon, finely chopped
1 lemon, zested
2 tsp freshly squeezed lemon juice
1 tbsp dill, finely chopped
salt and pepper

IN ADVANCE Flavored cream cheese stores for
about a week in the refrigerator.

TEA SANDWICHES

MAKES approx. 24
TIME approx. 15–25 minutes

12 slices sandwich bread of your choice
filling of your choice (*see the recipes below and on
    page 248*)

HAM, CHEESE & MUSTARD

1 tbsp Dijon mustard
1 tbsp honey
⅔ cup (150 ml) MAYONNAISE, store bought
    (**or** *see the recipe on page 74*)
5 oz (125 g) hard cheese, sliced
6 oz (175 g) smoked ham, sliced
½ cup (100 ml) finely chopped chives

Mix the mustard, honey, and ½ cup (100 ml)
mayonnaise and spread on one side of all the bread
slices. Cover half the slices with cheese and ham.
Put the remaining slices on top. Trim the edges and
then cut the bread into 4 triangles. Spread the rest of
mayonnaise on one side of each triangle and dip in
the chives.

See the photo on page 239.

TUNA & MANGO CHUTNEY

7 oz (185 g) canned tuna
⅔ cup (150 ml) MAYONNAISE, store bought (**or**
    see the recipe on page 74)
½ cup (100 ml) mango chutney
salt and pepper
½ cup (100 ml) toasted sesame seeds

Mix the tuna, ½ cup (100 ml) mayonnaise, and
mango chutney. Season with salt and pepper.
Spread a layer of tuna mixture on 6 bread slices.
Cover with the rest of the bread. Trim the edges and
then cut each sandwich into 4 triangles. Spread a
little mayonnaise on one side of each triangle, and
dip in sesame seeds.

See the photo on page 239.

CHÈVRE, RAISINS & PECANS

5 oz (150 g) chèvre
4 oz (100 g) cream cheese
1 tbsp finely chopped golden raisins
1 tbsp finely chopped dried cranberries
2 tbsp finely chopped pecans

Stir together the chèvre, cream cheese, raisins,
cranberries, and pecans. Spread the mixture on 6 of
the bread slices. Cover with the rest of the bread. Trim
the edges, and then cut each sandwich into 4 triangles.

See the photo on page 239.

CURRY CHICKEN & APPLE

7 oz (200 g) chicken fillet
approx. 1 tsp olive oil
½ apple, peeled and finely chopped
½ celery stalk, finely chopped
⅓ cup (75 ml) MAYONNAISE, store bought
    (**or** *see the recipe on page 74*)
½–1 tsp curry powder
1 tbsp sweet relish
salt and pepper

Cook the chicken in oil until it is cooked through.
Let it cool and chop finely. Mix it with the rest of
the ingredients. Season with salt and pepper.
Spread a layer of chicken mixture on the bread
slices. Cover with the rest of the bread. Trim the
edges, and then cut each sandwich into 4 triangles.

*See the photo on page 239. More sandwiches are listed
on the next page.*

CUCUMBER, RADISH & WATERCRESS
6 oz (175 g) cream cheese
7 oz (200 g) cucumber, thinly sliced
approx. 4 oz (100 g) radishes, thinly sliced
1 bunch baby watercress
poppy seeds for garnish

Spread 5 oz (150 g) of the cream cheese on one side of the bread slices. Cover half of the slices with the cucumber and radish slices. Sprinkle with the watercress, and cover with the rest of the bread. Trim the edges, and then cut each sandwich into 4 triangles. Spread a little cream cheese on one side of each triangle, and dip in poppy seeds.

See the photo on page 239.

EGG SALAD
3 hard-boiled eggs
3 tbsp MAYONNAISE, store bought (or *see the recipe on page 74*)
salt and black pepper
½ cup (100 ml) finely chopped dill for garnish

Chop the eggs finely and mix with 2 tbsp mayonnaise. Season with salt and pepper. Spread the mixture over half of the slices. Cover with the rest of the bread slices. Trim the edges and cut each sandwich into 4 triangles. Spread a little mayonnaise on one the side of each triangle and dip in the finely chopped dill.

See the photo on page 239.

IN ADVANCE All sandwiches can be made the day before. Wrap them in plastic wrap, and store in the refrigerator. Dip them in the garnish right before serving.

SCONES

MAKES approx. 24
TIME approx. 20 minutes

2 cups (500 ml) all-purpose flour
1 tbsp sugar
1 tsp baking powder + ¼ tsp baking soda
½ tsp salt
7 tbsp butter, cold
1 egg
½ cup (100 ml) buttermilk

Preheat the oven to 480°F (250°C).

Mix the dry ingredients.

Cut the butter into pieces and add to the flour mixture. Mix in a food processor or work it quickly by hand. Do not overwork the dough! Add the eggs and buttermilk.

Shape the dough into small balls or roll them out to a thickness of ⅔ inch (1 ½ cm), and punch out small rounds of about 1 inch (2 ½ cm) in diameter. Place them on a baking sheet, greased or lined with parchment paper. Bake for about 10 minutes.

Serve warm scones with CLOTTED CREAM (*see the recipe below*), whipped cream, jam, LEMON CURD (*see the recipe on the opposite page*), or plain or FLAVORED CREAM CHEESE (*see the recipes on page 246*).

See the photo on page 243.

RAISINS & DRIED FRUIT/NUTS
Mix ½ cup (100 ml) dried fruit and berries and/or ½ cup (100 ml) chopped nuts into the dough.

WHOLE WHEAT SCONES
Replace ¾ cup (200 ml) flour with whole wheat flour. Top with 3 tbsp sunflower seeds.

CHEESE SCONES
Mix 2 oz (50 g) of a grated cheese, such as Parmesan or Cheddar, into the dough.

IN ADVANCE Scones taste best freshly baked.

CLOTTED CREAM

MAKES approx. 3 tbsp
TIME approx. 1 ½–2 hours + 12 hours in the refrigerator

4 cups (1 liter) heavy cream

Pour the cream into a bowl, and place the bowl in a pan of simmering water. Let the cream simmer, without stirring, for about 1 ½ hours.

Let the cream cool down, and then refrigerate for least 12 hours. Use a spoon to scoop up the thickened cream on the surface and place in a separate bowl. Stir the thickened cream.

See the photo on page 243.

IN ADVANCE The clotted cream can be stored in the refrigerator for 2 days.

LEMON CURD

MAKES approx. 1 ¾ cups (400 ml)
TIME approx. 15 minutes

3 lemons, freshly squeezed juice of 3, zest of 2
⅔ cup (150 g) butter
1 ⅓ cups (300 ml) sugar
6 eggs, lightly beaten

Add the butter, sugar, eggs, lemon zest, and juice to a small saucepan or bowl. Place the pan or bowl over a larger pot of simmering water. Stir until the mixture thickens. Strain the lemon curd through a fine-mesh strainer. Pour into sterilized jars, cool, and seal.

See the photo on page 243.

IN ADVANCE Can be stored in the refrigerator for about a week.

MADELEINE CAKES

MAKES approx. 36
TIME approx. 1 hour

½ cup (100 g) butter, melted and cooled
2 eggs
½ cup (100 ml) sugar
1 tbsp brown sugar
⅔ cup (150 ml) all-purpose flour
1 tbsp honey
a pinch of salt

Preheat the oven to 440°F (225°C). Grease and flour a baking tray for mini madeleine cakes.

Beat the butter, eggs, sugar, and brown sugar until light and fluffy. Add the flour, honey, and salt, and mix until smooth. Refrigerate for 30 minutes.

Spoon the batter into the molds, filling no more than ⅔. Bake in the oven for about 5 minutes. Cool slightly and turn out the cakes to cool on a wire rack.

See the photo on page 242.

IN ADVANCE Once the cakes have cooled, they can be stored in a tightly sealed jar for 2 days or in the freezer for 3 months.

RUSSIAN CAKES

MAKES approx. 36
TIME approx. 1 ½ hours

1 ½ cup (350 ml) all-purpose flour
½ cup (100 ml) cornstarch
¼ tsp salt
1 cup (225 g) butter, unsalted
3 tbsp confectioner's sugar
1 tsp vanilla extract

confectioner's sugar for garnish

Preheat the oven to 350°F (175°C).

Mix the flour, cornstarch, and salt.

Beat the butter, confectioner's sugar, and vanilla extract until white and fluffy. Add the dry ingredients and mix into a smooth dough. Refrigerate for at least an hour.

Roll the dough into small balls and place them on a baking sheet, greased or lined with parchment paper. Bake in the oven for about 12 minutes. Place the cookies on a rack and let them cool for a few minutes.

Sprinkle some confectioner's sugar on a plate. Place the cookies on the plate and sprinkle more confectioner's sugar on top.

See the photo on page 242.

IN ADVANCE The cakes can be baked a week in advance and stored in a tightly sealed container when they have cooled, or in the freezer for 3 months.

MORE SWEETS FOR AFTERNOON TEA
In the chapter DESSERTS, see page 292, for many other sweets perfect for afternoon tea.

ORANGE, CARROT
& GINGER COOLER

BLUEBERRY, ALMOND &
COCONUT SMOOTHIE

FRUIT SALAD WITH PISTACHIOS

GRANOLA WITH YOGURT & BERRIES

SUMMER BERRIES
WITH LIME SUGAR

EXOTIC
FRUIT SALAD

AVOCADO, KIWI &
APPLE SMOOTHIE

250

The recipes are available on pages 259–261

FRENCH TOAST

PANCAKES

**YOGURT WITH HONEY,
POMEGRANATE & ALMONDS**

The recipes are available on pages 258–259

SALMON BAGEL

**EGGS BENEDICT
WITH ASPARAGUS**

SCRAMBLED EGGS & BACON

EGGS FLORENTINE

The recipes are available on pages 254–255 and 227 (mini-bagels)

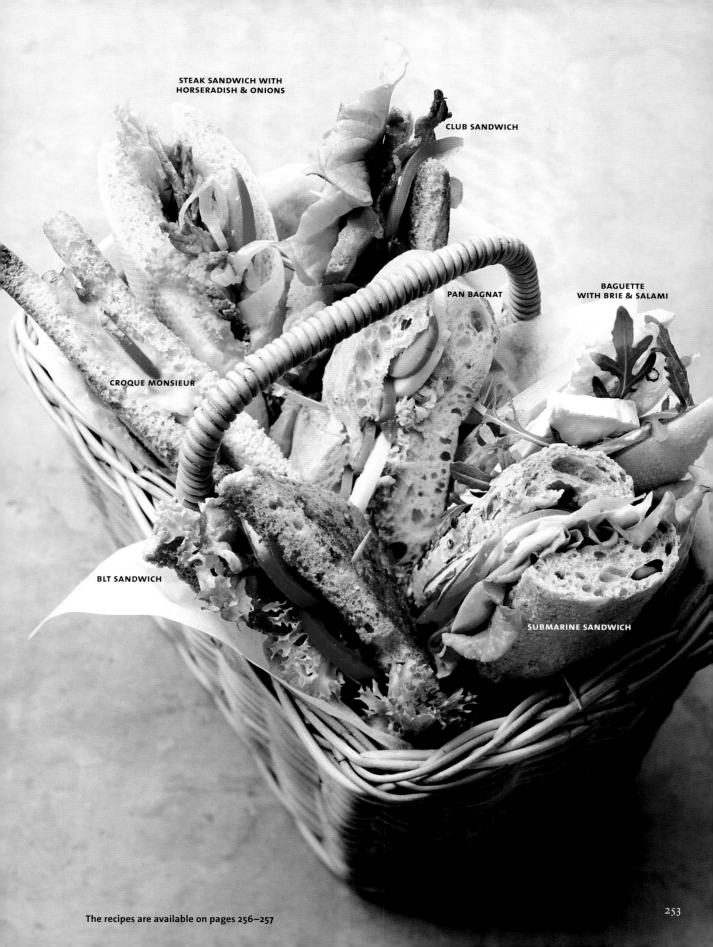

STEAK SANDWICH WITH
HORSERADISH & ONIONS

CLUB SANDWICH

PAN BAGNAT

BAGUETTE
WITH BRIE & SALAMI

CROQUE MONSIEUR

BLT SANDWICH

SUBMARINE SANDWICH

The recipes are available on pages 256–257

253

BRUNCH

Pancakes, eggs, and bacon as hors d'oeuvres? Why not?! Here we reinvent this
classic American meal into a miniature version, adding a touch
of whimsy to a popular favorite.

EGGS BENEDICT WITH ASPARAGUS

MAKES approx. 12
TIME approx. 40 minutes

4 oz (75 g) baked ham, sliced
12 asparagus buds
12 quail eggs or other small eggs
4 cups (1 liter) water
2 tbsp white vinegar

approx. ½ cup (100 ml) HOLLANDAISE SAUCE
   (*see the recipe on page 198*)

6 english muffins, toasted
fresh herbs for garnish

Make the sauce according to the recipe. Keep warm.

Cut both the bottoms and tops of the english muffins into squares. Cut the ham into similar size pieces, and place a piece of ham on each muffin.

Boil lightly salted water. Add the asparagus buds and simmer for 1–2 minutes. Keep warm.

Poach the eggs by boiling water and vinegar in a saucepan. Reduce the heat to a simmer. Crack one egg at a time into a cup and then gently slip into the water. Let the egg poach for 1–2 minutes or until the egg white has set. Carefully pick the egg up with a slotted spoon and drain it on paper towels. Poach a few eggs at the same time.

Place an egg on each slice of bread, then a dollop of warm Hollandaise sauce, and finally an asparagus bud. Garnish with some fresh herbs. Serve immediately.

See the photo on page 252.

IN ADVANCE Eggs Benedict taste best if cooked just before they are to be served.

EGGS FLORENTINE

MAKES approx. 12
TIME approx. 40 minutes

2 oz (60 g) baby spinach
1 tbsp butter
7 oz (100 g) smoked salmon, sliced
12 quail eggs or other small eggs
4 cups (1 liter) water
2 tbsp white vinegar

approx. ½ cup (100 ml) HOLLANDAISE SAUCE
   (*see the recipe on page 198*)

6 english muffins, toasted
fresh herbs for garnish

Cut both the bottoms and tops of the english muffins into squares.

Sauté the spinach in butter for about a minute, and arrange it on the muffin. Cut the salmon into similar size pieces. Top each muffin with the salmon.

Poach the eggs by boiling water and vinegar in a saucepan. Reduce the heat to a simmer. Crack one egg at a time into a cup, and then gently slip into the water. Let the egg poach for 1–2 minutes or until the egg white has set. Carefully pick the egg up with a slotted spoon, and drain it on paper towels. Poach a few eggs at the same time.

Place an egg on each bread slice, and top with a dollop of warm hollandaise sauce. Garnish with fresh herbs. Serve immediately.

See the photo on page 252.

IN ADVANCE Eggs Florentine taste best if cooked right before serving.

SCRAMBLED EGGS & BACON

MAKES approx. 10
TIME approx. 20 minutes

    5 slices bacon
    2 tbsp butter
    6 eggs
    ¼ tsp salt
    a pinch of black pepper

    fresh herbs for garnish

Cook the bacon until crispy, and drain it on paper towels. Halve each slice.

Melt the butter in a saucepan or skillet, and whisk the eggs. Add salt and pepper. Cook the eggs while stirring over low heat. Arrange the scrambled eggs in small glasses, and insert a piece of bacon. Garnish with fresh herbs. Serve immediately.

See the photo on page 252.

IN ADVANCE The bacon can be fried a few hours before serving, but the scrambled eggs should be freshly made.

SALMON BAGELS

MAKES approx. 20
TIME approx. 15 minutes

    7 oz (200 g) cream cheese
    1 tbsp chives finely chopped
    approx. 5 oz (150 g) smoked salmon, sliced
    10 cherry tomatoes, cut into wedges
    lettuce

    20 MINI-BAGELS *(see the recipe on page 227)*

Stir together the cream cheese and chives.

Halve the bagels. Spread the cream cheese and chive mixture on the bottom halves of the bagels, and add lettuce, salmon, and a tomato wedge. Cover with the other bagel halves, and fasten with a toothpick.

See the photo on page 252.

IN ADVANCE Bagels can be completed about 1 hour in advance.

CLUB SANDWICH

MAKES approx. 12
TIME approx. 45 minutes

    approx. 14 oz (400 g) chicken fillet
    salt and pepper
    6 slices bacon
    2 avocados, sliced
    ⅔ cup (150 ml) MAYONNAISE, store bought (or
        see the recipe on page 74)
    12 slices whole wheat bread
    lettuce

    MARINADE
    1 tbsp Dijon mustard
    1 tbsp apple cider vinegar
    1 tbsp brown sugar
    2 tbsp honey
    2 tsp sesame oil
    2 tsp soy sauce

Preheat the oven to 350°F (175°C).

Mix together the ingredients for the marinade.

Place the chicken in an ovenproof dish and brush it with half the marinade. Add salt and pepper.

Cook the chicken in the oven for about 30 minutes or until cooked through. Brush it with the rest of the marinade. Let it cool, and then cut it into thin slices. Cook the bacon until crispy. Let it drain on paper towels.

Trim the edges of the bread and toast the slices. Spread a little mayonnaise on the bread. Add lettuce, chicken, bacon, and avocado on half of the slices and cover them with the other halves. Cut each sandwich into 2 triangles, and fasten them with toothpicks.

See the photo on page 253.

IN ADVANCE The chicken can be cooked the day before and stored in the refrigerator. The bacon can be cooked several hours in advance.

BLT SANDWICH

MAKES approx. 12
TIME approx. 20 minutes

18 slices bacon
12 slices white sandwich bread
⅔ cup (150 ml) MAYONNAISE, store bought
   (**or** *see the recipe on page 74*)
lettuce
2 tomatoes, sliced

Cook the bacon until crispy. Let it drain on paper towels. Trim the edges of the bread and toast the slices. Spread a little mayonnaise on the bread. Add lettuce, bacon, and tomato on half of the bread slices, and cover with the other halves. Cut each sandwich into 2 triangles, and fasten with toothpicks.

See the photo on page 253.

IN ADVANCE The bacon can be fried a few hours before serving.

BAGUETTE WITH BRIE & SALAMI

MAKES approx. 12
TIME approx. 15 minutes

2 baguettes
arugula
6 oz (175 g) brie cheese, sliced
4 oz (100 g) salami, sliced
2–3 tomatoes, sliced
olive oil
course-ground sea salt and black pepper

Cut the baguettes into pieces about 3 inches (8 cm) long. Halve them lengthwise. Add the arugula, brie, salami, and tomato to the bottom piece. Drizzle with a little olive oil. Sprinkle with sea salt and black pepper. Cover with the other half, and fasten with a toothpick.

See the photo on page 253.

IN ADVANCE The sandwich can be prepared and kept cool for about 2 hours.

CROQUE MONSIEUR

MAKES approx. 12
TIME approx. 30 minutes

12 slices white sandwich bread
approx. 4 tbsp mayonnaise
5 oz (130 g) smoked ham, sliced
2–3 tomatoes, sliced

CHEESE SAUCE
1 tbsp butter
1 tbsp all-purpose flour
¾ cup (175 ml) milk
2 tsp Dijon mustard
2 ⅔ oz (75 g) Emmentaler or Gruyère, grated
1 egg yolk
salt and pepper

Preheat the oven to 440°F (225°C).

Melt the butter in a saucepan. Whisk in the flour. Add the milk little by little while whisking. Simmer while stirring until the sauce thickens. Remove from the heat and stir in the mustard and cheese. Stir until the cheese has melted. Whisk in the egg yolk, and season with salt and pepper.

Trim the edges of the bread and toast the slices in the oven until lightly browned. Spread mayonnaise on the untoasted sides of the bread. Arrange the ham and tomato on half of the slices. Top with the cheese sauce. Place in the oven, and broil for about 5 minutes or until sauce is golden brown.

Place the rest of the bread on top, and cut each sandwich into 2 triangles. Fasten with a toothpick. Serve warm.

See the photo on page 253.

TIP To make it easier, you can simply use a few slices of Emmentaler or Gruyère instead of making the cheese sauce.

CROQUE MADAME
Follow the recipe above, but top the ham with 6 fried eggs.

IN ADVANCE The cheese sauce can be made the day before. Everything should be assembled and grilled right before serving.

PAN BAGNAT

MAKES approx. 12
TIME approx. 25 minutes

approx. 3 ciabatta breads
lettuce
2 oz (60 g) green olives, pitted and sliced
4 hard-boiled eggs, sliced

TUNA SALAD
7 oz (185 g tuna, in oil
3 tbsp tomato, seeded and chopped
2 tbsp red onion, finely chopped
4 tbsp cucumber, seeded and diced
4 tbsp olive oil
2 tbsp white wine vinegar
course-ground sea salt and black pepper

Mix the tuna, tomato, red onion, cucumber, oil, and vinegar. Season with salt and pepper.

Cut each ciabatta into 4 pieces, then slice each piece lengthwise. Fill the ciabatta breads with lettuce, tuna salad, olives, and eggs. Fasten each sandwich with a toothpick.

See the photo on page 253.

IN ADVANCE The tuna salad can be mixed and the eggs boiled the day before. Store in the refrigerator.

SUBMARINE SANDWICH

MAKES approx. 12
TIME approx. 15 minutes

2 whole wheat baguettes
4 tbsp Dijon mustard
⅔ cup (150 ml) MAYONNAISE, store bought (or
  see the recipe on page 74)
lettuce
1 lb (450 g) cold cuts, such as ham, roast beef,
  mortadella, salami, and/or turkey
7 oz (200 g) aged cheese, sliced
2–3 tomatoes, sliced
½ red onion, sliced
¾ cup (200 ml) pickles, sliced

Halve the baguettes lengthwise. Spread the mustard and the mayonnaise on the bottom pieces. Arrange lettuce, cold cuts, cheese, tomatoes, red onion, and pickles on the bread slices. Cover with the top pieces, and slice the filled baguettes into 12 sandwiches. Fasten with toothpicks.

See the photo on page 253.

IN ADVANCE The lettuce can be rinsed and the cheese, tomatoes, and red onion can be sliced a few hours before serving.

STEAK SANDWICH WITH HORSERADISH & ONIONS

MAKES approx. 12
TIME approx. 30 minutes

1 onion, sliced
2 tbsp olive oil
2 baguettes
½ lb (250 g) sirloin steak
approx. 2 tbsp Dijon mustard
lettuce
approx. 2 tbsp grated horseradish
2–3 tomatoes, sliced

Sauté the onion in 1 tbsp olive oil over medium heat until it becomes translucent.

Heat 1 tbsp olive oil in a frying pan, and cook the steak for 3–4 minutes on each side, depending on how well done you want the meat. Let it rest in foil for about 5 minutes. Cut the meat into strips.

Cut the baguette into pieces of about 3 inches (8 cm) long. Halve the pieces lengthwise. Toast or grill the bread in the oven at 440°F (225°C) for a few minutes.

Spread mustard on the bottom pieces. Add the lettuce and the steak, and top with horseradish, tomatoes, and sautéed onions. Cover with the top pieces, and fasten with toothpicks.

See the photo on page 253.

IN ADVANCE Onions and beef can be sautéed a few hours in advance.

PANCAKES

MAKES approx. 20
TIME approx. 30 minutes

⅔ cup (150 ml) all-purpose flour
1 tbsp sugar
½ tsp baking powder
¼ tsp baking soda
½ tsp vanilla extract
a pinch of salt
¾ cup (175 ml) buttermilk
1 ½ tbsp canola oil
1 small egg, separated

butter and maple syrup for serving

Mix the dry ingredients. Add the buttermilk, oil, and egg yolk and whisk until smooth. Whisk the egg white until stiff, and fold it into the batter.

Heat a little butter in a skillet—make sure the pan isn't too hot. Pour about 1 tbsp of batter into the pan. Flip the pancake when bubbles form on the top.

Stack about 4 pancakes and fasten with a toothpick. Top with butter and maple syrup. Serve immediately.

See the photo on page 251.

WITH BANANA & PECANS
Mash half a banana and 1 oz (25 g) pecans. Mix into the batter.

WITH COCONUT & CHOCOLATE
Chop 1 oz (25 g) of dark chocolate, and mix into the batter along with 2 tbsp coconut flakes.

WITH BLUEBERRIES & LEMON
Mix 3 tbsp blueberries and the zest from half a lemon into batter.

IN ADVANCE The pancakes can be made a few hours in advance and then heated up in the oven at 300°F (150°C) for 5–6 minutes.

FRENCH TOAST

MAKES approx. 20
TIME approx. 20 minutes

2 eggs
2 tbsp milk
1 tbsp sugar
½ tsp ground cinnamon
10 slices day-old white sandwich bread
2 tbsp butter

whipped cream, fresh berries, and confectioner's sugar or butter and maple syrup

Whisk together the eggs, milk, sugar, and cinnamon.

Soak a slice of bread, one at a time, in the batter. Heat a little butter in a frying pan, and cook the bread on both sides until golden brown.

Cut each bread slice into 4 squares. Place 2 pieces of french toast on top of each other, and fasten with a toothpick. Top with a dollop of whipped cream and a few berries, and sift confectioner's sugar on top. Or add a dollop of butter and drizzle maple syrup over them. Serve immediately.

See the photo on page 251.

IN ADVANCE French toast can be prepared an hour in advance and then heated like **PANCAKES** *(see to the left)*.

ALMOND & APPLE FRENCH TOAST

MAKES approx. 16
TIME approx. 20 minutes

¾ cup (200 ml) applesauce
2 oz (50 g) almond paste
2 eggs
2 tbsp milk
2 tbsp heavy cream
butter
8 slices white sandwich bread

Mix the applesauce and the almond paste.

Trim the edges of the bread. Spread the apple mixture over half of the bread slices, and cover them with the rest of the slices. Beat the eggs and mix them with milk and cream. Cut the bread into squares, soak them in the egg the mixture, and cook them in butter.

Is not pictured.

IN ADVANCE *See* FRENCH TOAST *on the opposite page.*

YOGURT WITH HONEY, POMEGRANATE & ALMONDS

MAKES approx. 10
TIME approx. 15 minutes

½ cup (100 ml) heavy cream
2 tsp confectioner's sugar
½ tsp vanilla extract
¾ cup (200 ml) Greek yogurt
¾ cup (150 ml) honey
4 tbsp almonds flakes, roasted
seeds from ½ pomegranate

Whip the cream and the vanilla. Mix with the yogurt.

Pour the honey into the bottoms of small glasses. Fill the glasses with the yogurt mixture. Top with the roasted almonds and pomegranate seeds. Serve immediately.

See the photo on page 251.

IN ADVANCE The almond flakes can be roasted days before they are served. The pomegranate may be seeded the day before and stored in the refrigerator.

SEEDING A POMEGRANATE WITHOUT STAINING

Soften the pomegranate by rolling it on a hard surface. Halve it, and put one half at a time in a bowl of cold water. Under the water, turn the halves inside out so the seeds loosen and float to the surface.

GRANOLA WITH YOGURT & BERRIES

MAKES approx. 12
TIME approx. 30 minutes

2 ½ cups (600 ml) vanilla yogurt
¾ cup (200 ml) berries, fresh or frozen

GRANOLA
1 cup (250 ml) oats
2 tbsp sunflower seeds
2 tbsp pumpkin seeds
2 tbsp coconut flakes
1 tbsp flax seeds
2 tbsp chopped nuts (optional)
1 tbsp raw sugar
1 tsp ground cinnamon

2 tbsp water
1 tbsp canola oil
1 tsp honey

½ cup (100 ml) dried fruit, such as cranberries, raisins, banana, pineapple

lemon balm or fresh mint leaves for garnish

Preheat the oven to 400°F (200°C).

Mix the oats, seeds, coconut flakes, and nuts (if using) in a large bowl. Stir in the sugar and cinnamon.

Whisk together the water, oil, and honey. Blend the liquid mixture into the muesli.

Spread the granola in a roasting pan, and roast it for about 10–15 minutes. Stir the granola regularly to roast it evenly and to avoid burning. Let cool and mix in the dried fruit.

Fill small glasses with yogurt. Top with granola and fresh berries. Garnish with the lemon balm. Serve immediately.

See the photo on page 250.

IN ADVANCE The granola can be stored in a jar with a lid for up to 1 month.

BLUEBERRY, ALMOND & COCONUT SMOOTHIE

MAKES approx. 2 ½ cups (600 ml)
TIME approx. 10 minutes

    3 ripe bananas, peeled
    ¾ cup (200 ml) blueberries
    ½ cup (100 ml) almond milk
    1 tbsp almond butter
    2 tbsp organic coconut oil
    2 tsp crushed flax seeds
    ½ cup acai berry juice

Mix all ingredients in a blender to a smooth and creamy consistency. Pour into small chilled glasses, and serve.
See the photo on page 250.

IN ADVANCE The smoothie can be stored in the refrigerator for a few hours.

AVOCADO, KIWI & APPLE SMOOTHIE

MAKES approx. 2 ½ cups (600 ml)
TIME approx. 10 minutes

    1 avocado, peeled and pitted
    1 kiwi, peeled
    1 banana, peeled
    2 cups (500 ml) apple juice

Mix all ingredients in a blender to a smooth and creamy consistency. Add more juice if too thick. Pour into small chilled glasses, and serve immediately.
See the photo on page 250.

IN ADVANCE Because avocados discolor quickly, the smoothie should be made just before serving.

ORANGE, CARROT & GINGER COOLER

MAKES approx. 2 ½ cups (600 ml)
TIME approx. 10 minutes

    1 ¾ cups (400 ml) freshly squeezed
      orange juice
    ¾ cup (200 ml) carrot juice
    1 tsp grated fresh ginger
    approx. 6 ice cubes (optional)

Mix all the ingredients in a blender. Pour into small chilled glasses and serve immediately.
See the photo on page 250.

TIP If you are using a hand blender, you might want to crush the ice first.

IN ADVANCE The drink can be stored in the refrigerator for about 1 day.

SMOOTHIES
When it comes to choosing ingredients for a smoothie, the combinations are endless. A smoothie is so simple to make that you hardly need a recipe—just blend your favorite fruit and/or berries with juice, milk, or yogurt.

Frozen berries and fruit, bananas, and avocados thicken the consistency.

In addition to cow's milk and yogurt, consider a range of nut and grain milks such as oat, soy, rice, almond, and hazelnut.

EXOTIC FRUIT SALAD

MAKES approx. 12
TIME approx. 15 minutes

½ of a mango, diced
¼ of a honeydew, diced
2 kiwis, diced
½–1 starfruit, diced
4 oz (100 g) pineapple, diced

coconut chips or coconut flakes for garnish

Mix the fruit and fill small glasses. Sprinkle with coconut flakes.
See the photo on page 250.

IN ADVANCE Fruit salad tastes better if it is made a few hours before serving so the flavors can marry.

FRUIT SALAD WITH PISTACHIOS

MAKES approx. 12
TIME approx. 15 minutes

1 apple, cored and diced
1 pear, diced
10 grapes, halved
1 blood orange, peeled and diced

⅔ cup (150 ml) vanilla yogurt
approx. 3 tbsp chopped pistachios

Mix the fruit and fill small glasses. Top with a dollop of yogurt and some pistachios.
See the photo on page 250.

IN ADVANCE *See* EXOTIC FRUIT SALAD *above.*

SUMMER BERRIES WITH LIME SUGAR

MAKES approx. 10
TIME approx. 15 minutes

4 oz (100 g) strawberries, sliced
4 oz (100 g) raspberries
4 oz (100 g) blueberries
2 oz (50 g) redcurrants
3 tbsp sugar
zest of 1–2 limes

Mix the berries and fill small glasses. Mix the sugar and lime zest and sprinkle over the berries.
See the photo on page 250.

TIP Omit the lime sugar, and drizzle with a little balsamic syrup.

IN ADVANCE *See* EXOTIC FRUIT SALAD *to the left.*

MOJITO FRUIT SALAD

MAKES approx. 12
TIME approx. 15 minutes + 1 hour in the refrigerator

4 oz (100 g) watermelon, diced
4 oz (100 g) cantaloupe, diced
4 oz (100 g) strawberries, sliced
1 kiwi, diced
leaves from 3 sprigs of fresh mint
2 tsp sugar
3 tbsp freshly squeezed lime juice
a splash of rum (optional)

fresh mint for garnish

Mix the fruit in a bowl. Grind the mint leaves with lime juice, sugar, and rum (if using). Mix with the fruit, and refrigerate for about 1 hour. Arrange the fruit salad in small glasses. Garnish with a sprig of mint.
Is not pictured.

IN ADVANCE *See* EXOTIC FRUIT SALAD *to the left.*

**SALMON & MELON CUBES
WITH WASABI MAYO**

**WATERMELON
WITH BALSAMIC SYRUP**

The recipes are available on page 269

MINI-SKEWERS

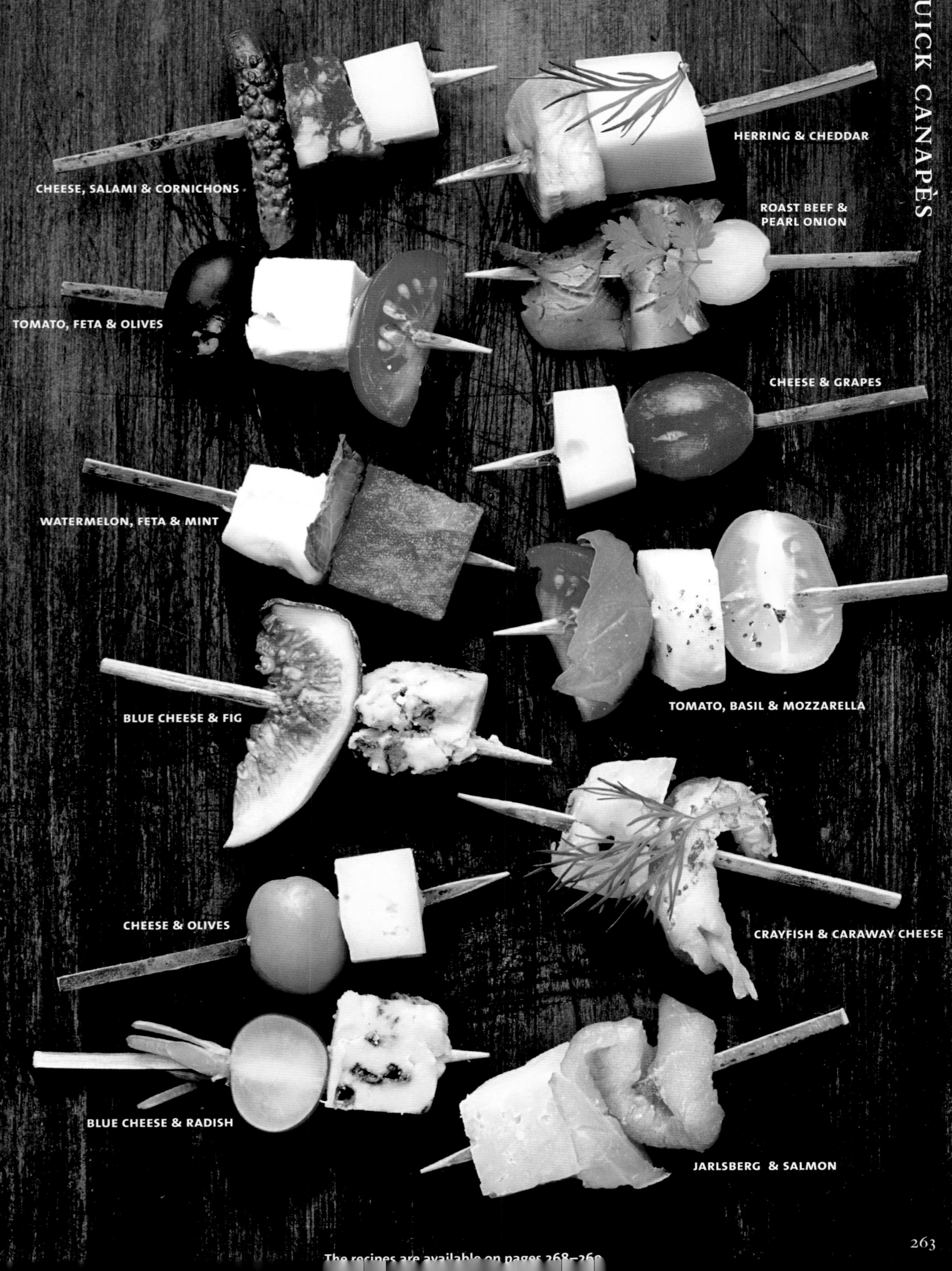
CHEESE, SALAMI & CORNICHONS
HERRING & CHEDDAR
ROAST BEEF & PEARL ONION
TOMATO, FETA & OLIVES
CHEESE & GRAPES
WATERMELON, FETA & MINT
TOMATO, BASIL & MOZZARELLA
BLUE CHEESE & FIG
CHEESE & OLIVES
CRAYFISH & CARAWAY CHEESE
BLUE CHEESE & RADISH
JARLSBERG & SALMON

The recipes are available on pages 268–269

CRUDITÉS

PROSCIUTTO-WRAPPED
ASPARAGUS

EDAMAME

BAGNA CAUDA

CREAMY HORSERADISH DIP

The recipes are available on pages 270–271

CREAMY SWEET CHILI DIP

CREAMY HERB DIP

NECTARINES WITH
CHÈVRE & MINT

GINGERBREAD COVERED
BLUE CHEESE

BLUE CHEESE
FILLED WALNUTS

CREAM CHEESE &
PECANS STUFFED DATES

The recipes are available on page 271

CRUDITÉ CANAPÉS

ENDIVE SALAD WITH BLUE CHEESE & WALNUTS

CARROT WITH WASABI CREAM CHEESE

CARROT WITH GARLIC & HERB CREAM CHEESE

CUCUMBER WITH SALMON, LEMON & DILL CREAM CHEESE

COCKTAIL TOMATO WITH BLUE CHEESE & BACON CREAM CHEESE

CELERY WITH BEETROOT & HORSERADISH CREAM CHEESE

SUGAR PEAS WITH CREAM CHEESE

267

The recipes are available on page 270

QUICK CANAPÉS

*A spontaneous celebration can sometimes be more successful than the
best-planned event. With these super-quick and delicious hors
d'oeuvres that only take ten minutes to prepare, all
that remains is to uncork the wine!*

MINI-SKEWERS

MAKES approx. 24
TIME approx. 10 minutes

24 toothpicks
ingredients of your choice (*see the recipes below*)
See the photo on page 263.

TOMATO, BASIL & MOZZARELLA
approx. 3 oz (75 g) mozzarella, diced
6 yellow cherry tomatoes, cut into wedges
6 red cherry tomatoes, cut into wedges
fresh basil
course-ground sea salt

Pierce a piece of mozzarella, a basil leaf, and
2 tomato wedges with a toothpick. Drizzle with
olive oil and sprinkle with sea salt.

TOMATO, FETA & OLIVES
24 olives, pitted
3 oz (75 g) feta, diced
6 cherry tomatoes, in wedges

Pierce an olive, a piece of feta, and a tomato wedge
with a toothpick.

CHEESE, SALAMI & CORNICHONS
12 cornichons, halved
2 oz (50 g) salami, diced
3 oz (75 g) aged hard cheese, diced

Pierce half a cornichon, a piece of salami, and a piece
of cheese with a toothpick.

BLUE CHEESE & FIG
4 fresh figs, in wedges
3 oz (75 g) blue cheese, diced

Pierce a fig and a piece of cheese with a toothpick.

CRAYFISH & CARAWAY CHEESE
24 cooked crayfish tails
3 oz (75 g) caraway cheese or other aged
cheese, diced
dill for garnish

Pierce a crayfish and a piece of cheese with a
toothpick. Garnish with dill.

CHEESE & GRAPES
24 small grapes, seedless
3 oz (75 g) aged hard cheese, diced

Pierce a grape and a piece of cheese with a toothpick.

CHEESE & OLIVES
24 olives, pitted
3 oz (75 g) aged hard cheese, diced

Pierce an olive and a piece of cheese with a
toothpick.

WATERMELON, FETA & MINT
3 oz (75 g) feta, diced
5 oz (125 g) watermelon, diced
fresh mint

Pierce a piece of feta, a leaf of fresh mint, and a piece
of watermelon with a toothpick.

HERRING & CHEDDAR
3 oz (75 g) Cheddar, diced
4 oz (130 g) pickled herring, halved
dill for garnish

Pierce a piece of cheese and a piece of herring with a toothpick. Garnish with dill.

ROAST BEEF & PEARL ONION

5 oz (125 g) sliced roast beef, in strips
24 pickled pearl onions

Pierce a pickled onion and a strip of roast beef with a toothpick.

JARLSBERG & SALMON

6 oz (125 g) sliced smoked salmon, in strips
3 oz (75 g) Jarlsberg, diced

Pierce a piece of salmon and a piece of cheese with a toothpick.

BLUE CHEESE & RADISH

12 radishes, halved
3 oz (75 g) blue cheese, diced

Pierce a radish and a piece of cheese with a toothpick.

IN ADVANCE All mini-skewers can be prepared a few hours before serving.

SALMON & MELON CUBES WITH WASABI MAYO

MAKES approx. 24
TIME approx. 10 minutes

approx. ½ lb (250 g) fresh salmon, diced
(see text box RAW FISH on page 75)
approx. ½ lb (250 g) melon, cubed
3 tbsp mayonnaise
½–1 tsp wasabi paste

Mix the mayonnaise and wasabi paste. Place a piece of salmon on a cube of melon. Dollop or pipe a little wasabi mayonnaise on top. Fasten with a toothpick.
See the photo on page 262.

IN ADVANCE Can be stored in the refrigerator for a few hours.

WATERMELON WITH BALSAMIC SYRUP

MAKES approx. 24
TIME approx. 10 minutes

approx. ¾ lb (350 g) watermelon
balsamic syrup
small basil leaves (optional)

Cut the watermelon into 1-inch (2 ½ cm) cubes. Make a hole (use the end of a chopstick) in each melon cube and fill it with balsamic syrup. Garnish with basil (if using). Serve immediately.
See the photo on page 262.

IN ADVANCE The watermelon can be prepared a few hours before it is served and filled with balsamic syrup right before serving.

EDAMAME

TIME approx. 10 minutes

edamame beans, still in pods
course-ground sea salt

Heat the beans as directed on the package. Sprinkle with sea salt and eat the beans warm by pushing them out of their pods.
See the photo on page 265.

IN ADVANCE Boil the beans right before serving. Serve directly.

CRUDITÉS WITH DIP

Preferably choose vegetables that are in season, and for an aesthetic touch, in a variety of colors.

Most vegetables can be served raw, like cucumber, carrots, cherry tomatoes, cauliflower, bell peppers, endive, and radishes. Broccoli, asparagus, green beans, wax beans, sugar peas, and baby corn taste best blanched in lightly salted water for one to two minutes and then rinsed in cold water. Serve with some of the dips below or see the Sauces and Dips sections in the index.

See the photos on pages 264–265.

CREAMY HERB DIP approx. 1 ⅓ cups (300 ml)
- ¾ cup (200 ml) sour cream
- 3 tbsp mayonnaise
- 2 tsp dill, finely chopped
- 2 tsp chives, finely chopped
- 2 tsp parsley, finely chopped
- 1 tsp herb salt

Stir the ingredients together.

CREAMY HORSERADISH DIP approx. 1 ⅓ cups (300 ml)
- ¾ cup (200 ml) sour cream
- 3 tbsp mayonnaise
- 1 tbsp grated horseradish
- 1 tsp dried parsley
- ½–1 tsp Worcestershire sauce
- 1 tsp freshly squeezed lemon juice
- 1 tbsp grated onion
- salt and pepper

Stir everything together. Season with salt and pepper.

CREAMY SWEET CHILI DIP approx. 1 ⅓ cups (300 ml)
- 1 cup (250 ml) sour cream
- 3 tbsp sweet chili sauce
- 1 tsp freshly squeezed lime juice
- few drops of sesame oil

Stir the ingredients together.

IN ADVANCE Chopped and blanched vegetables and dipping sauces can be stored in the refrigerator for a day. Rinse the vegetables in cold water right before serving.

BAGNA CAUDA

MAKES approx. ¾ cup (200 ml)
TIME approx. 10 minutes

- 4–5 cloves garlic, finely chopped
- 2 tbsp butter
- 4 oz (110 g) anchovies, chopped
- approx. ½ cup (100 ml) olive oil
- 2–3 tbsp capers, chopped

Sauté the garlic in butter for a few minutes. Add the anchovies and cook for another few minutes. Blend in a food processor or with a hand blender. Pour the oil in a thin stream while mixing to a smooth sauce. Pour it into a bowl and stir in the capers. Serve immediately with vegetables.

See the photo on page 264.

TIP The sauce is also delicious to dip toast in.

IN ADVANCE The sauce should be cooked right before serving.

CRUDITÉ CANAPÉS

These crudité canapés can be infinitely varied. Slice or cut vegetables of choice (see CRUDITÉS WITH DIP to the left). Decoratively pipe plain or flavored cream cheese (see page 246) onto the vegetables and top with garnish of choice.

See the photo on page 267.

SUGGESTIONS FOR GARNISH
- ⇢ chopped nuts
- ⇢ roasted sunflower seeds or pumpkin seeds
- ⇢ fresh herbs
- ⇢ crumbled PROSCIUTTO CHIPS (*see the recipe on page 286*)
- ⇢ crumbled PARMESAN CRISPS (*see the recipe on page 286*)
- ⇢ olives
- ⇢ sun-dried tomatoes in oil

IN ADVANCE The canapés can be prepared an hour before serving.

PROSCIUTTO-WRAPPED
ASPARAGUS

MAKES approx. 24
TIME approx. 10 minutes

  24 green asparagus stalks, halved
  12 slices prosciutto, split lengthwise

Blanch the asparagus in salted water for about
a minute. Rinse in cold water. Wrap a slice of
prosciutto around 2 asparagus stalks (one top and
one bottom). Serve as is or with hollandaise sauce
(*see the recipe on page* 198).
    See the photo on page 264.

IN ADVANCE The wraps can be prepared a few
hours before serving and stored in the refrigerator.

NECTARINES WITH
CHÈVRE & MINT

MAKES approx. 24
TIME approx. 10 minutes

  3 nectarines or 12 fresh apricots, pitted
  approx. 7 oz (200 g) chèvre
  1 bunch fresh mint

Cut fruit in smaller pieces. Place a piece of chèvre on
a piece of fruit. Garnish with mint.
    See the photo on page 266.

IN ADVANCE The fruit can be prepared and
refrigerated a few hours before serving.

CREAM CHEESE & PECAN
STUFFED DATES

MAKES approx. 24
TIME approx. 10 minutes

  24 dried dates, pitted
  approx. 4 oz (100 g) cream cheese
  20 pecans

Slit the dates without cutting through completely.
Pipe some cream cheese into the dates and press in
the pecans.
    See the photo on page 266.

IN ADVANCE The dates can be prepared and
refrigerated a couple of hours before serving. Add
the nuts just before serving.

BLUE CHEESE FILLED
WALNUTS

MAKES approx. 24
TIME approx. 10 minutes

  approx. 3 oz (75 g) cream cheese
  approx. 2 oz (50 g) blue cheese
  48 walnuts

Stir together the cream cheese and blue cheese until
smooth. Pipe some of the cheese on each walnut and
gently press together with another walnut.
    See the photo on page 266.

IN ADVANCE The cheese cream can be stored in
the refrigerator for about 2 days. Place the cream
between the walnuts right before serving.

GINGERBREAD COVERED
BLUE CHEESE

MAKES approx. 24
TIME approx. 10 minutes

  7 oz (200 g) blue cheese
  4 oz (100 g) cream cheese
  12 gingerbread cookies

Mix the blue cheese and cream cheese, and roll
into balls. Process the gingerbread cookies in a food
processor into fine crumbs. Roll the balls in the
crumbs.
    See the photo on page 266.

IN ADVANCE The cheese balls can be stored in
the refrigerator for about 2 days. Roll them in the
gingerbread crumbs right before serving.

MIMOSA

MARGARITA

BLUE LAGOON
VODKA

RAGNAR

GIMLET

The recipes are available on pages 278–280

CHAMPAGNE COCKTAIL

FROZEN DAIQUIRI

KIR ROYALE

SAKE MELON

TEQUILA
SUNRISE

RASPBERRY
PERNOD

273

SHIRLEY
TEMPLE

PINEAPPLE
PLEASURE

VIRGIN SEA
BREEZE

LEMONADE

ICED TEA

VIRGIN LYCHEE-TINI

274

The recipes are available on page 281

SPARKLING ELDERFLOWER
PUNCH

The recipe is available on page 280

COSMOPOLITAN

GIN & TONIC

AMARETTO
SOUR

SANGRIA

DRY MARTINI

HARVEY
WALLBANGER

MOJITO

BLOODY MARY

The recipes are available on pages 277–278

COCKTAILS

Part of the joy of planning a party is choosing beverages that complement the food. Here we offer some tried and true classics and a few modern twists.

COSMOPOLITAN

MAKES 1 drink

1 ⅓ oz (40 ml) vodka
⅓ oz (10 ml) Cointreau or triple sec
⅔ oz (20 ml) cranberry juice
½ lime, freshly squeezed juice

Pour all ingredients into a shaker filled with ice, shake, and strain into a chilled cocktail glass.
See the photo on page 276.

MOJITO

MAKES 1 drink

fresh leaves from 4 sprigs of mint
½ lime, wedged
⅓ oz (10 ml) SIMPLE SYRUP (*see the text box on page 280*)
1 ⅓ oz (40 ml) light rum
club soda
mint for garnish

Grind the mint leaves, lime wedges, and syrup in a glass. Pour in the rum and fill the glass with crushed ice. Top with club soda, and garnish with mint leaves.
See the photo on page 276.

DRY MARTINI

MAKES 1 drink

1 ⅔ oz (50 ml) gin
⅓ oz (10 ml) dry vermouth
1 green olive

Pour the gin and vermouth into a shaker filled with ice. Shake, then strain into a chilled martini glass. Add an olive.
See the photo on page 276.

TIP Make it a dirty martini by adding a dash of olive brine.

GIN & TONIC

MAKES 1 drink

1 ⅓ oz (40 ml) gin
tonic water
1 slice of lemon

Fill a highball glass with ice cubes and pour in the gin. Fill up the glass with tonic and garnish with the lemon slice.
See the photo on page 276.

BLOODY MARY

MAKES 1 drink

2 oz (60 ml) vodka
⅔ oz (20 ml) freshly squeezed lemon juice
3 ⅓–5 oz (100–150 ml) tomato juice
salt and pepper
celery salt
Tabasco
Worcestershire sauce
1 celery stalk

Mix the vodka, lemon juice, and tomato juice.
Season with salt, pepper, celery salt, and a few drops
of Tabasco and Worcestershire sauce. Pour the drink
into a glass, and fill with ice cubes. Garnish with a
celery stalk.

See the photo on page 276.

HARVEY WALLBANGER

MAKES 1 drink

1 ⅓ oz (40 ml) vodka
4 oz (120 ml) orange juice
⅓ oz (10 ml) Galliano
1 orange slice, cut in half

Pour all ingredients into a highball glass filled with
ice cubes. Stir.

See the photo on page 276.

AMARETTO SOUR

MAKES 1 drink

1 ⅓ oz (40 ml) amaretto
1 ⅓ oz (40 ml) freshly squeezed lemon juice
⅓ oz (10 ml) simple syrup (*see the text box on
    page 280*)
1 maraschino cherry

Mix the amaretto, lemon juice, and syrup in a glass
filled with ice cubes. Garnish with a maraschino
cherry.

See the photo on page 267.

SANGRIA

MAKES approx. 5 ¼ cups (1 ¼ liters)

½ lemon, halved and sliced
½ orange, halved and sliced
1 cinnamon stick
3 cloves
3 tbsp sugar
1 bottle red wine
¼ cup (60 ml) brandy
2 cups (500 ml) sparkling water or Sprite

Mix the fruit with the spices, wine, and brandy in a
large pitcher or bowl. Refrigerate for at least 1 hour.
Top up with sparkling water and ice.

See the photo on page 276.

FROZEN DAIQUIRI

MAKES 1 drink

*Choose your favorite fruit such as banana, mango,
strawberry, raspberry, or blackberry.*

1 ⅓ oz (40 ml) light rum
1 oz (30 ml) lemon or lime juice, freshly
    squeezed
⅔ oz (20 ml) SIMPLE SYRUP (*see the text box on
    page 280*)
4 oz (100 g) fruit or berry, of your choice
approx 8 ice cubes

Blend all ingredients in a food processor or blender,
to a smooth consistency. Pour into a chilled
cocktail glass.

See the photo on page 273.

KIR ROYALE

MAKES 1 drink

4 parts (40 ml) crème de cassis (blackcurrant liqueur)

15 parts (150 ml) chilled champagne or sparkling white wine

Pour the crème de cassis into a champagne glass. Top up with champagne or sparkling wine.

See the photo on page 273.

TEQUILA SUNRISE

MAKES 1 drink

1 ⅓ oz (40 ml) tequila

3 ⅓ oz (100 ml) orange juice

⅓ oz (10 ml) grenadine

1 orange slice for garnish

Pour tequila and orange juice into a highball glass filled with ice cubes. Stir. Carefully pour in the grenadine. Garnish with the orange slice.

See the photo on page 273.

MARGARITA

MAKES 1 drink

1 ⅓ oz (40 ml) tequila

⅔ oz (20 ml) Cointreau

⅔ oz (20 ml) freshly squeezed lime juice

salt

1 slice of lime

Pour the tequila, Cointreau, and lime juice into a shaker filled with ice cubes. Dip the rim of a chilled cocktail glass first in the lime juice and then in the salt. Shake the margarita mixture and strain into the glass. Garnish with a lime slice.

See the photo on page 272.

MIMOSA

MAKES 1 drink

3 oz (90 ml) chilled champagne or sparkling white wine

1 oz (30 ml) orange juice

Pour the champagne into a champagne glass, and top with orange juice.

See the photo on page 272.

CHAMPAGNE COCKTAIL

MAKES 1 drink

1 sugar cube

2 drops angostura bitters

⅔ oz (20 ml) Cognac

5 oz (150 ml) chilled champagne

Place a sugar cube in the bottom of a champagne glass, and add angostura bitters. Pour in the brandy and champagne.

See the photo on page 273.

RAGNAR

MAKES 1 drink

1 oz (30 ml) blackcurrant juice

2 oz (60 ml) Absolut Kurant (black currant vodka)

⅔ oz (20 ml) freshly squeezed lime juice

Sprite

Pour blackcurrant juice into a glass. Fill with crushed ice. Pour in the Absolut Kurant and lime juice. Fill up the glass with Sprite.

See the photo on page 272.

BLUE LAGOON VODKA

MAKES 1 drink

⅔ oz (20 ml) vodka
⅔ oz (20 ml) blue curaçao
⅔ oz (20 ml) freshly squeezed lemon juice

Mix the ingredients in a shaker filled with ice. Shake and strain into a chilled cocktail glass.

See the photo on page 272.

GIMLET

MAKES 1 drink

2 oz (60 ml) gin or vodka
1 oz (30 ml) Rose's Sweetened Lime Juice
1 lime peel

Pour gin or vodka and lime juice into a shaker filled with ice cubes. Shake and strain into a glass filled with ice cubes. Garnish with lime peel.

See the photo on page 272.

RASPBERRY PERNOD

MAKES 1 drink

1 ⅔ oz (50 ml) raspberry purée
⅔ oz (20 ml) vodka
1 ⅓ oz (40 ml) cranberry juice
⅓ oz (10 ml) Pernod or Ricard
⅓ oz (10 ml) simple syrup

Mix all ingredients and pour into a glass of crushed ice.

See the photo on page 273.

SAKE MELON

MAKES 1 drink

1 oz (30 ml) sake
1 oz (30 ml) Midori
⅔ oz (20 ml) freshly squeezed lemon juice
1 slice lemon

Pour the sake, Midori, and lemon juice into a shaker filled with ice cubes. Shake and strain into a cocktail glass. Garnish the lemon slice.

See the photo on page 273.

SPARKLING ELDERFLOWER PUNCH

MAKES approx. 6 ⅓ cups (1 ½ liters)

1 bottle sparkling white wine
2 cups (500 ml) Sprite
½ cup (100 ml) undiluted elderflower cordial
1 lemon, sliced
1 orange, sliced
1 starfruit, sliced
4 oz (100 g) green grapes

Mix all ingredients in a large bowl. Load with ice cubes.

See the photo on page 275.

SIMPLE SYRUP
Simple syrup is made of equal parts sugar and water. The longer it simmers, the thicker it becomes. Use in drinks such as MOJITO (*see the recipe on page 277*) and RASPBERRY PERNOD (*see the recipe to the right*).

NON-ALCOHOLIC DRINKS

MAKES 1 drink

SHIRLEY TEMPLE
4 oz (120 ml) Sprite or ginger ale
⅔ oz (20 ml) grenadine
1 maraschino cherry

Pour Sprite or ginger ale into a highball glass filled with ice. Pour in the grenadine, and garnish with a cocktail cherry.
See the photo on page 274.

VIRGIN SEA BREEZE
2 oz (60 ml) grapefruit juice
2 oz (60 ml) cranberry juice
⅔ oz (20 ml) grenadine

Pour the grapefruit juice and cranberry juice in a highball glass filled with ice. Top with grenadine.
See the photo on page 274.

VIRGIN LYCHEE-TINI
1 ⅓ oz (40 ml) apple juice
1 ⅓ oz (40 ml) lychee juice
⅔ oz (20 ml) cranberry juice
1 lychee for garnish

Pour the juices into a shaker filled with ice. Shake and strain into a chilled cocktail glass. Garnish with a lychee on a toothpick.
See the photo on page 274.

PINEAPPLE PLEASURE
2 oz (60 ml) pineapple juice
2 oz (60 ml) orange juice
⅔ oz (20 ml) freshly squeezed lime juice
⅓ oz (10 ml) Rose's Sweetened Lime Juice

Mix all ingredients and pour into a highball glass or wine glasses filled with ice.
See the photo on page 274.

LEMONADE

MAKES approx. ½ gallon (2 liters)

1 large lemon, sliced
2 cups (500 ml) sugar
approx 4 cups (1 liter) water
2 cups (500 ml) freshly squeezed lemon juice

Add the lemon slices to a bowl with sugar. Mash it together until the sugar begins to melt. Add water and lemon juice and mix until the sugar is dissolved. Strain the lemon slices. Taste and add more water if needed. Serve with lots of ice and a few slices of lemon.
See the photo on page 274.

TIP Replace the water with carbonated water, or the lemon with lime.

ICED TEA

MAKES approx. 4 cups (1 liter)

4–5 tsp Earl Grey tea leaves
   or 3–4 Earl Grey tea bags
4 cups (1 liter) boiling water
¼–½ cup (50–100 ml) sugar
1 lemon, freshly squeezed juice

Steap the tea leaves or tea bags in the boiling water for no more than 5 minutes. Strain the tea and stir in the sugar, to taste, until dissolved. Let cool to room temperature. Add the lemon juice to taste, and serve with lots of ice.
See the photo on page 274.

POTATO & ROOT VEGETABLE CHIPS

The recipes are available on page 288

BARBECUE NUTS

TRAIL MIX

SWEET & SPICY NUTS

ROASTED NUTS WITH ROSEMARY

CHILI & GINGER NUTS

ROASTED SEEDS WITH GOJI BERRIES

HONEY-ROASTED PECANS

MACADAMIA NUTS WITH COCONUT & EXOTIC FRUIT

PEANUTS, CHOCOLATE & CRANBERRIES

ROASTED SUNFLOWER & PUMPKIN SEEDS

SALT-ROASTED ALMONDS

DEEP-FRIED LENTILS, CHICKPEAS & NOODLES

The recipes are available on pages 288–291

FLAVORED POPCORN

SESAME SEED

BARBECUE

HONEY MUSTARD

OLIVE, HERB & LEMON

The recipes are available on page 287

FLATBREAD SNACKS

**PARMESAN &
PINE NUT CRISPS**

**CHEDDAR &
CARAWAY CRISPS**

PROSCIUTTO CHIPS

GRILLED POTATO SKINS

MINI GRISSINI

The recipes are available on pages 286–287

285

SNACKS

Surprise your guests with homemade chips and novel variations on flavored nuts and popcorn.
It's easier than you think, and adds a festive touch to any gathering.

PROSCIUTTO CHIPS

MAKES approx. 40
TIME approx. 10 minutes

approx. 7 oz (200 g) prosciutto

Preheat the oven to 440°F (225°C). Place the prosciutto on foil or parchment paper and roast in the oven for about 5 minutes or until crispy. Ensure that it doesn't burn. Let cool and break into smaller pieces.
See the photo on page 285.

TIP Replace the prosciutto with bresaola or salami.

IN ADVANCE The chips can be prepared a few days before serving and kept at room temperature.

PARMESAN & PINE NUT CRISPS

MAKES approx. 24
TIME approx. 15 minutes

5 oz (150 g) Parmesan, grated
1 oz (30 g) pine nuts

Preheat the oven to 440°F (225°C). Cover a thin rolling pin with aluminum foil.
Place the grated Parmesan in small piles on a baking sheet lined with parchment paper. Sprinkle pine nuts over the cheese. Don't make too many at once because each crisp needs to be shaped before the cheese hardens.

Melt the cheese in the oven for 3–5 minutes. Ensure that it doesn't burn. Let cool slightly until the crisps can be lifted up with a spatula and gently laid over the covered rolling pin. Allow to cool completely.
See the photo on page 285.

CHEDDAR & CARAWAY CRISPS
approx. 5 oz (150 g) Cheddar, grated
approx. 2 tsp caraway seeds

Follow the directions for Parmesan crisps above.
See the photo on page 285.

TIP You can also simply sprinkle all the cheese in an even layer on the baking sheet. After taking the melted cheese out of the oven, let it harden and then break into smaller pieces.

IN ADVANCE The crisps can be stored in a tightly sealed jar in the refrigerator for several days or in the freezer for about a month.

FLATBREAD SNACKS

Follow the recipe for FLATBREAD STRIPS on page 226, and simply cut the bread into small pieces. You can also bake the whole flatbread and then break into smaller pieces.
See the photo on page 285.

MINI GRISSINI

Follow the recipe for breadsticks on page 229, but cut the dough into smaller pieces before baking.
See the photo on page 285.

GRILLED POTATO SKINS

MAKES approx. 24
TIME approx. 1 ½ hours

> approx. 1 ½ lbs (700 g) potatoes
> 2 tbsp olive oil
> salt and pepper

Preheat the oven to 400°F (200°C).

Wash the potatoes. Pierce them with a fork, and bake in the oven for about an hour or until soft. Let cool.

Cut the potatoes into wedges. Scoop out the insides, leaving approximately ¼ inch (⅔ cm) on the potato skin.

Brush the potatoes with oil, and season with salt and pepper. Place on a rack and bake in the oven for about 10 minutes. Flip them over and return to the oven for approximately 5 more minutes or until crisp and golden brown. Serve immediately with dip, such as CREAMY HORSERADISH DIP or CREAMY SWEET CHILI DIP (*see the recipes on page 270*).

See the photo on page 285.

WITH ROSEMARY Sprinkle 1 tbsp fresh, finely chopped rosemary over the skins before baking.

WITH SESAME SEEDS Sprinkle 1–2 tbsp sesame seeds over the skins before baking.

WITH CHILI PEPPER Sprinkle about 1 tsp chili pepper flakes over the skins before baking.

IN ADVANCE Potato skins are crispiest when freshly baked.

FLAVORED POPCORN

MAKES approx. 8 ½ cups (2 liters)
TIME approx. 15 minutes

> 8 ½ cups (2 liters) popped popcorn
> 2 tbsp butter, melted
> seasoning of your choice (*see the recipes below*)

HONEY MUSTARD
> 1 tbsp honey mustard
> salt

Mix the butter and honey mustard into the hot popcorn. Season with salt.

See the photo on page 284.

OLIVE, HERB & LEMON
> ¾ cup (200 ml) pitted black olives, finely chopped
> approx. 1 tsp chili pepper flakes, crumbled
> 1 tbsp parsley, finely chopped
> 1 tbsp fresh oregano, finely chopped
> 1 lemon, zested
> salt

Mix the hot popcorn with the butter, olives, chili pepper, parsley, oregano, and lemon zest. Season with salt.

See the photo on page 284.

SESAME SEED
> 2 tbsp sesame seeds, white and/or black
> 1–2 tsp sesame oil
> salt

Mix hot popcorn with sesame seeds and sesame oil (omit butter). Season with salt.

See the photo on page 284.

BARBECUE
> see SPICE MIX *for the* BARBECUE NUTS *on page 289.*

Mix the hot popcorn with the melted butter and spices. Season with salt.

See the photo on page 284

IN ADVANCE Flavored popcorn can be made a few hours before serving.

POTATO CHIPS

MAKES approx. 4 cups (1 liter)
TIME approx. 40 minutes

   1 lb (500 g) potatoes, sliced paper thin
   4 cups (1 liter) oil for frying
   salt

Heat the oil in a heavy-bottomed saucepan to approximately 350°F (180°C). Fry the potato slices in batches until they are crispy and golden brown. Drain on paper towels. Sprinkle with salt, course-ground sea salt, or flavored salt.
   See the photo on page 282.

TIP Use Blue Congo potatoes to make chips that are a beautiful shade of purple.

ROOT VEGETABLE CHIPS
   1 lb (500 g) root vegetables, such as Jerusalem artichokes, beets, carrots, or parsnips, sliced paper thin
   4 cups (1 liter) oil for frying
   course-ground sea salt

Follow the recipe for potato chips above.

TIP Deep fry fresh herbs until crispy, and mix with the chips.

IN ADVANCE Both potato chips and root vegetable chips taste best freshly made, but can be stored for about a day if kept at room temperature.

PEANUTS, CHOCOLATE & CRANBERRIES

MAKES approx. 2 cups (500 ml)
TIME approx. 5 minutes

   ¾ cup (200 ml) salted peanuts
   ⅔ cup (150 ml) chocolate-covered peanuts
   ⅔ cup (150 ml) dried cranberries

Mix the salted peanuts with the chocolate-covered peanuts and cranberries.
   See the photo on page 283.

IN ADVANCE The mix can be stored for about 2 weeks in an airtight jar.

SALT-ROASTED ALMONDS

MAKES approx. 2 cups (500 ml)
TIME approx. 20 minutes

   2 cups (500 ml) almonds, unpeeled
   1 ⅓ cups (300 ml) water
   2–3 tbsp salt

Preheat the oven to 400°F (200°C).
   Boil the water and salt. Add the almonds, and let them cook for 1 minute. Drain the water and transfer the almonds to a baking sheet lined with parchment paper. Roast in the oven for about 10 minutes or until the almonds begin to darken slightly. Stir occasionally and ensure that they do not burn. Let cool.
   See the photo on page 283.

SMOKED ALMONDS Add 3 tbsp of liquid smoke in the water or use smoke flavored salt.

IN ADVANCE The mix can be stored for about 2 weeks in an airtight jar.

SWEET & SPICY NUTS

MAKES approx. 2 cups (500 ml)
TIME approx. 20 minutes

2 cups (500 ml) cashew nuts, unsalted
3 tbsp sugar
1 ½ tsp salt
approx. 1 tsp cayenne pepper
1 tbsp water
1 tbsp honey
1 tsp canola oil

Preheat the oven to 400°F (200°C). Roast the
nuts on a baking sheet for about 10 minutes. Stir
occasionally.

Mix the sugar, salt, and cayenne pepper in a bowl.

Mix the water, honey, and canola oil in a saucepan,
and bring to a boil. Stir the nuts into the honey
mixture, and then mix with all the spices in the bowl.
Stir until all nuts are coated. Transfer the nuts onto a
baking sheet covered with parchment paper to cool.

See the photo on page 283.

IN ADVANCE *See* CHILI & GINGER NUTS *on page 290.*

BARBECUE NUTS

MAKES approx. 2 cups (500 ml)
TIME approx. 20 minutes

2 cups (500 ml) mixed nuts
1 tbsp canola oil
1 tsp paprika
1 tsp oregano
1 tsp thyme
1 tsp onion powder
½ tsp chili powder

Preheat the oven to 400°F (200°C). Mix the nuts
with the oil and spices. Roast on a baking sheet for
about 10 minutes. Stir occasionally. Let cool.

See the photo on page 283.

IN ADVANCE *See* CHILI & GINGER NUTS *on page 290.*

MACADAMIA NUTS WITH COCONUT & EXOTIC FRUIT

MAKES approx. 2 cups (500 ml)
TIME approx. 20 minutes

¾ cup (200 ml) macadamia nuts
½ cup (100 ml) coconut flakes, toasted
¾ cup (200 ml) mixed dried exotic fruit, diced
salt

Preheat the oven to 400°F (200°C). Place the nuts
onto a baking sheet and roast in the oven for about
10 minutes or until they are golden brown. Stir
occasionally, and ensure that they do not burn.
Season with salt and let cool.

Mix the nuts, coconut, and dried fruit.

See the photo on page 283.

IN ADVANCE The mix can be stored for about 2
weeks in an airtight jar.

TRAIL MIX

MAKES approx. 2 cups (500 ml)
TIME approx. 25 minutes

1 ⅓ cups (300 ml) mixed nuts
3 tbsp sunflower seeds
3 tbsp pumpkin seeds
½ cup (100 ml) raisins and/or dried
   cranberries
salt

Preheat the oven to 400°F (200°C). Roast the nuts
on a baking sheet for about 10 minutes and the seeds
for about 5 minutes, or until golden brown. Season
with salt and let cool.

Mix the nuts and seeds with raisins and/or dried
cranberries.

See the photo on page 283.

IN ADVANCE The mix can be stored for about 2
weeks in an airtight jar.

ROASTED SEEDS WITH GOJI BERRIES

MAKES approx. 2 cups (500 ml)
TIME approx. 15 minutes

⅔ cup (150 ml) shelled pumpkin seeds
⅔ cup (150 ml) sunflower seeds
½ cup (100 ml) hemp seeds
½ cup (100 ml) goji berries
salt

Toast the different seeds separately in a dry skillet. Sunflower seeds are ready when they begin to brown, and pumpkin seeds and hemp seeds when they begin to "pop." Add salt, and let cool. Mix with the goji berries.

See the photo on page 283.

IN ADVANCE The mix can be stored for about 2 weeks in an airtight jar.

ROASTED SUNFLOWER & PUMPKIN SEEDS

MAKES approx. 2 cups (500 ml)
TIME approx. 30 minutes

¾ cup (200 ml) sunflower seeds
seeds from 1 small pumpkin
approx. 2 tbsp oil
approx. 1 tsp salt

Preheat the oven to 400°F (200°C).

Remove the seeds from the pumpkin, and rinse them in cold water. Mix them with the sunflower seeds and the oil on a baking sheet. Sprinkle with salt, and roast in the oven for 5–10 minutes or until the seeds begin to color. Let cool.

See the photo on page 283.

TIP Flavor with cayenne pepper, chili pepper flakes, or garlic salt.

IN ADVANCE The mix can be stored for about 2 weeks in an airtight jar.

CHILI & GINGER NUTS

MAKES approx. 2 cups (500 ml)
TIME approx. 30 minutes

2 cloves garlic, thinly sliced
1 tbsp sugar
2 tbsp brown sugar
1 tbsp water
2 tsp soy sauce
2 cups (500 ml) roasted cashew nuts
1 tbsp fresh ginger, grated
2 tsp chili pepper flakes
1 tsp lime zest
¼ tsp salt

Preheat the oven to 400°F (200°C).

Blanch the garlic for about 10 seconds in boiling water. Drain the water.

Boil the sugar, brown sugar, water, and soy sauce. Add the garlic, and then stir in the remaining ingredients. Spread the mixture on a greased or parchment paper–lined baking sheet and roast the nuts in the oven for about 15 minutes. Stir occasionally and watch carefully so it does not burn.

Let it cool slightly, and then put it on parchment paper to cool completely. Add more salt if desired.

See the photo on page 283.

IN ADVANCE The nuts can be stored for about 2 weeks in the refrigerator.

HONEY-ROASTED PECANS

MAKES approx. 2 cups (500 ml)
TIME approx. 25 minutes

2 cups (500 ml) pecans
½ cup (100 ml) honey
1 ½ tsp cinnamon

Preheat the oven to 400°F (200°C).

Mix all ingredients in a heavy-bottomed saucepan. Heat and stir until the nuts are covered with honey.

Spread the nuts on a baking sheet and roast in the oven for about 8 minutes. Stir occasionally and watch carefully so that they do not burn. Allow to cool.

See the photo on page 283.

IN ADVANCE *See* CHILI & GINGER NUTS *on the opposite page.*

ROASTED NUTS WITH ROSEMARY

MAKES approx. 2 cups (500 ml)
TIME approx. 20 minutes

¾ cup (200 ml) almonds, blanched and peeled
¾ cup (200 ml) pecans
approx. 2 tbsp butter, melted
1–2 tsp dried rosemary, crumbled
a pinch of cayenne pepper
course-ground sea salt

2 OZ (50 g) PROSCIUTTO CHIPS (*see the recipe on page 286*), crumbled
3 tbsp crispy fried onion
fresh rosemary for garnish

Preheat the oven to 400°F (200°C).

Mix the nuts with the butter, rosemary, and cayenne pepper to taste. Season with salt.

Spread the nuts on a baking sheet lined with parchment paper, and roast them in the oven for about 10 minutes or until they color. Stir occasionally, and watch that they do not burn. Remove and let cool.

Add more spices and salt if desired. Mix with prosciutto chips, crispy fried onions, and a few sprigs of fresh rosemary.

See the photo on page 283.

IN ADVANCE *See* CHILI & GINGER NUTS *on the opposite page.*

DEEP-FRIED LENTILS, CHICKPEAS & NOODLES

MAKES approx. 2 cups (500 ml)
TIME approx. 40 minutes + 2–3 hours of soaking

½ cup (100 ml) French Puy lentils
14 oz (400 g) canned chickpeas, drained
2 oz (50 g) thin egg noodles
2 tbsp anise seeds
½ tsp ground cumin
½ tsp curry powder
¼ tsp ground coriander
a pinch of cayenne pepper
salt
oil for deep frying

Soak the lentils for 2–3 hours. Drain the water, and boil the lentils in fresh water. Let them simmer for 5 minutes, then drain and dry on paper towels.

Break the uncooked egg noodles into smaller pieces. Heat the oil to 320°F (160°C). Fry the noodles for some seconds until golden brown. Drain on paper towels.

Fry the chickpeas in batches for about 5 minutes or until they are crispy. Be careful because the oil may splash. To avoid this, cover half the pot with a lid. Let the chickpeas drain on paper towels.

Fry the lentils until crispy and drain on paper towels.

Mix the spices. Add the chickpeas, noodles, and lentils to a bowl. Stir in the spices and mix well.

Season with salt.

See the photo on page 283.

IN ADVANCE Can be stored at room temperature in an air tight jar for a couple of days.

FIG & HONEY
PASTRY

RASPBERRY & PASSIONFRUIT TARTLET

NECTARINE PASTRY WITH
LIME & CARDAMOM CREAM

APPLE PASTRY
WITH CANDIED NUTS

CARROT CUPCAKE

CHOCOLATE TRUFFLE
PIE

BROWNIE

LEMON
CUPCAKE

CHOCOLATE
CUPCAKE

KEY LIME
PIE

STRAWBERRY
SHORTCAKE

The recipes are available on pages 296–300

STRAWBERRY & LIMONCELLO TRIFLE

BERRY MOUSSE

CHOCOLATE PANNA COTTA

VANILLA PANNA COTTA

TIRAMISU

BLACKBERRY & WHITE CHOCOLATE PANNA COTTA

BAILEYS PANNA COTTA WITH CANDIED NUTS

293

The recipes are available on pages 301–303

VANILLA CUSTARD

LIME SUGAR

FRUIT SKEWERS

CHOCOLATE TRUFFLES

The recipes are available on pages 295–296

DESSERTS

*Honestly . . . who doesn't have a sweet tooth? Some of our most
popular parties consisted of little more than champagne and a
sumptuous buffet of mini desserts. Sheer decadence!*

CHOCOLATE TRUFFLES

MAKES approx. 25
TIME approx. 45 min. + 4 hrs. in the refrigerator

8 oz (225 g) semisweet or bittersweet chocolate
⅔ cup (150 ml) heavy cream
2 tbsp butter
cocoa powder

Chop the chocolate finely and add to a bowl.

Boil the cream and pour it over the chocolate. Let
it stand for a few minutes without stirring. Add the
butter in small pieces, and mix gently to a smooth
cream. Let stand in the refrigerator until the mixture
has thickened and set—at least 4 hours.

Dip a spoonful of the truffle in the cocoa powder—
so it does not stick in your hands—and roll into a
ball. Roll the truffles in the cocoa powder or another
garnish of your choice (*see below*).

See the photo on page 294.

GARNISH
→ melted dark chocolate
→ finely chopped nuts
→ finely chopped/crushed candy canes or
   hard caramel candies
→ finely chopped or grated dark or white
   chocolate
→ coconut flakes
→ equal parts sugar and brown sugar
→ confectioner's sugar

CHILI PEPPER TRUFFLES
Add a pinch of dried chili flakes to the
chocolate cream.

LIQUORICE TRUFFLES
Add 3 tbsp of crushed salted licorice hard candies to
the chocolate cream.

COGNAC TRUFFLE
Add 2–3 tsp cognac and brandy to the
chocolate cream.

ORANGE TRUFFLES
Add the zest of ½–1 orange to the chocolate cream.

MINT TRUFFLES
Add a few drops of peppermint extract to the
chocolate cream.

IN ADVANCE Truffles can be stored in the
refrigerator for several days or in the freezer for
3 months. Garnish before serving.

TRUFFLES TIPS
To add a handmade touch to truffles, instead
of rolling them, slightly pinch them into
uneven balls.

When preparing a large amount of truffles,
let the chocolate cream set in a small square
mold that has been lined with plastic wrap. Then
use the plastic wrap to lift the hardened truffle
onto a cutting board. Cut into squares and cover
with cocoa powder or powdered sugar.

FRUIT SKEWERS WITH LIME SUGAR

MAKES approx. 24
TIME approx. 20 minutes

1 ⅓ lbs (600 g) fruit of your choice, in pieces, and/or berries of your choice

LIME SUGAR
½ cup (100 ml) sugar
1 lime, zest

whipped cream or vanilla yogurt for serving

Mix the sugar with the lime zest. Pierce the fruit with the wooden skewers. Serve with the lime sugar, whipped cream, or vanilla yogurt as dips.
See the photo on page 294.

IN ADVANCE Prepare the skewers on the same day they are to be served.

BROWNIES

MAKES approx. 40
TIME approx. 40 minutes

2 eggs
1 cup (250 ml) sugar
⅔ cup (150 g) melted butter, cooled
½ cup (100 ml) all-purpose flour
⅔ cup (150 ml) cocoa powder
1 tsp vanilla extract
½ cup (100 ml) chopped walnuts (optional)

4 oz (100 g) melted semi-sweet chocolate for garnish

Preheat the oven to 300°F (150°C). Grease and flour an ovenproof dish, approximately 8 inches × 12 inches (20 cm x 30 cm). Beat the eggs and sugar until light and fluffy. Stir in the melted butter. Mix the flour, cocoa powder, and vanilla extract into the batter. Add the walnuts. Pour the batter into the dish, and bake for 25–30 minutes. Let cool and cut into squares. Drizzle with melted chocolate.
See the photo on page 292.

IN ADVANCE Brownies can be stored in an airtight container for about 3 days, or frozen for about 3 months.

STRAWBERRY SHORTCAKE

MAKES approx. 40
TIME approx. 1 hour

SPONGE CAKE
2 eggs
¾ cup (200 ml) sugar
1 cup (250 ml) all-purpose flour
1 tsp baking powder
2 tsp vanilla extract
5 tbsp butter, melted and cooled
½ cup (100 ml) milk

¾ cup (200 ml) heavy cream
1 tsp confectioner's sugar

1 ¾ cup (400 ml) VANILLA CUSTARD (*see the recipe on page* 299).
10 strawberries, cut in wedges

lemon balm for garnish

Preheat the oven to 350°F (175°C). Grease and flour an ovenproof pan approximately 8 inches × 12 inches (20 cm × 30 cm).

Beat the eggs and sugar until light and fluffy. Mix the dry ingredients, and stir into the egg mixture together with the butter and milk.

Spread batter evenly in the pan and bake for about 20 minutes. Remove from the oven, and let it cool.

Whip the cream with the confectioner's sugar.

Punch out small rounds or cut the sponge cake into squares. Pipe or dollop a little vanilla custard and whipped cream on each piece. Add a strawberry and garnish with lemon balm.
See the photo on page 292.

IN ADVANCE The sponge cake can be stored in an airtight container for about 3 days or in the freezer for about 3 months.

CHOCOLATE CUPCAKES

MAKES approx. 30
TIME approx. 45 minutes

4 oz (100 g) butter, at room temperature
⅔ cup (150 ml) sugar
2 eggs
1 cup all-purpose flour
½ cup (100 ml) cocoa powder
½ tsp baking powder
½ tsp baking soda
1 tsp vanilla extract
a pinch of salt
⅔ cup (150 ml) water

CHOCOLATE FROSTING

2 cups (500 ml) confectioner's sugar
3 tbsp cocoa powder
4 oz (100 g) cream cheese
2 oz (60 g) butter, unsalted
1 tsp vanilla extract
1 tbsp coffee or espresso

Preheat the oven to 350°F (175°C).

Fill a mini cupcake baking tray with paper liners, or grease and flour the tray.

Beat the butter and sugar until fluffy. Add the eggs one at a time. Mix the dry ingredients and add them to the batter together with the water. Mix until smooth.

Pour the batter into the tray and bake for 7–10 minutes, or until a toothpick comes out dry. Allow to cool. Mix the ingredients for the chocolate frosting, and stir it until smooth. Spread or pipe the frosting on the cupcakes.

See the photo on page 292.

IN ADVANCE The cupcakes, without the frosting, can be stored in an airtight container for about 3 days or in the freezer for about 3 months.

LEMON CUPCAKES

MAKES approx. 30
TIME approx. 45 minutes

4 ½ oz (125 g) butter, at room temperature
⅔ cup (150 ml) sugar
1 ½ cup (350 ml) all-purpose flour
1 tsp baking powder
½ tsp baking soda
2 eggs
½ cup (100 ml) buttermilk
1 lemon, zested and freshly squeezed juice

LEMON FROSTING

7 oz (200 g) cream cheese
⅔–⅔ cup (150–200 ml) confectioner's sugar
½ lemon, zested

Preheat the oven to 350°F (175°C).

Fill a mini cupcake baking tray with paper liners, or grease and flour the tray.

Beat the butter and sugar until fluffy. Combine the dry ingredients and stir them into the mixture. Add the eggs, one at a time, and then the buttermilk and lemon. Mix to a smooth batter.

Pour the batter into the tray and bake for 7–10 minutes, or until a toothpick comes out dry. Allow to cool. Mix the ingredients for the frosting and stir until smooth. Spread or pipe the frosting on the cupcakes.

See the photo on page 292.

IN ADVANCE *See* CHOCOLATE CUPCAKES *to the left.*

CARROT CUPCAKES

MAKES approx. 30
TIME approx. 45 minutes

½ cup (100 ml) puréed cooked carrots
  (2 medium sized carrots)
¾ cup (200 ml) all-purpose flour
¾ cup (200 ml) sugar
¼ tsp salt
½ tsp baking soda
½ tbsp ground cinnamon
1 tsp vanilla extract
⅓ cup (75 ml) canola oil
2 eggs
½ cup (100 ml) chopped pecans
3 tbsp applesauce

FROSTING
7 oz (200 g) cream cheese
⅔–¾ cup (150–200 ml) confectioner's sugar
1 tsp vanilla extract

Preheat the oven to 350°F (175°C). Fill a mini cupcake baking tray with paper liners, or grease and flour the tray.

Mix the dry ingredients. Add the carrot purée, oil, eggs, and applesauce and mix to a smooth batter. Add the pecans.

Pour the batter into the tray and bake in middle of the oven for about 15 minutes, or until an inserted toothpick comes out dry. Let cool.

Mix the ingredients for the frosting and stir it until smooth. Spread or pipe the frosting on the cupcakes

See the photo on page 292.

IN ADVANCE *See* CHOCOLATE CUPCAKES *on page 297.*

CHOCOLATE TRUFFLE PIE

MAKES approx. 15
TIME approx. 1 ½ hours

CHOCOLATE PIE CRUST
⅔ cup (150 ml) all-purpose flour
1 tbsp confectioner's sugar
1 ½ tbsp cocoa powder
2 ½ oz (75 g) butter, cold
½ egg yolk
1 tsp cold water

TRUFFLE FILLING
½ cup (125 ml) heavy cream
3 tbsp sugar
7 oz (200 g) bittersweet chocolate, finely
  chopped
1 oz (35 g) butter

½ cup (100 ml) heavy cream, whipped

Start with the pie crust. Combine the flour, sugar and cocoa powder in a food processor. Add butter and pulse until mixture resembles a coarse meal. Add the egg yolk and water just until the dough pulls together. Refrigerate for at least 30 minutes.

Preheat the oven to 400°F (200°C).

Grease a mini pie or mini muffin tray. Line the forms with dough. Prick the bottom of the dough with a fork. Refrigerate for another 15 minutes.

Bake the crusts for about 7 minutes. Let cool.

To make the truffle filling, bring the heavy cream and sugar to a boil in a saucepan. Remove the pan from the heat and add the chocolate. Stir until the chocolate has melted, then add the butter in small pieces. Mix to a smooth cream, and pour the filling into the crust. Let it cool and then refrigerate until set.

Dollop or pipe the whipped cream onto the pies shortly before serving.

See the photo on page 292.

IN ADVANCE The pies can be made about 2 days in advance and stored in the refrigerator or in the freezer for about 3 months.

RASPBERRY & PASSIONFRUIT TARTLETS

MAKES approx. 12
TIME approx. 1 ½ hours

PIE CRUST
⅔ cup (150 ml) all-purpose flour
2 ½ tbsp sugar
2 ½ oz (75 g) butter, cold
1 egg yolk

VANILLA CUSTARD
1 egg
2 tbsp sugar
2 tbsp butter
2 tbsp cornstarch
1 ⅓ cup (300 ml) milk
2 tsp vanilla extract

2 passion fruit
12 raspberries

Preheat the oven to 350°F (175°C). Grease a mini pie or mini muffin tray.

Start with the pie crust. Combine the flour and sugar in a food processor. Add butter and pulse until mixture resembles a coarse meal. Add the egg yolk until the dough pulls together. Refrigerate for at least 30 minutes.

Line the forms with dough. Prick the bottom of the dough with a fork. Refrigerate for another 15 minutes.

Bake for about 13 minutes. Allow to cool.

Mix all the ingredients except vanilla extract for the custard in a heavy-bottomed saucepan. Heat over medium heat and continue whisking. Remove the pan from the heat as soon as the first bubble appears. When the custard has cooled, stir in the vanilla extract.

Halve the passion fruit, and scoop out the pulp. Fill the crusts with the vanilla custard. Top each with passion fruit and a raspberry.

See the photo on page 292.

IN ADVANCE The crust can be baked about 2 days in advance and stored in the refrigerator or in the freezer for about 3 months. The vanilla custard can be stored in the refrigerator for 1 day.

KEY LIME PIE

MAKES approx. 12
TIME approx. 1 hour and 45 minutes

1 batch PIE CRUST (*see recipe to the left*)

FILLING
2 egg yolks
½ cup (100 ml) condensed milk
3 tbsp lime juice, freshly squeezed
2 tsp lime zest

MERINGUE
2 egg whites
½ cup (100 ml) sugar
¼ tsp cream of tartar

Preheat the oven to 350°F (175°C). Grease a mini pie or mini muffin tray. Make the pastry crust and let it rest for 30 minutes.

Beat the egg yolks until creamy. Whisk in the condensed milk, lime zest, and lime juice.

Line the forms with dough. Refrigerate for 15 minutes.

Fill the forms with the lime filling. Bake in the oven for 10–15 minutes or until the filling has set.

In the meantime, whisk the egg whites with the cream of tartar until stiff. Spoon in the sugar while whipping to form a firm meringue batter.

Pipe the meringue onto the pies, and bake for another 5–10 minutes or until the meringue is slightly golden brown. Let cool before serving.

See the photo on page 292.

IN ADVANCE The pies can be prepared without the meringue the day before and stored in the refrigerator or in the freezer for about 1 month. Bake the pies with the meringue on the serving day.

NECTARINE PASTRIES WITH LIME & CARDAMOM CREAM

MAKES approx. 24
TIME approx. 30 minutes

  6 oz (170 g) puff pastry sheets
  1 egg yolk, lightly beaten

  1 nectarine, peeled and cored
  2 tbsp butter
  ½ cup (100 ml) almond flakes

  LIME & CARDAMOM CREAM
  ½ cup (100 ml) heavy cream
  1 tbsp sugar
  ½ lime, zested
  ½ tsp ground cardamom

Preheat the oven to 440°F (225°C).

Cut the nectarine into slices.

Roll out the puff pastry sheets. Brush with the egg, and punch out small circles with a round cutter, or cut into squares.

Arrange the nectarines on top of the pastry, brush with butter, and sprinkle with the almond flakes. Bake for approximately 10 minutes or until the pastry begins to brown. Let it cool slightly.

Whip the cream with the sugar, lime zest, and cardamom. Put a dollop on each tartlet.

See the photo on page 292.

IN ADVANCE The tartlets taste best freshly baked, but can be made a few hours in advance. The cream may be mixed the day before and stored in the refrigerator. Add the cream right before serving.

FIG & HONEY PASTRIES

MAKES approx. 24
TIME approx. 20 minutes

  6 oz (170 g) puff pastry sheets
  1 egg yolk, lightly beaten
  2 figs, cut into thin wedges
  2 tbsp butter, melted
  approx 3 tbsp honey

Preheat the oven to 440°F (225°C).

Roll out the puff pastry sheets. Brush with the egg, and punch out small circles with a round cutter or cut into squares.

Arrange the fig wedges on top of the pastry, and brush with butter. Bake for about 10 minutes or until the pastry begins to color.

Drizzle with a little honey right before serving. *See the photo on page 292.*

IN ADVANCE The tartlets taste best freshly baked, but can be made a few hours in advance.

APPLE PASTRIES WITH CANDIED NUTS

MAKES approx. 24
TIME approx. 30 minutes

  6 oz (170 g) puff pastry sheets
  1 egg yolk, lightly beaten

  1 apple, peeled and cored
  2 tbsp butter, melted

  approx. ½ cup (100 g) vanilla yogurt
  CANDIED NUTS (*see the recipe on page* 303)

Preheat the oven to 440°F (225°C).

Halve the apple and slice thinly. Roll out the puff pastry sheets. Brush with the egg, and punch out small circles with a round cutter or cut into squares.

Arrange the apple slices on top of the pastry and brush with butter. Bake for about 10 minutes or until the pastry begins to color. Let it cool.

Add a dollop of vanilla yogurt to each tartlet and sprinkle with candied nuts.

See the photo on page 292.

IN ADVANCE The tartlets taste best freshly baked, but can be made several hours in advance. Add the yogurt and nuts right before serving.

TIRAMISU

MAKES approx. 12
TIME approx. 20 minutes

2 egg yolks
3 tbsp sugar
9 oz (250 g) mascarpone
½ cup (100 ml) heavy cream
⅔ cup (150 ml) strong coffee or espresso
2 tbsp brandy, amaretto, or dark rum
approx. 4 oz (100 g) ladyfinger cookies

cocoa powder for garnish

Beat the egg yolks and sugar until light and fluffy. Blend in the mascarpone. Whip the cream, and stir it into the mascarpone mixture.

Mix the coffee and liqueur. Break the cookies into smaller pieces, and dip them in the coffee and liqueur mixture.

In small glasses or bowls, layer the cookies with the mascarpone cream. Finish with the mascarpone cream on top and dust with cocoa powder.

See the photo on page 293.

IN ADVANCE Tiramisu can be made the day before and stored in the refrigerator. Dust with cocoa powder right before serving.

STRAWBERRY & LIMONCELLO TRIFLE

MAKES approx. 12
TIME approx. 15 minutes

9 oz (250 g) SPONGE CAKE (*see the recipe on page* **296**)
¼–½ cup (50–100 ml) limoncello
9 oz (250 g) fresh strawberries, sliced
1 lb (500 g) vanilla custard
⅔–¾ cup (150–200 ml) LEMON CURD (*see the recipe on page* **249**)

Cut the sponge cake into small pieces. Drizzle with limoncello. Layer the cake, strawberries, vanilla custard, and lemon curd into small glasses or bowls until they are filled. Top with strawberries.

See the photo on page 293.

IN ADVANCE The trifle can be made the day before and stored in the refrigerator. Garnish with strawberries right before serving.

BERRY MOUSSE

MAKES approx. 12
TIME approx. 15 minutes + 1 hour in the refrigerator

½ tsp unflavored gelatin powder
1 tbsp cold water
¾ cup (200 ml) fresh berries, such as raspberries, strawberries, blueberries, or blackberries
2–3 tbsp confectioner's sugar
½ tsp vanilla extract
¾ cup (200 ml) heavy cream

berries and lemon balm or mint for garnish

Soften the gelatin in a bowl with the cold water.

Mix the berries with the confectioner's sugar to a purée. Strain the purée through a fine mesh sieve to remove the seeds.

Heat a tablespoon of purée in a saucepan. Stir in the softened gelatin until dissolved. Remove the pan from the heat, and stir in the rest of the purée.

Whip the cream with the vanilla extract, and carefully fold it into the purée. Pipe the mousse into small glasses and chill until set—at least one hour.

Garnish with fresh berries, lemon balm or mint.
See the photo on page 293.

TIP Make this dessert even more scrumptious by sprinkling crushed hard candies on top.

IN ADVANCE The mousse can be made the day before and garnished right before serving.

VANILLA PANNA COTTA

MAKES approx. 12
TIME approx. 10 minutes + 3 hours in the refrigerator

2 tsp unflavored gelatin powder
4 tbsp cold water
1 vanilla pod
2 cups heavy cream
3 tbsp sugar

fresh berries for garnish

Soften the gelatin in a bowl with the cold water.

Cut the vanilla pod lengthwise, and scrape the seeds into a saucepan. Pour in the cream, vanilla pod, and sugar, and let the mixture simmer on low heat for about 3 minutes.

Whisk the gelatin into the warm cream until completely dissolved. Remove the vanilla pod, and pour the cream into small glasses. Refrigerate for about 3 hours or until the panna cotta has set.

Top with fresh berries before serving.

See the photo on page 293.

CHOCOLATE PANNA COTTA

Follow the recipe for vanilla panna cotta, but use only ½ tsp gelatin powder dissolved in 1 tbsp cold water. Add 4 oz (100 g) bittersweet chocolate to the hot cream and let it melt. Garnish with grated chocolate or chocolate spirals. The spirals can be done by gently grating the edge of a white or dark chocolate bar with a vegetable peeler.

See the photo on page 293.

IN ADVANCE The panna cotta can be stored in the refrigerator for 1 day.

BLACKBERRY & WHITE CHOCOLATE PANNA COTTA

MAKES approx. 12
TIME approx. 20 minutes + 3 hours in the refrigerator

1 batch VANILLA PANNA COTTA (*see the recipe to the left*)
½ cup (100 ml) puréed blackberries

WHITE CHOCOLATE CREAM
½ cup (100 ml) heavy cream
2 oz (50 g) white chocolate, finely chopped

12 blackberries
zest of 1 lime
1 tbsp sugar

Follow the recipe for VANILLA PANNA COTTA, and mix with the puréed blackberries before the cream is poured into the glasses. Leave room for the white chocolate cream. Refrigerate.

After about an hour, when the panna cotta has begun to set, prepare the white chocolate cream. Heat the cream, and stir in the white chocolate until completely melted. Let cool slightly. Pour the white chocolate cream on top of the blackberry panna cotta. Refrigerate for about 3 hours.

Mix the blackberries, lime zest, and sugar. Top each panna cotta with a blackberry before serving.

See the photo on page 293.

IN ADVANCE The panna cotta can be stored, without berries, in the refrigerator for a day. Garnish right before serving.

BAILEYS PANNA COTTA WITH CANDIED NUTS

MAKES approx. 12
TIME approx. 20 min. + 3 hrs. in the refrigerator

1 batch VANILLA PANNA COTTA + ¼ tsp gelatin
  powder (*see the recipe on the opposite page*)
approx. 1 ½ tbsp Baileys Irish Cream

CANDIED NUTS
½ cup (100 ml) mixed nuts, chopped
2 tbsp sugar
1 tbsp water
1 tsp butter

Follow the recipe for vanilla panna cotta, adding the additional gelatin powder and the Baileys before the panna cotta is poured into glasses.

Grease a baking sheet. Boil the sugar and water in a saucepan until slightly golden brown. Add the nuts and butter and stir. Spread nut mixture onto the greased baking sheet, and allow to cool. Crush the candied nuts into smaller pieces.

Sprinkle candied nuts over the panna cotta right before serving.

See the photo on page 293.

IN ADVANCE The panna cotta can be stored in the refrigerator for 1 day. The candied nuts can be stored dry for several days before they are to be served. Garnish right before serving.

PAVLOVA WITH BERRIES

MAKES approx. 24
TIME approx. 1 ½ hours

2 egg whites
¼ tsp cream of tartar
½ cup (100 ml) sugar
½–¾ cup (100–200 ml) heavy cream
⅔ cup (150 ml) LEMON CURD (*see the recipe on page 249*) or Nutella

fresh berries, such as strawberries, blueberries, blackberries, redcurrants, and/or raspberries for garnish

Preheat the oven to 350°F (175°C).

Beat the egg whites in a clean bowl until stiff. Add the sugar a little at a time. Continue to whisk until the meringue is glossy and firm. Spoon out the batter into circles of about 1 inch (2 ½ cm) in diameter onto a baking sheet with parchment paper. Form the meringue as small bowls.

Place the meringues in the oven, and immediately lower the heat to 260°F (125°C). Bake for about 45 minutes. Turn the oven off, and let the meringues stand and cool with the oven door slightly open.

Whip the cream.

Dollop the lemon curd or Nutella onto the meringues, and top with the cream. Garnish with fresh berries.

Is not pictured.

IN ADVANCE The meringue can be stored at room temperature for 2 days. Prepare the pavlovas right before serving.

PROPOSED MENUS

Here is a proposed selection of hors d'ouevres for various occasions.
These are merely suggestions—feel free to choose and combine
from the 565 recipes offered throughout this book.

BABY/BRIDAL SHOWER
Carrot Omelet Roll with Feta (*see recipe on page 30*)
Caviar Cheesecake with Shrimp (*see recipe on page 94*)
Vol-Au-Vents with Mushroom & Cognac Filling
   (*see recipe on page 28*)
Crème Ninon with Shrimp (*see recipe on page 46*)
Quiche Lorraine (*see recipe on page 41*)
Orange, Fennel & Olive Salad (*see recipe on page 53*)
Salmon Mousse With Cucumber & Celery Salad
   (*see recipe on page 65*)
Watermelon with Balsamic Syrup (*see recipe on page 269*)
Crudités (*see recipe on page 270*)
Key Lime Pie (*see recipe on page 299*)

GRADUATION PARTY
Baked New Potatoes with Sour Cream & Prosciutto Chips
   (*see recipe on page 33*)
Chicken Terrine With Apricot & Pistachio
   (*see recipe on page 25*)
Carrot Rösti with Feta (*see recipe on page 38*)
Corn Soup with Chili & Crab (*see recipe on page 49*)
Beet, Chèvre & Pine Nut Salad (*see recipe on page 52*)
Chicken, Sage & Lemon Skewers (*see recipe on page 55*)
Cheese Wheel (*see recipe on page 214*)
Puff Pastry Baked Olives (*see recipe on page 184*)
Flatbread Strips with Cheddar & Caraway
   (*see recipe on page 226*)

FOURTH OF JULY
Omelet Roll with Salmon & Chives (*see recipe on page 30*)
Canapé with Crab & Apple (*see recipe on page 81*)
Chilled Avocado & Grapefruit Soup (*see recipe on page 48*)
Asian Potato Salad with Beef & Sweet Chili
   (*see recipe on page 52*)
Fish Tacos with Fried Cod & Coleslaw (*see recipe on page 145*)
Tuna Sliders with Mango Salsa & Wasabi
   (*see recipe on page 130*)
Green Pea & Cashew Spread (*see recipe on page 237*)
Garlic Bread with Parsley (*see recipe on page 226*)
Crudités (*see recipe on page 270*)
Summer Berries with Lime Sugar (*see recipe on page 261*)

SUPER BOWL SUNDAY
Flavored Popcorn (*see recipe on page 287*)
Grilled Potato Skins (*see recipe on page 287*)
Prosciutto Chips (*see recipe on page 286*)
Classic Hamburger Sliders (*see recipe on page 129*)
Buffalo Chicken Wings (*see recipe on page 131*)
Pizza with Salami, Olives & Arugula (*see recipe on page 189*)
Sesame-Crusted Salmon Skewers (*see recipe on page 57*)
Grilled Mushrooms with Mozzarella (*see recipe on page 182*)
Roasted Pita with Cumin & Sesame (*see recipe on page 228*)
Potato & Almond Dip (*see recipe on page 235*)

NEW YEAR'S PARTY
Blinies with Caviar (*see the recipe on page 37*)
Crème Ninon with Shrimp (*see the recipe on page 46*)
Potato Purèe with Lobster & Herb Butter
   (*see the recipe on page 62*)
Scallops in Champagne Sauce (*see the recipe on page 63*)
Cauliflower Mousse with Prosciutto Chips
   (*see the recipe on page 64*)
Shrimp with Dipping Sauces (*see the recipe on page 74*)
Canapé with Salmon Tartar (*see the recipe on page 79*)
Canapé with Caviar, Sour Cream & Red Onion
   (*see recipe on page 80*)
Oysters or Oyster Rockefeller
   (*see the recipe on page 73* and 82)
Croutons with Foie Gras & Raspberry Onion Chutney
   (*see the recipe on page 201*)
Salmon Rillette (*see the recipe on page 204*)
Mini-skewers with Blue Cheese & Fig (*see the recipe on page 268*)

COCKTAIL PARTY

Puff Pastry Sticks, Wheels & Palmiers *(see the recipe on page 29)*
Carrot Omelet Roll with Feta *(see the recipe on page 30)*
Flatbread Roll with Ham & Spinach *(see the recipe on page 33)*
Carrot Soup with Curry, Ginger & Cumin
   (see the recipe on page 47)
Patatas Bravas *(see the recipe on page 103)*
Quesadillas with Tuna Filling *(see the recipe on page 147)*
Pizza with Zucchini, Mushrooms & Tomato
   (see the recipe on page 190)
Potato & Almond Dip *(see the recipe on page 235)*
Mini-skewers with Cheese & Olive *(see the recipe on page 268)*
Roast Beef & Pearl Onion Toothpicks
   (see the recipe on page 269)

FANCY COCKTAIL

Vol-Au-Vents with Brie & Crab Filling
   (see the recipe on page 28)
Carpaccio Roll with Parmesan & Arugula
   (see the recipe on page 29)
Chanterelle Soup with Truffle Oil *(see the recipe on page 50)*
Oysters with Sauces *(see the recipe on page 73)*
Canapé with Caviar, Sour Cream & Red Onion,
   (see the recipe on page 80)
Oysters Rockefeller *(see the recipe on page 82)*
Croutons with Foie Gras & Raspberry Onion Chutney
   (see the recipe on page 201)
Snails with Garlic & Parsley *(see the recipe on page 203)*
Steak Tartare *(see the recipe on page 205)*
All recipes in the chapter AMUSE-BOUCHES

VEGETARIAN

Gougères *(see the recipe on page 27)*
Crêpe with Mushroom & Blue Cheese Spread
   (see the recipe on page 32)
Baked Potatoes with Sour Cream & Deep-Fried Capers
   (see the recipe on page 33)
Ricotta & Spinach Pie with Sun-dried Tomatoes
   (see the recipe on page 41)
Beetroot Soup with Apple & Blackcurrants
   (see the recipe on page 48)
Asparagus Mousse with Parmesan Crisps
   (see the recipe on page 65)
Tortilla de Patata con Zucchini *(see the recipe on page 101)*
Stuffed Mushrooms *(see the recipe on page 104)*
Falafel *(see the recipe on page 117)*
Artichokes with Dipping Sauce *(see the recipe on page 198)*
Grilled Mushrooms with Mozzarella
   (see the recipe on page 182)
Grilled Marinated Vegetables *(see the recipe on page 183)*
Crudités *(see the recipe on page 270)*

GARDEN PARTY

Ajo Blanco—Chilled Garlic & Almond Soup
   (see the recipe on page 50)
Asian Potato Salad with Beef & Sweet Chili
   (see the recipe on page 52)
Chicken, Sage & Lemon Skewers *(see recipe on page 55)*
Sesame-Crusted Salmon Skewers *(see recipe on page 57)*
Ceviche *(see the recipe on page 75)*
Tortilla de Patata *(see the recipe on page 100)*
Gazpacho *(see the recipe on page 109)*
Buffalo Chicken Wings *(see the recipe on page 131)*
BBQ Baby Back Ribs *(see the recipe on page 131)*
Corn on the Cob *(see the recipe on page 133)*

CHILDREN'S PARTY

Quiche Lorraine *(see the recipe on page 41)*
Chicken & Prosciutto Skewers *(see the recipe on page 55)*
Classic Hamburger Sliders *(see the recipe on page 129)*
Pizza with Potatoes, Bacon, Rosemary & Parmesan
   (see the recipe on page 190)
Muffins with Feta & Spinach *(see the recipe on page 230)*
Croque Monsieur *(see the recipe on page 256)*
Mini-skewers with Watermelon, Feta & Mint
   (see the recipe on page 268)
Flavored Popcorn *(see the recipe on page 287)*
Potato & Root Vegetable Chips *(see the recipe on page 288)*
Fruit Skewers with Lime Sugar *(see the recipe on page 296)*

ACKNOWLEDGMENTS

This book took over two years to complete, and many people have helped us along the way.

Thanks to our talented photographer Roland Persson. You put in many hours of hard work. It's always inspiring to work with you, and once again, together, we've created a fantastic book!

We are grateful to everyone at Bonnier Fakta, especially our editor Anna Paljak. Your patience is infinite. Thanks also to Birgit Hemberg for sharing your extensive knowledge of food, as well as Constance Renfrow at Skyhorse Publishing for helping to bring this labor of love to an English speaking audience.

Thanks to Bruka Design, Hertzman Fruit & Vegetables, Mikaela Willers, Lagamati, Cordon Bleu, Tabbouli House, and Lexington.

Thanks also to our wonderful and patient friends who served as models.

Special thanks to mom. We would have never been able to write this book without your unconditional support, which has involved everything from washing dishes to test cooking the same recipes over and over again—often with grandchildren tugging at your apron.

Thanks to our beloved Lars and Henrik for changing diapers and cooking meals while we worked on the book.

To our big brother Teddy, to whom we are especially grateful—what would we have done without you?

And thanks to little Benjamin for waiting in your mommy Lisa's tummy until the book was finished.

INDEX

The Eisenman sisters' other works include the following titles, which are available in Swedish from Bonnier Fakta.

Two Sisters' Sweets (Två systrars söta) 2005
Awarded Dessert Book of the Year by Måltidsakademien
Prize for Best Cookbook Cover at the Gourmand Cookbook Awards

Soups, Breads & Spreads (Soppor, bröd & röror) 2006

Winter Sweets (Vinterns söta) 2007

Summer Sweets (Sommarens söta) 2009
Awarded Pastry Book of the Year by Måltidsakademien

Monica Eisenman's Asian Noodles and Snacks (Monica Eisenmans asiatiska nudlar och smårätter) 2010

Please visit the Eisenman sisters' website www.eisenmansisters.com

Skyhorse Publishing books may be purchased in bulk at special discounts for sales promotion, corporate gifts, fund-raising, or educational purposes. Special editions can also be created to specifications. For details, contact the Special Sales Department, Skyhorse Publishing, 307 West 36th Street, 11th Floor, New York, NY 10018 or info@skyhorsepublishing.com.

Skyhorse® and Skyhorse Publishing® are registered trademarks of Skyhorse Publishing, Inc.®, a Delaware corporation.

www.skyhorsepublishing.com

10 9 8 7 6 5 4 3 2 1

Library of Congress Cataloging-in-Publication Data

Frisk, Lisa Eisenman.
  [Systrarna Eisenmans minglemat. Englsh]
  The party food bible : 565 recipes for amuse-bouches, flavorful canapes, and festive finger food / Lisa Eisenman Frisk & Monica Eisenman ; photography by Roland Persson ; translated by Anette Cantagallo.
     pages cm
  Includes index.
  ISBN 978-1-62636-085-3
1. Appetizers. 2. Entertaining. 3. Parties. I. Eisenman, Monica. II. Title.
  TX740.F68513 2013
  641.81'2--dc23

                          2013033319

Printed in China